D1548829

The Asian American Experience

Series Editor
Roger Daniels, University of Cincinnati

Books in the Series

The Hood River Issei: An Oral History of Japanese Settlers
in Oregon's Hood River Valley
Linda Tamura

Americanization, Acculturation, and Ethnic Identity:
The Nisei Generation in Hawaii
Eileen H. Tamura

Sui Sin Far/Edith Maude Eaton: A Literary Biography
Annette White-Parks

Mrs. Spring Fragrance and Other Writings
*Sui Sin Far; edited by Amy Ling and
Annette White-Parks*

The Golden Mountain: The Autobiography
of a Korean Immigrant, 1895–1960
*Easurk Emsen Charr; edited and with
an introduction by Wayne Patterson*

The Golden Mountain

Easurk Emsen Charr, 1923

THE
GOLDEN
MOUNTAIN,

The Autobiography
of a Korean Immigrant,
1895–1960

Easurk Emsen Charr

*Edited and
with an Introduction by*
Wayne Patterson

Second Edition

University of Illinois Press
Urbana and Chicago

This book is printed on acid-free paper.

Frontispiece photograph of Easurk Emsen Charr, on his
graduation from Park College in 1923, was provided by
the Park College Photographic History Collection,
Park College Library.

Library of Congress Cataloging-in-Publication Data
Charr, Easurk Emsen, 1895–1986.
   The golden mountain : the autobiography of a Korean
immigrant, 1895–1960 / Easurk Emsen Charr ; edited and
with an introduction by Wayne Patterson. — 2nd ed.
      p.   cm. — (The Asian American experience)
   Includes index.
   Originally published: Boston : Forum, 1961.
   ISBN 0-252-02217-3 (cloth : alk. paper). —
   ISBN 0-252-06513-1 (pbk. : alk. paper)
   1. Charr, Easurk Emsen, 1895–1986. 2. Korean Americans—
Biography. I. Patterson, Wayne, 1946– . II. Title.
III. Series.
E184.K6C462   1996
973'.04957—dc20   95-17504
                                                          CIP

Contents

Illustrations follow page 162

Foreword

Roger Daniels

American immigrant autobiographies are a special genre, and *The Golden Mountain*, by Easurk Emsen Charr, is typical of that genre, even though Charr himself was an improbable immigrant author. As Wayne Patterson, the outstanding historian of first-generation Korean Americans, makes clear in his introduction, Charr was a unique member of his generation of Korean immigrants, managing to serve in the United States Army and getting a college education. As far as we know, he is the only one who wrote and published an autobiography.

William Boelhower, the leading scholar of immigrant autobiography, has written that the "specialty" of American ethnic autobiographical writing "largely consists in consciously elaborating or simply rewriting the received behavioral script of the rhetorically well-defined American self."[1] Similarly, if less elegantly, my mentor, the late Theodore Saloutos, used to say that when an immigrant became a "patriot," he or she often became a "200 percent" American. Although Boelhower is speaking of immigrants generally and Saloutos was speaking particularly of Greek Americans, their observations fit Charr's memoir quite well. The great myths of American immigration—Plymouth Rock, the Statue of Liberty, and the Melting Pot—reverberate in *The Golden Mountain*, as they do in most works by immigrants.

Immigrants from Asia suffered under special constraints, chiefly, their inability to become naturalized citizens until the World War II–cold war era. That Charr could eventually surmount this obstacle because of his brief stint as a World War I doughboy does not obviate the discrimination he faced. Some readers may wonder that this and other discrimination figures so little in Charr's book, but for him to have dwelt upon this would have meant a departure from the traditional "script." He spends much more time thanking those who helped him than complaining about the wounds he suffered.

Charr's life is neither distinguished nor particularly dramatic. His is a story of endurance, of survival, and, as Patterson indicates, of descendants who, in typical American fashion, achieved higher socioeconomic status than the first generation. Readers will note that Charr devotes many more pages to his family and background in Korea and to his army and college years than to his wife and family in America. This, too, it seems to me, is part of the received "script." Although he dedicated his book to Park College and the American Legion, no one should doubt that Charr really wrote it to leave a record of his life for his children and their descendants.

We, its nonfamilial readers, have other uses for this autobiography that helps bring to life the earliest complement of Korean Americans, so different in circumstance from the Korean Americans who populate contemporary Koreatowns. Even more important, *The Golden Mountain* shows how an Asian immigrant's recollection can resonate with the same themes and myths as do other immigrants' autobiographies. We are much in debt to Wayne Patterson, not only for his

"discovery" of a little-known piece of Asian America-
na, but also for his clear and insightful introduction.

Note

1. William Boelhower, "The Making of Ethnic Autobiography in the United States," in *American Autobiography: Retrospect and Prospect,* ed. Paul John Eakin (Madison: University of Wisconsin Press, 1991): 123–41.

Introduction

Wayne Patterson

Easurk Emsen Charr (Cha Ŭi-sŏk) was born in 1895 in northern Korea. At the improbable age of ten and on his own volition he emigrated without his parents to Hawaii and then to the continental United States, where he lived until his death in 1986 at the age of ninety-one. This book, a twenty-year project that Charr completed in 1960, represents the life story of one of the seven thousand Koreans who came to the United States between 1903 and 1905. Because he had such a clear recollection of his life, readers of his autobiography learn not only about the life of a Korean immigrant in early twentieth-century America but also much about late Yi Dynasty Korea at the turn of the century.

While there is no such thing as a "typical" immigrant account, Charr's story is rich in detail about many experiences and events similar to those of many other early Korean immigrants to the United States. Indeed, personal accounts such as his enrich our understanding of the immigration process as it was experienced at the individual level. At the same time, it is well to remember that immigrants like Charr remained largely unaware of other aspects of the immigration process that occurred on a different level involving diplomats, politicians, and businessmen. For this reason Charr's autobiography contains no discussion of these issues.[1] However, a brief introduction that outlines this other level will serve to place Charr's individual experience within a broader context. It will also serve to fill in some of the blanks in Charr's story, using information based on interviews with his children and documents collected by the editor.

* * *

By the 1870s, sugar had become the mainstay of the Hawaiian economy and the demand for laborers had become so great that the Hawaiian Sugar Planters' Association (hereafter referred to simply as the planters) had to look for plentiful and cheap labor from abroad. In Asia the planters found what they were looking for. At first, Chinese were imported to work in the fields; then, by the mid-1880s, Japanese were brought in, the planters consciously mixing the races to prevent any one race from achieving a labor monopoly. If not for political developments in Hawaii and on the American mainland, this immigrant flow might have continued unchanged for some time.

Hawaii was annexed by the United States in 1898 and American statutes became the law there at the turn of the century. The issue of Asian labor in Hawaii now came to the forefront under a new set of political and legal considerations. On the one hand, the planters in Hawaii had institutionalized the policy of mixing the races on the plantations. On the other hand, Chinese could no longer come to Hawaii to offset the now more numerous Japanese because of the Chinese Exclusion Act, in effect in the United States since 1882. Moreover, since U.S. law prohibited contract labor and Hawaii was now part of the United States, nothing prevented Japanese sugarcane workers from quitting their jobs and moving to California, where wages were about twice those in Hawaii.

Also, since strikes were now legal, those Japanese who remained in Hawaii on the plantations vigorously exercised their newfound freedom during the first three years of the twentieth century. As a result, Koreans were brought in to work the Hawaiian sugarcane fields.

Hawaiian sugar planters knew little about Korea except that it was in Asia and was potentially a source of cheap labor. But their precarious labor situation dictated that they explore the possibility of Korean immigration. Fortuitously, just as the planters decided to inquire about Koreans, they learned that the American minister to Korea, Horace Allen, was en route to Korea from home leave in Ohio. Meeting Allen in San Francisco and Honolulu, representatives of the planters asked him for information and help in arranging for Korean laborers to come to Hawaii. Allen was more than happy to oblige. For nearly two decades, he had been active in Korea, first as a medical missionary and, after 1897, as the ranking American diplomat in that country.[2]

Allen was profoundly unhappy about the official American policy of neutrality and nonintervention in Korean affairs. To him, this policy meant that the United States would stand idly by if and when Japan decided to take over Korea. Realizing that such a hands-off policy was due at least in part to the miniscule American economic involvement in Korea, Allen set about to promote American business interests there in the hopes that Washington would then pay more attention to the political situation. The chance to send Korean laborers to Hawaii thus represented for Allen an opportunity to advance his efforts to increase Washington's interest in the area and indirectly to help Korea maintain its independence in the face of mounting Japanese pressure. But it was one thing for Allen to applaud the venture and quite another to bring it to fruition.

There were several obstacles Allen had to overcome, and in doing so he disobeyed orders not to interfere in Korean affairs. The first obstacle was potential opposition from the Korean government. Luckily, Allen was a personal friend of the emperor, Kojong,[3] and was able to appeal to his pride by telling him that Koreans could go to the United States while the Chinese, whom Koreans had traditionally admired, could not. Allen also knew that Kojong wanted closer relations with the United States to preserve Korea's independence and, like himself, saw emigration as a prelude to closer political ties with Washington. Second, Allen had to find a recruiter who would have no scruples about violating U.S. laws against contract labor. Allen had been told in Hawaii that Korean workers would sign agreements to work in the cane fields before leaving Korea and that their passage would be prepaid by the planters, both of which were illegal. He selected David Deshler, the stepson of Governor George Nash of Ohio,[4] who had intervened with President McKinley to get Allen appointed to his ministerial post; thus, Allen was repaying a political favor.

Third, Allen had to figure out a way for Deshler, the planters, and himself to evade the laws against contract labor—laws that Allen was sworn to uphold. He did so by arranging for Deshler to set up a "bank" in Korea that would have only one "depositor"—the Hawaiian Sugar Planters' Association—and whose only business was to "loan" passage money to intending immigrants. (Readers will notice that Charr never mentions how he was able to pay the fifty-dollar passage to Honolulu—a small fortune for most Koreans at the turn of the century.) Fourth, Allen had to intercede on the planters' behalf in Washington, where there was growing nervousness about Japanese immigration. He knew that the venture would fail if Washington—and organized labor—found out that there was about to be a new, potentially large-scale wave of immigration from Asia, and he especially wanted to hide the fact that it had been organized by the American minister to Korea. So in a carefully worded letter to the Department of State, he declared that the impending arrival of Koreans was not organized in any way, that he had only secondhand knowledge of the project, and that the Koreans were good people who would not come in any great numbers. The ruse worked and Washington offered no objections.

Finally, Allen needed to help the Korean government set up the actual mechanism for sending Koreans to Hawaii since Korea had little experience with legal emigration. He did so by first obtaining a copy of Japanese emigration rules and regulations and having the Korean government adopt them. He then arranged for the creation of a Department of Emigration within the Korean government to process passports. Allen clearly had no qualms about ignoring his diplomatic instructions not to interfere in Korean politics.

Allen's efforts having succeeded, the first Koreans departed from Inch'ŏn harbor on December 22, 1902; after transferring to a transpacific steamer in Japan, they arrived in Honolulu on January 13, 1903. Allen had been successful in initiating the project; now the challenge was to keep it going.

As Allen, Deshler, and the planters looked ahead, they were encouraged that there seemed to be no shortage of immigrants. Times were bad in Korea, and one American missionary there remarked that "we can't blame them for wanting to go to America."[5] To many Koreans, it was obvious that the five-hundred-year-old Yi Dynasty was on its last legs, with famine, disease, poverty, oppression, maladministration, rebellion, and war stalking the peninsula. These conditions uprooted many from their rural homes and their occupation as farmers and sent them fleeing to the cities and to urban occupations. As refugees of a sort, dislocated from familiar surroundings, these new arrivals lived on the margins of society and were more interested than most Koreans in the message carried by American missionaries who were located in the cities. (Readers will note that Charr's family was forced to move to the city of P'yŏngyang in the wake of the Tonghak Rebellion and the Sino-Japanese War [1894–95]. In P'yŏngyang they met the American Presbyterian missionaries who converted them to Christianity.)

As Korean converts interacted with American missionaries they naturally became acquainted not only with Western religion but also with Western customs, language, food, habits, medicine, houses, and clothing. When the opportunity to emigrate to Hawaii presented itself, the thought of leaving Korea was not quite as daunting as it might have been for those who had little contact with Christian missionaries and Western culture. Although the number of Korean converts to Christianity was few at the turn of the century (perhaps 100,000 out of a total population of eight million), a considerable majority of the Koreans who went to Hawaii were connected in some way with Christianity and with American missionaries. In a prizewinning college essay in 1921, Charr wrote about his own experience with American missionaries:

When I was a little boy of about twelve, I felt
like many an American boy today who reads the
famous story of "Sinbad the Sailor" in the "Ara-
bian Nights Entertainments" and dreams of setting out on an adventurous voyage and of reaching a mysterious island of hidden treasures and of
many strange things. O, how eagerly I tried to
secure information concerning America, the land
of untold opportunities, a promised land flowing
with freedom and happiness, and how desirous I
was to see it once in my lifetime! I can still remember that I used to sit right in front of the
church platform. Can anyone imagine how closely I watched and observed Dr. Moffett, my pastor? O, how anxiously I wished that I could wear
a suit of clothes like he did! And O, how greatly
I admired Dr. Wells, a medical missionary who so
kindly cured my sore eyes and removed my sore
tooth! The services of these two missionaries
were impressed so deep into my sensitive and
acquisitive young mind that I have desired to be
a medical missionary ever since, to carry the Bible in one hand and a medicine case in another
to render a similar service to my own people.[6]

David Deshler, the recruiter chosen by Allen, took
full advantage of this sentiment by locating his offices in the major port cities and hiring Korean converts
to advertise the Hawaiian opportunity. Needless to
say, his advertising painted a bright picture of life in
the United States, so it is not surprising that Charr
and others would believe reports that said that work
in America was like "taking a nap under a pear tree."
    For the first six months of the newly organized
migration, until the late spring of 1903, nearly six

hundred Koreans proceeded to Hawaii without a hitch. Then, an incident occurred that threatened to stop the flow altogether. The interpreter ("a damned fool," according to one of the planters[7]) who accompanied the 142 Koreans aboard the *Nippon Maru*, which arrived on April 30, 1903, admitted that they had indeed contracted to work for the planters prior to their departure from Korea. Immediately, the U.S. immigration authorities ordered that further shiploads of Koreans be held back while an investigation ensued. The planters were thrown into a tizzy as they scrambled to get their story straight. After a nerve-wracking summer, which included the bribing of a federal judge,[8] the flow of immigrants was permitted to resume. The planters had to agree not to hire Korean workers until after they arrived in Honolulu. Luckily for the planters, the authorities never found out that they were also paying the Koreans' passage.

In 1904, the second full year of immigration, conditions in Korea worsened, primarily because the Russo-Japanese War had begun and Korea was the scene of much of the fighting. It was at this point, in the fall of 1904, that Charr left Korea. He was lucky, because in the spring of 1905 the opportunity for Koreans to emigrate to America ceased and would not resume until after World War II. The reasons for this had much to do with the outcome of the Russo-Japanese War and Japanese-American relations.

The Russo-Japanese War represented the second war that Japan had fought in a decade over who would control Korea. Having first ousted China in 1895 and now Russia, Japan was certainly not about to fight over Korea a third time. Largely for reasons of security, Japan began to take steps to control Korea so that it could not attach itself to a foreign power that might threaten Japan. In 1905 Japan placed a protectorate over Korea; five years later it annexed the country.

Before Japan could establish a protectorate over Korea, it had to consider the attitude of the United States. The Japanese managed to convince President Theodore Roosevelt that their takeover of Korea would benefit the Korean people; as a result, in the Taft-Katsura Memorandum issued in the summer of 1905, the United States gave Japan a free hand in Korea in exchange for Japan giving the United States a free hand in the Philippines.

As Koreans continued to arrive in Hawaii, reaching nearly seven thousand by early 1905, Japanese from Hawaii streamed into California at the rate of about one thousand per month. Public opinion, inflamed by the words of labor leaders, politicians, and newspaper publishers, began calling for a Japanese Exclusion Act similar in scope to the Chinese Exclusion Act of 1882. In March 1905 the California legislature explicitly called on Washington to pass such an act. For Japan, which considered itself the equal of the major Western nations, the prospect of such an act was psychologically devastating as it would call into question Japan's standing and place it in the same undesirable category as China. Japan felt that it was one thing to exclude the lowly Chinese but quite another to exclude the Japanese. It became imperative to head off such legislation.[9]

The foreign minister of Japan, a Harvard graduate named Komura Jutarō, saw that the problem was caused by the thousands of Japanese moving from Hawaii to California. Further investigation revealed that Japanese sugarcane workers were making the move because wages in California were twice those in Hawaii. Why? Because low-paid Koreans were being imported to prevent Japanese from striking successfully for higher wages. If Koreans could be prevented from emigrating to Hawaii, Japanese could regain their monopoly over labor and could successfully strike for higher wages. As a result, the wage disparity between the two areas would be reduced or eliminated, and the threat of an exclusion act against Japan would recede.

With its troops occupying the entire Korean peninsula in early 1905, Japan could simply have flexed its considerable muscle and prevented Koreans from leaving for Hawaii. But Japan had assured the United States that its takeover of Korea would result in a more efficient and humane government, and so it could not use brute force to stop Koreans from emigrating. Instead, Japan needed to find a deterrent consistent with its contention that it had only humanitarian concern for the welfare of the Korean people.

Japan already knew a great deal about the inner workings of the Korean government, including that it was weak and incompetent. Furthermore, Japan quickly found that Korea was particularly incompetent in its handling of emigration matters. For example, the Japanese learned about an incident in early April 1905 in which the Korean government had allowed a thousand Koreans to depart for Mexico aboard a chartered ship. These emigrants were put to work on hennequin plantations in the Yucatan peninsula under slavelike conditions, they had departed Korea without passports, and there was no Korean consul in Merida to look after the new arrivals. In fact, Korea did not enjoy diplomatic relations with Mexico. Even in places like Honolulu and Vladivostok, where thousands of Koreans now lived, the Korean government had neglected to assign consuls to look after their welfare—

something that any competent government would have long since done. What about the rules and regulations that had been brought directly from Japan and that Korea supposedly was following? They had been abolished by imperial decree, along with the Department of Emigration, when an opponent of the project happened to get the ear of Emperor Kojong. Clearly, the Korean government had lost control of the emigration process.[10]

This damaging information was a gold mine for the Japanese since they could use it to stop Koreans from going to Hawaii and, at the same time, express their "humanitarian concern" for the Koreans. All the Japanese had to do was go to the Korean government and "suggest" that it would be a good idea to stop all emigration until suitable rules and regulations were drawn up, knowing that the Korean government, in extremis, was unlikely to do so. When Japan did exactly that, the Korean government, in a last-ditch effort to retain its freedom of action and sovereignty, ordered the vice minister of foreign affairs to go to Hawaii and Mexico in the summer of 1905 to visit Koreans living there, and then to return to draw up suitable regulations governing emigration. If the vice minister succeeded, Japan would have been forced to resort to bullying Korea, and that would have sullied its reputation with countries such as the United States. So, when the Korean official finished his inspection tour of Hawaii and was preparing to leave for Mexico, the Japanese government refused to allow the Korean government to send him money for his passage to the Yucatan, forcing him to return to Korea. The mission thus did not succeed, and the Japanese now argued that because the Korean government was unable to draw up suitable rules on emigration, the Japanese government should henceforth take responsibility for "protecting" Koreans abroad. Later, in November 1905, Japan placed a protectorate over Korea, effectively dooming any chance for Koreans to emigrate to Hawaii since Korea's foreign affairs were now in the hands of the Japanese foreign ministry.

*   *   *

Easurk Emsen Charr was able to leave Korea just before the window of opportunity, open for a little over two years, closed completely. Of those Koreans who reached Hawaii, the vast majority (nearly five thousand) opted to stay, while a thousand returned home. Charr and over a thousand like him viewed Hawaii as merely a stopover on the way to California and the mainland. In fact, Charr spent less than six months in Hawaii before moving on to California, arriving in San Francisco in the summer of 1905. Once again Charr was able to leave just in time, for in March 1907 President Roosevelt issued Executive Order 589 preventing Japanese and Korean laborers from moving from Hawaii to the mainland. Although Charr swore that he would return to Korea upon completing a medical education, he never saw his homeland again.

At the tender age of ten, Charr found himself in San Francisco, alone except for his older cousin, without a job, without a place to stay, and with no competence in the English language. Japan was taking over Korea and his father was dying. For the next eight years, Charr recounts a dizzying pattern of employment, education, and geographic mobility. During this period he met two men who sustained him and helped set his direction in life. One of these was An Ch'ang-ho, a leading figure in the Korean nationalist movement who assisted Charr on several occasions. The other was the Presbyterian missionary George Shannon McCune, who suggested in 1913 that Charr attend the high school attached to Park College near Kansas City, Missouri.

In the fall of 1913, Charr enrolled at Park College's academy and, except for his senior year, which he spent at Claremont High School in California, completed his high school education at Park in 1917. Because his admissions application of September 1913 still exists in the alumni office of Park College, we can get a glimpse of Charr at the age of eighteen. He was 5'5" and 125 pounds, smoked cigarettes, and attended the theater. A Presbyterian, he averred that he was neither profane nor played cards. His subjects in high school, gleaned from his transcript, included Latin, mathematics, history, English, zoology, botany, geometry, physics, typing, and German.

As Charr was preparing to enroll as an undergraduate in Park College, the United States entered World War I. Charr wanted to demonstrate his loyalty to his new country, so in April 1918 he enlisted in the U.S. army as a private first class and served for more than eight months in the medical corps near Washington, D.C. When he was discharged in late December, his military record listed his character as "Excellent," with the additional remarks of "Service honest and faithful. No A.W.O.L. No sick in hosp. Hon. discharged."[11] He was given travel pay of $133.21 to return to California. Although his service in the American armed forces was brief and uneventful, it proved to be an important interlude in his life. Indeed, the American Legion, an organization formed by service veterans of World War I, assisted him later with his naturalization and helped resolve his wife's immigration problems. Charr was so grateful that he dedicated his book in part to the American Legion.

The war over, Charr could begin his education at Park College, and it was there that his concern for his native land manifested itself. He began his freshman year in 1919 when the anti-Japanese March First Movement of that year occurred in Korea, galvanizing many Koreans, including Charr, into action. He wrote an essay calling for Korea's independence, and we know (since his children still have the admission ticket) that he attended a dinner in November 1919 at the First Presbyterian Church in Kansas City where Philip Jaisohn (Sŏ Chae-p'il) and Kuisic Kimm (Kim Kyu-sik), delegates to the Versailles Peace Conference, were the guest speakers. Charr joined the Missouri branch of the League of the Friends of Korea, formed in 1920 in response to a visit to the campus by Homer Hulbert, whom Charr had first met in 1908.[12] After his graduation in 1923, Charr continued to concern himself with Korea's predicament, serving as an advisory member of the Korean delegation at the Conference on Pacific Problems held at the University of Chicago in the spring of 1925 (his credentials card is among his collected documents). Charr, like most other overseas Koreans, was deeply concerned about the fate of Korea.

Charr's main preoccupation at this time was to obtain a college education. All the available evidence seems to indicate that his four years (1919–23) at Park College were productive ones. He took courses in the Bible, biology, chemistry, economics, English, ethics, French, German, history, religious education, mathematics, philosophy, psychology, sociology, Spanish, and library science. Not only did he have a solid liberal arts education, but he was also a good student, with grades mostly in the 80s and 90s. Evidently, he was very interested in history, winning two prizes for essays on history awarded by the Daughters of the American Revolution.

Charr was well accepted by his classmates and was well integrated into college life. He worked at the college printing office, was a member of Lowell (a social club), served as vice president of the Cosmopolitan Club, and illustrated the college yearbook. His scrapbook is replete with notices of parties, gatherings, plays, and so on, indicating that he was an active participant in the social and cultural activities of the college. One of Charr's classmates reminisced: "As I recall Emsen, he was pleasant, an easy conversationalist, and mixed well with those of similar interests."[13]

After four years at Park College, Charr had fulfilled all the requirements necessary for graduation. His photo in the 1923 yearbook included a quote from Tennyson that read: "A courage to endure and obey; a hate of gossip, parlance, and of sway." Charr was ready to face the world with a college degree in his hand. Evidently, he felt that his education had served him well because nearly forty years later he dedicated his book in part to his alma mater.

After graduation, Charr moved thirty miles west to Lawrence, Kansas, and enrolled in medical school at the University of Kansas for the fall 1923 semester. The archives of the university still have a brief record of Charr's matriculation, showing that he withdrew on February 13, 1924. Returning briefly to Park College to work, he soon left for Chicago, where he enrolled in the School of Pharmacy of the University of Illinois Medical College. At this time he met his future wife, Evelyn Kim, who had come to the United States on a student visa in 1926 at the age of eighteen and was studying in Dubuque, Iowa, to become a nurse.

Emsen and Evelyn were married in Chicago in

1928. Unlike many "picture" marriages that first-generation Koreans entered into, theirs was a "love" marriage.[14] Although Charr does not mention it in his book (the information comes from interviews with his children), he had at one point sent for a picture bride, but the woman had jilted him, keeping the passage money and remaining in Korea. His wife often joked that Charr had gotten her "on the cheap" because no money had changed hands. Soon their first child, a daughter, arrived. But before this young family could settle down to enjoy life together, the Depression hit, and Charr lost his job with the mapmaker Rand McNally in Chicago.

In 1931 Charr returned with his wife to California, where he found work in his nephew's barbershop in San Francisco's Chinatown; he remained there for most of the 1930s. J. Paul Goode, a professor at the University of Chicago who had befriended the Charrs while they lived in Chicago, wrote to Charr in early 1932: "You are very fortunate to have a nephew with a barber shop. It seems that no matter how low the depression people must have the barber's attention, so there is a possibility of a living in it, and that after all is the important thing for several million people in this country, at the present moment."[15] Still, life was difficult. His cousin died, two more of his children were born (a girl and a boy), and the immigration authorities started deportation proceedings against his wife.

During the 1920s and 1930s Charr had doggedly pursued the dream of obtaining U.S. citizenship; the last part of his book is devoted to this single-minded quest, spurred initially by a law that stated that anyone who had served in the U.S. armed forces during World War I was eligible for citizenship. However, in

1922 the courts ruled that this law did not apply to Asians. Nonetheless, Charr continued to seek naturalization and enlisted the aid of the American Legion, of which he was now a member. His wife's predicament was more serious, because in 1932 she was threatened with deportation as her student permit had expired. With help from the American Legion, her deportation order was lifted, and she was given an indefinite permit to remain in the United States. Finally in 1936, Charr was naturalized as a result of a new law passed the previous year.[16]

Now that he was an American citizen, Charr took and passed the civil service examination; and for the remainder of his working life, until his retirement in 1964, he was employed by the government. In 1940 he was assigned to work in Nevada, and two years later he moved to Portland, Oregon. His book concludes at this point.

*   *   *

When reading *The Golden Mountain*, one does not sense the racism and discrimination that permeated the West Coast in the early twentieth century and that Charr undoubtedly had to endure. He does mention that someone threw a rock at him in San Francisco just after he arrived there in 1905, and he comments critically on the passage of California's anti-Asian Alien Land Law. Also, an undertone of bitterness and resentment pervades Charr's account of his struggle to obtain American citizenship. When he seeks, for example, to invoke the law that made anyone who served in the armed forces eligible for citizenship and is told by his interviewer that *he* is not eligible, he replies that the law means "anyone but me." To keep this in perspective, it is perhaps relevant to point out that Charr was the beneficiary of many acts of kindness and generosity by Caucasians at crucial points in his life, and not only from Christian clergymen, a quarter from which such acts might have been expected. His sergeant, for example, encouraged him to seek naturalization, and the American Legion exerted great efforts to save his wife from deportation. The positive experiences may in his mind have greatly outweighed and overshadowed the negative.

Still, Charr's experience with racial discrimination is muted in this book. For example, an incident that he omits, but one that can be reconstructed from interviews with his children, occurred when the family moved to Portland in 1942. Charr wanted to purchase a house in a nice neighborhood, but the neighbors circulated a petition not to sell the house to him. As a result, the Charr family had to settle for a home in a less-desirable section of town. His former nationality, as noted on his naturalization certificate, was "Japanese and/or Korean," and there was considerable anti-Japanese feeling on the Pacific Coast only a few months after the Japanese attacked Pearl Harbor. Since many Americans were unable to distinguish between Japanese and Koreans, this racist incident may have had anti-Japanese overtones as well.

Nonetheless, the question remains: Does this book reveal Charr's real feelings or is it a "positive tract" that glosses over anti-Asian racism? As one specialist in Asian-American studies commented after reading Charr's book: "Charr is not a critical observer of his life. . . . His work is infused with love of the U.S. and love of his church. Of course there is nothing wrong with these emotions, but it inhibits his ability to provide the analysis that scholars would find useful."[17] To a certain extent this is true. Many first- and second-generation Asian Americans bore racism and discrimination stoically and without complaint. Indeed, Charr himself remembered when the tables were turned and American missionaries were harassed in turn-of-the-century Korea. Yet such stoicism has often been viewed critically by third-generation Asian Americans and contemporary scholars in Asian-American studies. Often active in campaigns against racism, many in these groups criticize silence in the face of outrages. Even the grandchildren of Easurk Emsen Charr were more likely to give voice to such concerns than their grandfather did.

Amanda Charr, a granddaughter of Charr, wrote a short reminiscence when she was seventeen, entitled "The Final Visit," in which she remembers her grandfather:

At the puerile age of nine, visiting my dying grandfather was almost dreaded as much as eating brussel sprouts. I was too young to understand the significance of these visits. All I ever thought about were his awful stench and senility. I now regret being so naive and immature as to ignore and be disgusted by such an incredible man. It wasn't until after his death that I started to acknowledge the fact that I didn't know my grandfather at all. He had written a published autobiography and knowing that this would be the closest to ever truly meeting my grandfather, I cracked open the book. As I read, I cried. I had uncovered the life of a man who had become my idol. His book, *The Golden Mountain*, reveals a story about a young man, nearly fifteen [*sic*], who bravely decides to discover America in search of

a life of milk and honey. The irony is that he dis-
appointingly is beleaguered by a world replete
with racism and minute opportunity for a non-
English speaking Korean immigrant. Before the
great departure, he made a promise to his mother and father: to return as soon as he could afford
to. No one imagined that the goodbyes that he
exchanged with his family would be the goodbyes forever. He simply could not afford to return
to his home while supporting a wife and three
children. When he did have enough, his parents
had already passed away. If I had the chance of
ever speaking with Easurk Emsen Charr, I would
begin by apologizing for being such a selfish and
ignorant granddaughter. I would want to speak
solely about the pain and anguish that he en-
dured in this land regarding acceptance based on
race and culture. I would ask him how he coped
with the wounding racial prejudices that he experienced and in turn ask for advice on how I could
cope with mine. I know that he would be very
hurt by the fact that racism still exists and that it
sometimes prevails in today's society. In the
book, he stated how he wished that his dear
grandchildren would never have to endure such
hatred. It would be hard telling him that his wish
is quite far from coming true. To finish off the
conversation, I would commend him on his great
bravery, diligence, and selflessness whether he
was seeing off his family in North Korea, cutting
sugar cane in Hawaii, picking grapes in California, sharing wedding vows with Grandma in Chicago, or pleading against her deportation. It
would bring me much joy to see him again for
only one minute. But, if I had too little time to

say all that I wished, I would condense it into a hug and an "I love you."[18]

* * *

The Golden Mountain was originally published in 1961 by a private publishing firm that no longer exists—a vanity press. Only a few hundred copies were printed, relegating a fascinating life history to almost complete obscurity. That Charr had to resort to self-publishing is understandable given the times. Stories such as Charr's were not in demand then because the fields of Korean studies and Asian-American studies were in their infancy. In recent years, however, interest has increased dramatically in works of this type, so it is indeed fortuitous that this book is being made available to a larger audience.

A few words are in order concerning the title of the book. Because the phrase "the golden mountain" (*chin shan* in Chinese, *kŭm san* in Korean) is usually associated with Chinese immigrants as a nickname for the United States, a subtitle has been added to identify this as a book by and about a Korean immigrant. With this one exception, not a single word of the author's has been changed. Thus the reader will note that Charr does not follow the standard McCune-Reischauer romanization system for transliterating Korean words and names into English, nor does he always follow the usual convention of placing Korean family names first. The original text has been supplemented with photographs, annotations (asterisks in the outer margins of the autobiography will alert readers to the existence of a note at the end of the book), this introduction, and an index.

Charr's book joins several related titles on early Korean immigrants. One is an account written by a woman who was five years old in 1905 when she was brought to the United States by her family. That account, written by Mary Paik Lee and edited by Sucheng Chan, is entitled *Quiet Odyssey: A Pioneer Korean Woman in America* (Seattle: University of Washington Press, 1990) and deals almost entirely with Lee's experience in the United States. Charr's book delves more deeply into his life prior to leaving Korea; indeed, more than a third of the story deals with his life in Korea from birth through age ten. The second account, by Younghill Kang, is *East Goes West* (Chicago: Follett, 1965), a more literary autobiographical account of a Korean who arrived in the United States as one of a small contingent of students and political refugees and who was thus different from the seven thousand agricultural laborers who arrived at the turn of the century. Readers will also be interested in the two autobiographical books by Peter Hyun: *Mansei! The Making of a Korean American* (1986) and *In the New World: The Making of a Korean American* (1995), both published by the University of Hawaii Press. Other titles that might be of interest include Younghill Kang's *The Grass Roof* (book 2) (Chicago: Follett, 1966), which contains autobiographical information, and No-Yong Park's *Chinaman's Chance: An Autobiography* (Boston: Meador, 1940), about a Korean who was raised in Manchuria as a Chinese. Il-Han New's *When I Was a Boy in Korea* (Boston: D. Lothrop, 1928) and Induk Pahk's *The Cock Still Crows* (New York: Vantage Press, 1977) are other books worthy of notice.

After his book was published, Charr sent complimentary copies to friends, relatives, and important political figures, including Harry Truman, Dwight Eisenhower, and Hubert Humphrey. He donated fifty copies to the American Legion in Oregon, twenty-five copies to the Presbyterian church, and fifty copies to Park College and its library. He also sold his book in the Interior Building where he worked in Portland. Lacking the resources of a major press, Charr essentially had to be his own agent.

Later in life, his two main interests remained Park College and the American Legion. He returned to Park in 1963 for his fortieth reunion and donated annually and generously to its alumni fund. He also remained an active member of the Portland American Legion Post Number One. Although he never managed to return to his Korean homeland, he maintained a connection with Korea through the Foster Parents Plan, which helped find homes for Korean orphans in the 1960s.

On December 30, 1964, Charr retired from the U.S. civil service. Two years later, in 1966, his wife and son moved to a better neighborhood in Portland, though Charr continued to live in the old house. Twelve years later, at age eighty-four, he fell out of a tree in his backyard while picking fruit and was found unconscious. His family believes that this injury hastened the onset of Alzheimer's disease. Charr was moved to a nursing home in 1978, where he lived for the last eight years of his life. He died at the Portland Veterans Administration Hospital on May 13, 1986. His wife, Evelyn, preceded him in death in June 1984. Both are buried in Willamette National Cemetery in Portland, Oregon.

Notes

I would like to acknowledge Carolyn Elwess, Director of Alumni Relations at Park College; Harold Smith, Park College Archivist; the children of Easurk Emsen Charr: Professor Anna Pauline Charr Kim and her husband, An-

drew Kim, in Chicago, and Dr. Philip Y. Charr in Portland, Oregon. I conducted interviews with Dr. Charr on
August 15, 1992, and with Professor Kim on February
23, 1992, and February 14, 1993. Both were generous in
sharing their time, their memories, their documents, and
their photographs. I also appreciated the hospitality of
Richard and Dess Babal while doing research for this
volume in Portland. The introduction benefitted from
the insightful comments and suggestions of Roger
Daniels of the University of Cincinnati and Charles
McClain of the University of California at Berkeley. I
would also like to acknowledge the University of Kansas, whose invitation to teach Korean history during the
spring semesters of 1992 and 1993 allowed me to under-
take some of the research at nearby Park College. Finally, I would like to thank the Faculty Personnel Committee of St. Norbert College, which provided me with a
sabbatical leave and funding from the Faculty Personnel
Fund.

1. Readers who want to delve more deeply into those
aspects are directed to Wayne Patterson, *The Korean
Frontier in America: Immigration to Hawaii, 1896–1910*
(1988; rpt., Honolulu: University of Hawaii Press, 1994).
2. Readers interested in Allen's long career in Korea
should consult Fred Harvey Harrington's pioneering
work, *God, Mammon and the Japanese: Dr. Horace N. Allen
and Korean-American Relations, 1884–1905* (Madison: University of Wisconsin Press, 1966). For Allen and the issue of immigration, see Wayne Patterson, "Sugar-Coated
Diplomacy: Horace Allen and Korean Immigration to
Hawaii, 1902–1905," *Diplomatic History* 3, no. 1 (Winter
1979): 19–38.
3. Kojong (1852–1919) reigned from 1864 to 1907.
His death in 1919 helped spark the anti-Japanese March
First Movement.
4. Nash served two terms as governor of Ohio, from
1899 to 1903.
5. The missionary was Sallie Swallen, posted to the

Presbyterian Mission in P'yŏngyang. See Sallie Swallen
to Jennie Ashbrook, Oct. 9, 1903, Mrs. William L. (Sallie) Swallen Letters, 1901–3, Samuel H. Moffett Documents, no. 6 (1890–1903). In the possesion of the Reverend Samuel A. Moffett, Seoul.

6. "A Korean Student Writes," Park College *Record*,
11 and 12 (Mar. 12 and 19, 1921).

7. Walter M. Giffard to William G. Irwin, May 12,
1903, Walter M. Giffard Papers, University of Hawaii
Archives.

8. The federal judge in question was Morris M. Es-
tee. An account of this episode can be found in Patterson, *The Korean Frontier,* 86–90.

9. For a thorough treatment of this issue, see Roger
Daniels, *The Politics of Prejudice: The Anti-Japanese Movement in California and the Struggle for Japanese Exclusion,*
2d ed. (Berkeley: University of California Press, 1977).

10. For more information on the Mexican affair, see
Wayne Patterson, "The Early Years of Korean Immigration to Mexico: A View from Japanese and Korean
Sources," *Seoul Journal of Korean Studies* 6 (1993): 87–
104.

11. See Charr's Enlistment Record under "Remarks,"
on the reverse of his discharge papers (in the possession
of Anna Charr Kim).

12. Homer Hulbert (1863–1949) was a missionary,
educator, editor, publisher, linguist, publicist, and sometime diplomat who lived in Korea for twenty-one years
(1886–1907).

13. Wallace Edgar to Carolyn Elwess, director of
Alumni Relations at Park College, Mar. 21, 1992. It was
also at this time that Charr added Emsen to his name
because, according to his children, he thought it sounded vaguely Scandinavian in origin. So by his twenties, he
was known as Easurk Emsen Charr, and from that time
on signed his name E. Emsen Charr.

14. That is, many Korean single men who came to
the United States made arrangements for a "picture
bride" to be sent from Korea after an exchange of pho-

tos and passage money through a go-between. Indeed, this system prevailed from 1910 to 1924 when it was ended by the Immigration Act of 1924.

15. This letter is in the possession of Charr's children.

16. In 1935 Congress passed a law, 49 STAT 397, allowing naturalization of aliens otherwise ineligible for citizenship who had served in the armed forces between April 6, 1917, and November 11, 1918. The major push for the law came from Japanese Americans. The American Legion, as Charr's book makes clear, was also a strong supporter of the measure.

17. This assessment comes from a report provided by an anonymous reader as part of the manuscript review process prior to publication of this reprint edition.

18. Amanda Charr's essay is in the possession of her father, Philip Y. Charr.

Preface

This is my life story, of deep interest and of wide experience in the two different worlds—the very old and the very new. A former missionary to my native land once suggested to me that I should tell the thrilling story of the immigrant lad whose wonderful dream came true in more ways than he had ever dreamed. Hence, the life story of a Korean-American.

At the turn of the century, during the Russo-Japanese war, in 1904, I left the ancient "Hermit Kingdom" and sailed westward in quest of the BEAUTIFUL COUNTRY, poetically called "The Land of the Golden Mountain," and better known as the home of the Statue of Liberty, proclaiming, "Liberty Enlightening the World." Indeed, this is the New Promised Land that I found flowing with milk of wisdom and honey of freedom. I am exceedingly glad that I came to America, and I am humbly proud that I am an American citizen. May God bless America, my country, my home!

E.E.C.

Acknowledgments

Acknowledgments of my sincere appreciation for their kindly assistance given in preparing the manuscript for publication: to Prof. W. F. Sanders, Dean Emeritus of Park College; to Mrs. Betty Pearce, formerly of Soil Conservation Service; and to Mrs. Freda-Bobbs Adams, Miss Helena Rupert and Mrs. Catherine McNealy of the Bonneville Power Administration.

The Golden Mountain

1
War Refugees
in the Mountains

It was during the Sino-Japanese War of 1894, when *
the battle was being waged in Pyeng-An-Do, the northwestern province of Korea, centering around the
ancient capital city of Pyeng Yang, that my father's
ancestral home was broken up and scattered. Fleeing
the scene of battle between the two contending forces
of foreign powers close to his native village, in Sun-
chun, north of Pyeng-Yang, my father, as a youth,
went north to find a temporary shelter there among
the strangers, while his two older brothers sought
refuge among the proverbial mountains to the east, in
the district of Mangsan, taking along with them their
families, including my grandmother whom I later met
and loved most dearly.

As a refugee among the strangers in the northern-
most district on Yalu River, bordering Manchuria,
called Kang-gay, or River Border, my father found
favor and married my mother who gave me birth to
this world. In the meantime, my two uncles, who had
fled to the Great White Mountains, located in an ideal
place of peace and safety from the ravages of war
and seclusion from the outside world—the life of a
perfect hermit in the "Hermit Kingdom."

The one thing which I can remember most clearly

now is that, as a child, I was being carried upon my
father's back, mile after mile, day after day, over the
mountains and across the rivers we traveled south-
eastward, and my mother carrying a bundle on her
head, trudging along behind. It must have been a long
and wearisome journey over the good roads and bad,
trails and byways, and across the many streams, some
with only stepping stones, some with single log bridges,
and some with no bridges at all.

At last we had come to our journey's end! We
arrived at my grandmother's home, high and deep in
the bosom of the Tai-bak-san or the Great White
Mountains. My father must have told me of my
grandmother, how wonderful and how kindly she was
to him as he was the youngest son of hers, and now
how much more so she would be to me as the first born
son of her youngest son she had not yet seen. Of
course, I was then too young and too small to understand him.

Indeed, as soon as the war was over, my grandmother had sent for me and my parents to come to
see her, to live with her, and to love her and be loved
by her. And, now, here I was on my grandma's lap!
No doubt there must have been a great feast, cele-
brating the family reunion at which I myself must
have been the hero and the particular object for rejoicing by my grandmother!

The house in which my grandmother lived was the
only human habitation there in the mountain which
was surrounded by still higher and rugged mountains
on all sides. The place was called Jargen Goodee, or
Small Hollow, situated on a small depression on the
slope of the mountain facing south and a small valley
down below. It must have been built by my second
oldest uncle, whom I called Middle Uncle, with the

help of the three oldest cousins of mine, the sons of my oldest uncle whom I always called Big Uncle.

It was a big house built solidly for a permanent residence. The house had five large rooms in a row, with paper-windowed doors in front and back. The roof was covered with "chung-suk", or bluestone slate, quarried from the spot, like the timber that was cut and used in building. Under another roof in the front of the house there were a cow shed, a pig sty, a chicken perch, and a dog house in separate compartments, but all in one structure, strongly caged in, with a long narrow courtyard separating it from the main building. Both the buildings were enclosed by a strong, inter-woven fence from fifteen to twenty feet high of which closely placed fence post tops had sharp pointed spikes made of both hard wood and iron to keep the tigers out by days as well as by night.

It was a big house, indeed, yet it was not quite large enough for all of us. There were already fifteen persons in the house, including a lady visitor, from Pyeng Yang, who was also a war refugee. My Big Uncle and aunt had four sons, the three oldest newly-married, and a daughter. My Middle Uncle and aunt had one of their two daughters living with them, and my grandmother. And our coming had added three more souls into the already over-crowded house.

And, how did they manage to accommodate the eighteen persons in a five-room dwelling? It was a big housing problem even in those by-gone days of long ago. But my carpenter uncle solved that prob-lem. He began to partition off the large rooms, one by one, until he made the five-room house into a ten-room one when we moved in, thus giving a room to each couple in the family.

Then, too, both my uncles had many of their friends

come visiting them from time to time. When they came, they usually stayed several days. And whenever they found there were not enough rooms to go around, it was customary for the female members of the household to share their rooms together, making more rooms available for the menfolk and their visiting friends. Sleeping on the matted floor, as is the custom in Oriental countries, and shoving over a little, every inch and foot of the floor space could be utilized at will. And, did anybody complain? No, never. "The more the merrier" was the right slogan for them all in that tiger-infested lonely mountain recess. Yes, they, and myself included, had fled from the fearful war to the nest of the ferocious tigers of the mountains.

Tigers' nest it was, indeed. Why, only a short time after we arrived there a tiger had jumped in over that high spiked fence one night and carried off the only and the last dog there was left in the house. It was a giant of a dog, too. Poor dog! It must have been playing outside the cage, depending too much, perhaps, on that high fence as did the Chinese on their Great Wall. The year before, on one summer day, yes, in daylight, a tiger had come and killed a calf feeding out in the stockyard while everybody was out in the fields down in the valley. Only the bones of the poor calf and a length of the rope with which it was tied to a stake were found left behind!

In the middle of one night I was awakened by the report of a gunshot. Sensing that a tiger had jumped in over the fence, since suddenly there was a noise and confusion in the cow shed and the pig pen, my oldest cousin had grabbed a gun, cocked the gun, and fired a shot through the paper window in order to scare the prowling beast away. We had three matchlocks in the house all the time, besides the one owned by my Middle Uncle who was also a huntsman and was away on a hunting trip at the time. And, one day, a giant eagle swooped down from his usual perch on a topless old pine tree on a distant cliff into our front yard and carried off a puppy dog which was given to us by one of my uncle's visiting friends only a short time before.

The house was well-supplied with fresh water gushing out of the spring at a cozy nook, at the farther end of the stockyard, and also with cereals, vegetables, fruits and meat. Barley, corn, buckwheat and potatoes were grown down in the valley by my cousins. They also grew a few rows of cabbage and turnips for winter pickles that every family must put up in the fall. More than that was not necessary, for kindly nature had provided them aplenty with all kinds of edible plants—herbs, sprouts, shoots, nuts, grapes and fruits all over the valley and the mountain sides, more than we could take care of. I used to follow my cousins out hunting these wild fruits and pitch pine which we used for matches in the house and for torches outside at night. And, wasn't I afraid of tigers out in the woods? Oh, yes, but my cousins always carried guns and spears with them every time we went out, firing a shot or two as a warning to any tiger that might be sneaking around. We were always vigilant and prepared.

It was, therefore, a very good hunting ground for my huntsman uncle who was very fond of big game hunting. From late fall, when the snow began to fall, all through the winter, and up to late spring until all the snow melted down from the mountains, was open hunting season for him. And he was a hunter of no mean proportion. He had the best hunting outfit as well as being one of the best marksmen among his

half-dozen companions gathered from distant points
of the great mountain range.

He was then a handsome man, tall and well-built,
of some thirty years, I should judge, with a black
mustache. A black scarf was tied around his head
over his top-knot, a leather belt worn around his middle, over the roomy native costume in huntsman's dark
brown from which hung a ten-inch knife in rawhide
sheath by his side, a powder horn, a bagful of fuse, a
small pouchful of round bullets he himself manufac-
tured at home, and a matchlock, with all the brass and
nickel trimmings, slung over his shoulder, made him
look like one of the five hundred huntsmen who were
called up to Seoul by the king to keep away the "Oce-
anic" invaders, (the French in 1866 and the American expedition in 1871), from the Kang-wha forts on
* the Yellow Sea coast.

Several times during the season he and his companions would come home loaded with deer and
pheasants which they killed. At night, there would
be a big feast, eating, drinking, playing cards, and
my uncle would relate to the rest of the family all
the adventures and thrilling experiences which he and
his friends had had during their hunt. Had any of
those many tigers been killed, too? Sure enough. I
saw them many a time. That is, the skins of leopards
that were spotted, and those of the tigers that were
striped which they had brought home with them. No
one ever cared for their carcasses, though. The tiger
killed for food, and man killed it for its skin.

Honestly, that was about the closest I had ever
come to anything of a tiger in that tiger-infested place
where I spent my childhood days. As soon as a tiger
had been killed, it was flayed, and the skin was taken
to the magistrate of the district who paid a handsome

reward to the marksman for destroying the beast which was a great menace to the people and their cattle in his district.

I remember seeing one of the huntsman friends of my uncle's who had only his left hand. He was a dead shot, I heard them say. He lost his right hand in tiger's jaw when he was tussling with it when an accident happened to his gun and he missed his aim somehow. And, just for that he vowed to kill more tigers, all that he could, to avenge his trigger finger which was lost along with his right hand. He learned to use his left hand even more expertly and deftly than he did his right hand. He was known as the "Killer King" of the "Mountain King," meaning the ferocious tiger, and was rewarded and decorated many times by the magistrate of Mang-san, I heard them say. He lived on the government bounties.

Going back to the story, they would enjoy eating at their feast, eating the favorite dish of buckwheat noodles with pickles and fried pheasant meat so finely chopped up and strongly seasoned, which was, according to their taste and tradition, the best dish in the world. Really, that was the national dish, at least, in that part of the country, then as now. That was my favorite dish, too. I would awaken in the middle of the night to devour a man-size bowl of them. The noodles were a sort of panacea for all my ailments! Whenever I was sick, the noodles were the first and last thing I could think of, and a bowl of noodles seemed to have cured me of every sickness except a sore eye which an American missionary doctor in Pyeng Yang treated.

And all the venison we had stored up in the house! The meat taken from at least three or four deer at a time was sliced into fine strips like bacon, salted and dried in the sun on the slate roof, or over the fireplace. My dear grandmother used to broil it for me over the charcoal fire at night, and I certainly loved to eat it. It makes my mouth water to think of it even now. Yes, the venison tasted so good to me and my grandmother was so kind to me. Indeed, she was the grandest grandmother who ever lived, and she certainly knew how to cook the venison for me and to tell me the most fascinating fairy tales!

2
Man of the Soil

"Man is ruled from the soil;
Sow and reap by his toil.
The south rows' laden grain
I'll gather in again."
—From the *Book of Thousand Characters*.

My father was a farmer from his boyhood and had never gone to school as did Big Uncle who was a learned scholar and traveler. In this respect, he was like my Middle Uncle who learned carpentry instead of going to school. In those days, only boys were sent to school in order to learn Chinese literature . . . the classics, history, and poetry. My father and my Middle Uncle were both ignorant of Chinese learning. I never asked to know how it came about in that way, but my belief is that my grandfather had died rather early in life, for I had never seen him, and there was no one to send the younger sons to school, nor anyone else to support the family. That is how they had started their respective trades, one as a carpenter and another as a farmer.

Being driven away from his native village by the war, my father went North and found a landowner who hired him as a farm hand. He was an honest and conscientious man, as I have known him to be all his life. And, consequently, he was trusted and loved by his employer. Soon the man gave him his daughter . . . his only child—for a wife, making him a "live-with" son-in-law. That is why I was born in my mother's home and lived there until my parents took me to my grandmother's house where we lived for some time before moving to my father's new farm in the lowlands.

Now my father, a farmer, with a little savings of his own, wanted to buy a farm in the lowlands to the west, not far from my grandmother's home. And he did find such a one right at the foot of the mountain and just across the river, about three mountain miles down from the "Big House." An Elder's house is so-called whether really big or small. In this case, though, the "Big House" was really big.

The farm was situated on the west bank of the river, which is the north fork of the famous Dai-Dong-kang that flows through the city of Pyeng Yang. This river valley, lying between the two chains of mountains on either side of it, was rather narrow, as it was less than a mile in width at the widest point where my father's farm was located. The fertile fields in this valley had long been in cultivation, and the soil on his farm was rich and good. "All's well when soil's well" to a farmer. Wheat, corn, millet, beans, sesame, potatoes, and other crops thrived; kitchen vegetables grew in the garden just outside the gate, and the summer squash vines covered up the fence all around the house.

Our thatch-roofed house on the farm, facing north, located some 500 feet from the river, was really snug and comfortable. There were two rooms and a kitchen, all in a row. In winter, the house was heated by flues beneath the floor which drew the heat from the hearth in the kitchen at one end of the house, and emitted the smoke out the chimney at the opposite end of the house. In summer, cooking was done outside in order to keep cool inside.

We had a barn in front of the house, too. Half of

it was for our cow, and the other half was used as a
store room. We also had a dog which was kept with
the cow at one corner for our protection. Even down
here on the lowlands, the nocturnal prowlers, the
tigers, were seen abroad at nights, especially in winter,
when their food was scarce in the mountains. Their
unmistakable tracks in the snow betrayed their presence. So here, too, we put up a high fence around the
house, and the cow shed was locked and bolted at
night.

And the worst menace here, as I remember it, was
the weasels that often killed our chickens. My in-
genious father trapped some of them. He had a two-
fold purpose in doing so, one was to get rid of them
and another to use their hair in making brush pens
for me. He couldn't do that himself, of course, but
then there were brush-makers going around from
school to school, from time to time, and my father
had them give me so many brushes for each weasel
tail offered him. In that way, I was very well supplied
with brushes. Weasel hair is called "chung-mo," or
blue hair, the best that there was for small, fine
brushes, while "whang-mo," or brown hair of fox or
cow was used in making large brushes.

A cousin of my father's moved in and lived nearby.
He was a tall man with fiery eyes, who brewed rice
wine in his courtyard for a living. I called him New
Uncle. It was he who brought my mother's widowed
mother home lately. The house beyond that of my
New Uncle was a large tile-roofed mansion of the
well-to-do gentry who owned most of the landed property in the valley. The owner, called Kim Gamyuk,
or Superintendent Kim, had two sons, one married. I
used to go up there and play in his garden which was
full of beautiful peonies, and greatly admired his fine

horses. His youngest son liked me very much—so much, that he promised to give me a horse to ride as soon as I was big enough. We were good friends, indeed, he and I, until a regrettable thing happened between his people and mine, some time later.

Yes, I had to move down to my father's new house. Nevertheless, I remained with my grandmother at the Big House until I was big enough to go to a village school some distance down the other side of the river. They say I started school when I was only six years old, and began to learn Chinese, which was very difficult, right from the start. The first reader I studied was called *"Chun-ja-mun,"* or the *"Book of a Thousand Characters."*

There was a remarkable story attached to this primer. Ju Heung was the name of the author, a Chinese courtier and scholar, who was being falsely accused of a treasonable crime which he was said to have committed, and was about to be executed. And because he was an honorable man and a famed scholar, the emperor-king was petitioned by a great number of men of letters and by his own cabinet ministers, that a reprieve be granted him on one condition, that if he could compose a book of rhymes of a thousand characters picked at random, in one night's time, he would be pardoned, but if he failed, he was doomed to die a traitor's death the following morning at sunrise.

He was a scholarly enough man to do it, but in doing so with such strain and stress imposed upon him, his raven-black hair turned completely white overnight, it was said. And that is why the book was also known as *"Bak-su-mun,"* or the *"Book of White Head."*

But why was I required to learn Chinese, which was so hard to acquire, instead of the native Korean alphabet, which was as easy as it was natural? Well, it was for the same reason that European and American scholars still study Greek and Latin for those roots which make up the important part of their languages. To the Koreans, as well as to the Japanese who also have their own written and spoken language, Chinese is a classical tongue, and the verbs and most of the nouns, especially the abstract nouns and the names of persons and of places and all the official documents were written in that language; only the popular story books were written in Korean. But with the coming of Christianity, this old system was changed. All the Christian literature was translated first into pure Korean, and later on some of them were printed in mixed script of Korean and Chinese, as was done with the secular books and magazines. Chinese, therefore, is the integral part of their language and the vocabulary of the learned persons. An educated Korean can communicate with either a Chinese or a Japanese in written Chinese, although he understands not a word of either of their spoken languages.   *

The teacher always had a bundle of sapling sticks standing in the corner near his seat, ready to whip the boy on the calf of his bare leg for tardiness and misconduct in and out of school. As a matter of fact, learning manners was of primary importance. "Sun-nei-hu-hak," or "manners first, studies next," was the basic principle in the educational system. For a well-behaved person is a well-educated person, and vice versa.

I was never whipped, though, either for misconduct or for failing in my studies. Indeed, I was a well-behaved and studious boy to tell the truth. Usually I came out at the top of my class with coveted prizes from the general examinations given at the end of every season or year, or at the time I had finished a text book sooner than others with excellent grades. Usually a prize consisted of a ream of paper, which was highly valued in that mountainous district; a set of brush pens, large and small; and a few cakes of best-quality black ink.

3

The Spirit Worshippers

"King Yo went to Hwa, and a man of Hwa said,
'I pray thee, O thou holy man, let the people have
longevity, riches, and many sons.' And Yo said, 'Wish
them not. For many sons, many fears; rich, much work;
long life, long abused.' "—*History of China,* First Book.

My Big Uncle was a scholar. Of three brothers, he
alone was educated in the Chinese classics, and having
passed the government examination, he attained the
title of "Cho-sey," equivalent to the college degree of
Bachelor of Arts.

He was a poong-soo or geomancer by profession,
and travelled all over the 338 goon or districts of the
original eight provinces of the country. For that reason, he was called "Charr-Pal-do," or Eight Provinces
Charr, the Charr Poong-soo. But more generally he
was called Charr Chosey, always the surname preceding the title and the given name. My ancestors had
their birthplace in Yun-an district in the Yellow Sea
province, north of the Capital Province where Seoul
is located and south of my home province of Pyen-
an-do with its capital at Pyeng Yang, my hometown.

In the country where ancestor worship was a religion, the science of selecting the most desirable site
for a burial ground for one's deceased parents or
grandparents was indeed in demand. And a geomancer
was an honored guest and was well-paid by well-to-do
families who required his services. My Big Uncle
was well-versed in the science of geomancy and was an
expert diviner of grave sites which would insure the

finest, the cleanest, the driest, and the safest depth of the earth where the remains of the departed shall find rest in peace and comfort. And by the virtues of that state of happiness that had been secured for the deceased, his or her children and their children's children shall be blessed. As a reward, they shall receive one or more of the five primary happinesses: Longevity, riches, fame, honor, and posterity; especially along the male line.

Such a highly-prized cemetery must be one that had a gently sloping mountain or hill as a background, a stream or river in the foreground, and on either side protecting arms or ramparts. That would be the general topography. The more immediate surroundings of the tomb should have the four great guardians —the Blue Dragon on the left, the White Tiger on the right, the Red Bird in front, and the Black Giant in the rear. Usually, carved stone images of the guardians were placed around the mound to insure protection against the elements and evil spirits. They were also symbolic of the four directions—east, west, south, and north respectively, and of the four seasons of the year as well—spring, summer, autumn and winter, in that order. I had seen two famous royal tombs, one of King Kija just outside the Chilsungmun, or Seven-Star gate at the north end of the city of Pyeng Yang whose capital it was; and another that of Tong-Myeng Wang, or the King East Light, of Kokuryu dynasty, at Moo-jin, some twenty miles east of Pyeng Yang. They were impressive enough to be kings' tombs, indeed. They were majestic and steeped in tradition. Evidently all private tombs follow the pattern of these and other royal tombs.

My Big Uncle, with the magnetic compass in his left hand and a magic wand in his right hand, could

tell you all there was to know about the geomantic
science. In lines and figures he would point out to you
that the mound or hill on which you stood resembled
the general shape of a tortoise, one of the Four Sacred
Creatures; therefore, it held the potency of longevity.
Pointing at a hollow spot at the base of the mountain
yonder, which resembled a scoop or a vessel, he would
tell you that it would be a fine burial ground for someone whose posterity would enjoy immense riches. And
of that flat-topped foothill among the pine trees yonder, halfway between the steep mountain above and
the lowlands below, with a stream in front of it, he
would point out to you saying that whosoever's body
be buried there would surely find rest in peace, and
by virtue of it, out of his descendants would come
three generations of prime ministers and six generations of the king's cabinet ministers in succession. With
his magic wand waving toward that prominent point
on the tableland overlooking the rice fields to your
right, he would prophesy that by virtue of having
buried one's dead there, some day soon out of the
next generation a man would come forth to claim his
fame and honor as a scholar or a statesman, or both.

Thus prophesying future for the virtuous sons and
grandsons and preaching the merits of the geomantic
science, of which he was a master, and the mystic power
and the magic influence which the science possessed,
my Big Uncle traveled the length and breadth of the
peninsula. He was constantly abroad on his travels,
and he came home only a few times in the year, but
he never missed his mother's birthday and his father's
memorial day. Going from place to place, he became
acquainted with the life and customs of the people of
the different provinces and localities which were
slightly in variance, owing to the lack of transportation

facilities and to the acquired habits of the majority
of the people who lived and died generation after
generation in the same hamlets, in the same districts
and provinces for thousands of years. He became
acquainted with scholars and officials and people with
means and influence. So he had come to know people
and places everywhere.

Especially was this true in his own district and
province. I knew that he was a good friend of Kim
Doong-goon and his brother Kim Gam-yuk, both high
officials at the seat of the local government of Mangsan, and Kim Jusa, the Secretary of State of Pyeng-an
Province, who lived in Pyeng Yang. The wife of the
Secretary was the lady visitor who had come to stay
with us at the Big House during the Chinese-Japanese
War.

Now, selecting grave sites for others all his life,
it seemed to have occurred to my Big Uncle that he
should do the same for his own parents, like the virtuous son that he was. His father's tomb was in the
district of Yung-heung, near the village of Yang-jang-
dong, in the northeastern province of Hamkyung, just
over on the other side of his mountain home. Evidently, that site must have looked good when he selected it. But now he found a better-looking site than
that, and decided to "chun-jahng" or move it to
another place right near our house.

And what a big fight we had with Kim Gamyuk
and his son, our closest neighbors, over a burial place!
Kim Gamyuk had his father's tomb on the mountainside near our corn field, and my Big Uncle, the expert
geomancer, being so covetous of the grave site, transferred his long-dead father's bones from over the
Great White mountains and buried them right close
to Kim's tomb by force in broad daylight. Nuk-jahng,

or cemetery invasion, was considered as a major crime, and a major cause for many bloody feuds between the parties involved in that land of the spirit worshippers.

Man for man, in a hand-to-hand fight we would outnumber them by seven to two, and the high officials of the district government, who were present, were my uncle's personal friends and legal, social, and political allies. Realizing the situation, the Kims dared not oppose us in the open, so no actual fighting resulted at the time. My Big Uncle won the burial war easily, but my father almost lost the battle for his life in that war. One early morning, shortly afterward, while my father was out weeding a ditch close to New Uncle's house, Kim Gamyuk's eldest son sneaked up from behind and dealt a blow with a rock on my father's skull and stole away. Luckily, however, my New Uncle, who happened to be up early that morning, heard my father's cry for help and saw the assailant stealing away. Dashing down to the ditch, he rescued my father and brought him home on his back. For over three months, my father was critically ill, his life hanging in balance, and there were ominous signs of real trouble brewing in the air. We were so worried, especially my mother and my grandmother, and I was really frightened.

But our worries were soon to be over as my father began to recover. It makes me wonder if any of the old superstitious folk imagined that it was the manifestation of powers of the spirit of their long-dead father's bones just buried on that mountainside that had so readily performed such a miracle in restoring the life of the virtuous son that my father was, rather than due to the virtue of the cure-all herbs that my Big Uncle had administered to him. At any rate, my father's condition had turned for the better, and in another three months, he was completely restored to normal health. Wasn't I happy! And wasn't everybody else happy! And the ever-so gracious and kind-hearted grandmother of mine was so very happy, that she persuaded her three sons to forget any idea of seeking vengeance, but to make peace with the Kims if they were really virtuous sons trying to make their parents happy in life as well as in death, and reasoning with them that they were the offenders in the first place, and, therefore, were responsible for all that had happened.

Obeying their mother's wishes and guided by their better judgment, they made peace with Kim Gamyuk at a banquet prepared for the occasion in front of our house on a September afternoon, with Kim Doong-goon of the district magistrate's office as a mediator. Kim Gamyuk was invited to this outdoor feast of peace, and the statesman-like Kim Doong-goon received him cordially, expressing his pleasure in participating in a friendly gathering of the old neighbors together. Filling up the cups in front of each man at the table with the rice wine plentifully supplied by my New Uncle, he proposed a toast:

"Drink, my friends, drink.
Let us all drink.
Let me be a friend
True to the end."

Overjoyed in thinking of the restoration of peace among good old neighbors, Kim Gamyuk, himself, re-filling each cup to the brim, and then lifting up his cup of white wine, said:

"Happy is the man
Who makes others happy.
To have peace is happiness . . .
You and yours blessed be."

And spontaneously, my Big Uncle arose from his
seat holding up his cup, and clicking it with that of
Kim Gamyuk's, replied:

"What I've done I regret,
What you've done I'll forget.
Our fathers yonder rest in peace.
Let us too have our peace.
Blessed alike their spirits be,
Blessed alike their children be!"

And the two men were locked in embrace, and cried
with joy and laughed through tears. Looking from
a distance, as my cousins and I and the womenfolk
were not allowed to sit with the elders, according to
the custom of the land, I thought they looked very
funny. But I was really happy, too.

4
The Legend of Prince Jung

Now it can be told. Now it can be told that my Big Uncle was a member of the Dong-Hak-Dang (and who wasn't?), a revolutionary party professing the overthrow of the corrupt and incompetent government of the Yi dynasty. Such being its objective, and in order to carry on the movement unsuspected and unmolested by the government, it had stood behind the curtain of a religious cult called Dong-Hak, or the Cult of the East, versus the Cult of the West, meaning Christianity.

It was made up of the three prevailing religions of the land, Confucianism, Buddhism and Taoism. Buddhism, which was the state religion during the Wang dynasty of Koryu, (hence Korea), preceding that of the ruling sovereign at the time, was a religion for the philosophically minded. Confucianism, the teachings of the great sage of China, was a religion chiefly for the ruling class society, while Taoism, with its practice in conjuring up magic powers, was the closest ally of the old native religion of Spirit Worship, or Shintoism.

Down through the centuries, these separate cults or religions have been blended together into a sort of an amalgam of religions, so that it was really a difficult thing for a common man to point out which was which. Besides, the people themselves believed and practiced the essential parts of all three of them and did not care to distinguish which was which. For to them there was some good in all three of them, and all of them were recognized as their own by now. And, that being the case, why not just combine them all into one and call it Dong-Hak? Precisely, that was the idea, and a bright one at that. And to unite the people, unite the religions which they believed in!

In Dong-Hak were represented the scholars of the school of Confucianism, the philosophic monks of Buddhism and the mystic confounders of Taoism. Together with the sorcerers and geomancers of the Spirit worshippers and the followers of each cult, the common people were all combined into one, and there was the whole thing in a nutshell. And how fast the movement grew! It grew like the green things in the river valley in summer time and its followers multiplied like the waters in a flood season. In two decades it had grown up to be the greatest compact organization of the common people ever formed in the land. Its organization was called the Dong-Hak-dang (dang or party).

Dong-Hak had started soon after Catholicism had made its inroads into the anti-foreign kingdom and was being persecuted by the royal decrees, fobidding Occidental foreigners and their religion which they tried to propagate in that Hermit Kingdom. And, in the heat of persecution of the foreign religion, the Dong-Hak had its fine chance to grow and prosper under the cloak of being a native religion.

The Dong-Hak-dang's places of meeting and worship were found, invariably, in the most secluded spots in the mountains, like the Buddhist monasteries, and chanting like the Buddhist monks, praying like the Spirit Worshippers and lecturing like the Confucian scholars, the new native religion spread like wild fire into the remotest corners of the peninsula. Inner circle was formed around the head of the cult called Do-ju. Provincial and local headquarters were established. Membership dues were collected in the form of three spoonsful of rice each day. Resident and itinerant teachers or propagandists were at work making new converts to the new born religion.

It had its beginnings in the South, and soon it had spread throughout the land. Its membership had reached to the aggregate of a hundred thousand within a few years' time.

Like John the Baptist before Christ, the Dong-Hak promised the coming of Prince Jung-Do-Ryung who was to become the founder of an enlightened new dynasty of new order superseding the Yi dynasty of decadence and incompetency.

Near the Big House there was a secret place where my Big Uncle had the rendezvous with his Dong-Hak teachers whom I had often seen coming and going. It was a little shack built under an overhanging cliff just around the next turn of the big gully to the east of the house, about a mile away. I saw some of those strange looking persons come visiting with my Big Uncle and disappearing together into that secret hideout place for days and nights at a time. And, weren't we youngsters curious about these comings and goings! We wanted to have a "looksee." So one day three of us little ones started out, following a trail leading to that out-of-the-way place to find out what was going on over there.

What a nice little cottage we found there hidden among the trees and brushwood, so quiet and so secluded a place where one could make all the noise he wanted to and not be heard, and where one could plot a rebellion and not be detected! But, no such thing was being done there, however. All we heard of what they were doing inside there was chanting the Dong-Hak creed, "Si-tien-ju jo-wha-jung, yung-sei-bul-mang man-sa-ji; ji-ki-gum-ju won-y dai-kang." Translated, "Believe in the heavenly lord the creator, forgetting never and knowing all things; self-denial, temperance, and shun foreignism; that is the great doctrine."

One can readily see that it contains the Biblical terms of Lord, the Creator, showing that the creed was influenced by the very foreignism which it professed to abhor. Their general headquarters was established in Bak-San, or the White Mountain, in the southernmost province of Chullado and called it The Salvation Institute.

And, why should there have been any revolution at all? The reason is simple. When the leaves of trees stir and the surface of the water agitated, we know that the wind is blowing there. So with revolution. Revolution is the result of misrule. Where there is misrule there will be revolution. The same was true in the Land of Morning Calm at the time of which I am writing. Political intrigues were going on within the palace gates in Seoul, the capital city, accompanied by murder, banishment and confiscation. Official jobs were bought and sold, bribery went rampant, life and property of the people were taken outright by the corrupt officials on one pretext or another. Rival factions were formed in the ruling class society, such as No-ron (Older Set), So-ron (Younger Set), and *
Dong-in (Easterner), Su-in (Westerner), Nam-in (Southerner), Buk-in (Northerner).

The people in general were divided into two main groups of Yang-ban or the aristocrats and Sang-nom or the commoners, with the former licensed to mistreat the latter who had no place to go for redress. The royal household itself, was divided into two opposing parties. The young king and his father, the regent prince Tai-won-goon, on one side, and the queen and her kinsmen of the Min clan on the other. The former was known for a time as the Progressive Party backed by Japan, and the latter, the Conservative Party, influenced by China. And here entered the third party, which was the Dong-Hak-Dang of the common people in the great majority.

There were some progressive leaders, among them were Kim-Ok-gune and Park yung-heo, who advocated enlightenment in government policies, laws and institutions of new order in governing the people along the lines of modern civilization. And in order to do this, they had advised the king to encourage modern education exemplified by the Japanese government as they were educated in Japan themselves and that the government should provide the means to send students abroad for the purpose of acquiring knowledge which would benefit the country.

Taking the advice, the Emperor Gwang-mu had sent several students abroad, some to Japan, and others to the United States. Jaipil Sur, Tchiho Yun, Gwangbum Sur,* Kiusik Kim, and others came to America. Sur and Yun had returned to Korea upon completion of their studies, but the former had been exiled back to America, became an American citizen, and lived here ever since under the name of Dr. Philip

---

*All but one of the five of these distinguished gentlemen had I the honor of meeting in person here in this country. Soon after the Republic of Korea was established in 1948, Prof. Hulbert paid a flying visit to Seoul, and died and buried there where he taught and labored long before the coming of the Japanese rule. And Dr. Jaisohn also made a trip to his native land, and soon after his return home in Philadelphia, he died and was buried in the soil of his adopted country and home for more than half a century.

Jaisohn. The government of the United States, at the request of the king, had sent Prof. Homer B. Hulbert as an advisor on education to his majesty's government. He is the author of *"History of Korea"* and *"The Passing of Korea,"* a sequence of all the internal and international intrigues that finally destroyed the ancient kingdom as a political entity and as a nation by Japan in 1910.   *

Now, it was about that time when the party of the queen and her kinsmen was at the zenith of political power with China's emissary Yuan Shi-Kai's troops stationed in Seoul as a bulwark of conservatism. The queen was the power behind the throne and the regent prince in front of it, and the king tried to rule from in between, his queen back of him and his father in front of him who were deadly enemies to each other and equally ambitious for political power. And, like the king himself, the Dong-Hak-Dang leaned toward the progressive leaders, and it rebelled against the queen and her allies for the murder of Kim Ok-gune in Shanghai and for the attempted murder of Park Yung-heo and also the treacherous murder of Choi Jay-woo, their own leader and the founder of Dong-Hak. Rumors of more contemplated bloody deeds grew and spread, and the Dong-Hak-dang rose up against the Mins for usurping the royal power and prerogatives by a clan other than that of Yi of the reigning house.   *

The adherents of Dong-Hak-Dang, throwing off their religious cloak of disguise and taking up the true role of the revolutionary, rose up in a body. Beads around their necks, matchlocks slung over their shoulders and swords and spears in their hands, chanting the Dong-Hak creed and singing their battle song called Tai-Pyung-Ga, like the summer clouds they gathered in from all directions, sweeping the southern provinces and marching on to Seoul, declaring to protect the king and to clear the palace of the traitors. The capital was in danger of capture.

That was when Japan showed her treacherous hand. The erstwhile friend of progressivism turned against the Dong-Hak-Dang in murdering Choi Si-hyung, its new leader. The revolutionary movement died with him and his followers scattered to the four winds. The remaining two factions, Japan-sponsored Progressive and China-backed Conservative, brought about the Sino-Japanese War, resulting in the murder of the Korean queen and the ousting of the Chinese influence by the Japanese. As a consequence, the country was declared as an independent nation for a decade until the Russo-Japanese War when the victorious Japanese made themselves the master and oppressor in Korea for forty long years until the end of the World War II.

Indeed, the people were looking for and longing for Prince Jung-Do-Ryung, as did the Israelites of old for the Messiah, to come to claim the kingship of the land and enthrone himself in his new capital to be built at the base of the Gay-Riong Mountain in Choong-Chung province in the south. A man named Jung-Gam had long ago prophesied that the "Yee-In" (Wonder Man) or the "Jin-In" (True Man) will come out of the island of the sea to claim the throne of Korea to succeed the then reigning dynasty which will have come to an end at the conclusion of its fifth century mark marked with decadence and incompetence. And this man's name was to be "Jung-Do-Ryung, Prince Jung-Do-Ryung."

Such a romantic name and fame of one who had not yet appeared, but had caught the fancy of many and captured imaginative appeal of the populace for

several generations. It was only natural for the mis-
governed and mistreated people to wish for a general
change. They dreamed of a change in the hands of
this romantic figure of Prince Jung-Do-Ryung who
would give them a panacea for all their ills and make
their country a land of grandeur and tranquility.

And, that small shack was still standing there where
my Big Uncle and his teachers were still chanting the
Dong-Hak creed long after the Dong-Hak cause had
been lost until it was destroyed by the forces of nature some time later. There was a night of severe
rainstorms accompanied by thunder and lightning. On
the following day, it was found that a boulder had
hurtled down from the overhanging cliff above it,
crashing through the roof, demolished the shack to its
foundation. Fortunately, no one was in it that night,
my uncle having been away for quite some time.

Today, some Koreans are inclined to believe that
this centuries-old prophecy has been fulfilled and that
both the Wonder Man and the True Man had come
at last. It may sound fantastic, yet it proves to be
literally true, word for word. If the term coincidence
is preferred to that of prophecy, well, it is the most
remarkable coincidence that ever occurred in history.
The Wonder Man was thought to be the late President Franklin D. Roosevelt himself who had promised
Korea's independence at the Cairo Conference in 1943,
paving the way for the True Man who proved to be
none other than President Harry S. Truman himself.

For it is a proven fact that during the administration
of President Truman that the Japanese were driven
out of Korea by the Allied Forces, and that it was
under his guidance, with the United Nations representatives as witnesses, that Korea has become once
more an independent nation in the memorable year of

grace of our Lord 1948. It is also a proven fact that President Truman has fulfilled not only the Korean prophecy, he has also fulfilled the time-honored promise of mutual assistance contained in the Korean-
* American Commercial Treaty of 1882!

The treaty had provided that "If other powers deal unjustly and oppressively with either government, the other will exert its good offices, on being informed of the case, to bring about an amicable arrangement, thus showing its friendship." Indeed, Americans were the first foreigners to visit and open up the Hermit Kingdom to Western civilization; first to conclude a commercial treaty with Korea; first to send Protestant missionaries; first to introduce a modern educational system. They built Korea's first railroads; first street railways; first electric light plant; first water works; started her first street paving, sewers, macadamized roads; and installed the first modern mining plants.

The Statue of Liberty, on Bedloe's Island, in New York harbor was a gift from the sister Republic of France to commemorate the 100th anniversary of American independence. Some day soon I would like very much to see another Statue of Liberty rise on the Golden Gate, a gift from the new sister Republic of Korea, proclaiming, "Liberty Encircling the World."

5

The Prince of Peace

My Big Uncle had been away for quite some time, and one day in late fall he returned. He stopped at my home on his way to the Big House. He came back a changed man! I could see that readily in his countenance and in his bearing. The wrinkles on his forehead seemed to have disappeared and the corners of his mouth lifted. He used to look proud and sullen with the big heavy-rimmed spectacles accentuating his rather domineering personality. I used to get scared of him—not that he was unkind to me or scolded me or anything like that, though. Now he looked humble and happy with radiant smiles all over his visage, greeting us so kindly and talking to us so happily excited about something, and acting as though he had received an appointment as a district magistrate recommended by his influential friend while he was away.

After mutual greetings, he told my father that he had so much good news to tell everybody in the family that he wanted us to go up with him to the Big House. And telling us to get ready, he personally went over to my New Uncle's house to bring his family along with him so that we could all go up to my grandmother's house together. Wasn't I excited that I was going up to see my grandmother whom I had not seen for a long time!

At the Big House that evening he gathered every member of the big family about him and said he had a very good piece of news which he wanted to tell

them. He said he had been out to Pyeng Yang and clear up to Seoul while he was away, and had seen many wonderful things which he had never before seen in all his life. He met for the first time some of the American missionaries who could talk like Koreans, and through them he found Yesu, or Jesus, the Savior of the world! He met Won-Moska, (or the Rev. Horace Underwood) in Seoul and Mah-Moksa (or the Rev. Samuel Moffitt) in Pyeng-Yang, the two prominent pioneer missionaries who had come from Me-Gook (Short for AMERICA; "Me" means
* BEAUTIFUL and "Gook" means COUNTRY).

"Yesu," he said, "was the Savior of the world, and he had come just in time to save our people from the old superstitions and ignorance and sins that had held us down so long. Hopelessly we have been groping in the dark and in vain we have been looking for a Savior from a wrong direction. I was one of them. So were you all. Now I found the real and true Savior of our people and of all mankind who is called Yesu Christo. He was born of Virgin Mary in a small village of Bethlehem in the land of Judea nearly two thousand years ago. His coming was prophesied long before that by the prophets of old and he was called "the Wonderful Counsellor, Almighty God, Everlasting Father, the Prince of Peace."

"The Prince of Peace!" exclaimed my Middle Uncle. "What a romantic name! Why, it sounds like Prince Jung-do-ryung himself whom we've been looking for all this time!"

"Oh, no, my dear brother, nothing like that at all," exclaimed my Big Uncle. "The Prince of whom I am telling you about is the Savior of the soul of man, but not of the tottering thrones and kingdoms of this world. Christo's mission was of spiritual and not of temporal kingdom when He came to the land of Judea which was just about in the same condition as is our own. I know what you are talking about, and I sympathize with you. And you are not the only one who thought of Yesu Christo in that way. When He was yet on this earth his followers asked him saying, "Lord, wilt Thou at this time restore again the kingdom to Israel?" and Yesu answered and said, "It is not for you to know the time or the seasons, which the Father hath put in His own power!" Yes, the Israelites were patriots just like we are, and they, too, were looking for their Messiah, who was Yesu himself, to come and restore their kingdom of Judea, the house of David and Solomon, again from the yoke of the Roman conquerors. That was their first and last thought of Him from the time of His birth to the very moment of His ascension.

"So you see that Yesu was not an earthly prince like Prince Yi or Prince Jung. Yesu was the Prince of Peace . . . peace of mind and of heart with God when man or woman is free from sin. And what is Sin? Sin is anything done contrary to the Ten Commandments which God had given to the children of Israel through Moses long before Yesu was born. The Ten Commandments read: "Thou shalt have no other Gods before me; Thou shalt not worship idols; Thou shalt not take my name in vain; Thou shalt keep the Sabbath holy; Thou shalt honor thy father and mother; Thou shalt not kill; Thou shalt not commit adultery; Thou shalt not steal; Thou shalt not covet; Thou shalt not tell a lie." In other words, "Worship God and love thy neighbor as thyself," as Yesu taught His disciples.

"I am a sinner. My sins are many. I have worshipped false gods. I did steal and hated my neigh-

bors. I was wicked. Men were wicked. The world
was wicked. Their hearts were wicked. They all
sinned against God and against their neighbors."

"But, My Big Cousin," interrupted my New Uncle,
"You said you did steal. I think you meant you stole
that grave site from Kim Gam-Yuk. But that could
not be a sin because you did it for your departed father and not for yourself. Didn't you read one of
the Ten Commandments which said, 'Honor thy father and mother?' "

"Yes, it said that, my dear cousin," said my Big
Uncle. "Of course, we've honored our parents more
than any other people on earth, perhaps. And, I suppose that was the primary purpose in selecting a place
for their burial after they had died. That part is all
right, according to the Christian ideals. But we had
gone too far in superstitious belief that the very site
and ground where they were buried had the virtue of
actually giving happiness to their posterity. And,
naturally, we believed and practiced it chiefly for our
selfish purpose, that we ourselves wanted to be en-
riched by it. In America, I hear, they have public
cemeteries where they bury their dead, side by side
with others, and they are all blessed alike!

"Yes, Yesu was the Prince of Peace in the hearts
of people everywhere who will only believe on Him
and obey His Commandments. Yesu was King of
kings and Lord of lords. Earthly kings cannot make
man good. Man is good when his heart is right. And
Yesu alone can give man the right kind of heart that
will make for peace and happiness by freeing him from
besetting sins. And how could a man be like that? He
said man must be born again!

"Peace was proclaimed by the angels at His birth.
Peace He left with His followers when He ascended

to Heaven. So you see, that's the great Gospel of
Peace and Truth. The heart is the main thing, and
Yesu had come to take care of the hearts of men
everywhere. All the worldly troubles had come out
of the hearts that were proud and selfish, greedy and
filthy, cruel and intolerant. And He taught humility,
kindness, meekness, righteousness, purity and peace-
making as the greatest virtues that human beings can
attain and the rewards promised are greater than
any earthly kingdoms and empires that ever existed.
A change of heart from wickedness to godliness will
change the whole complexion of this world in which
we live. The Christ had come into this world to trans-
form it into the Kingdom of God in the hearts of
every man, woman, and child who will only believe in
Him.

"He lived and preached the great truths for thirty-
three years and performed miracles by curing incurable
diseases, driving devils out of the devil-possessed,
and raising the dead from the grave and giving back
the life again. And, do you know what the people
thought of Him? Some believed on Him as the God-
sent Messiah, but others were so hard-hearted that
they still asked Him for a surer sign that He was the
Messiah after having witnessed all the miracles He
had performed and heard all His teachings. And still
others of his fellow-countrymen were so wicked in their
hearts that they accused Him as a rebel leader against
their Roman masters. And one of His own disciples
betrayed Him and sold Him for thirty pieces of silver!

"Yes, Yesu told them a sign which they asked for.
He said that the sign will be that the Son of Man
shall die on the cross for the sinful men of wicked
heart, and He did die on the cross of Calvary as de-
manded by His own people. And the wicked Roman

soldiers stabbed His side with their spears that the pure blood of the Holy Man flowed! This was the red blood of Christo which will wash the crimson sins of wicked men who will only believe on Him. God is love, and God so loved the world, in spite of its wickedness, He gave His only begotten Son to die and to rise again from the grave that whosoever believed on Him shall not perish but have everlasting life!

"I believe on Him. I accepted Christianity. I was baptized by Won-Moksa (Rev. Horace G. Underwood) while I was in Seoul. Now I am a Christian. I want you all to believe on Yesu as I do. Now let me ask all of you. Do you believe in Yesu also?"

With tears in their eyes, everybody said, "I do. He must have been the Son of God. He was so holy, so kind, so loving. He was the Prince of Peace, indeed!"

And, with his face full of radiant smiles, my Big Uncle said, "This is the happiest day in my life for I know that we are all saved by Yesu this very night. I have been a great sinner through ignorance and superstition. And, as the head of the family, I had led you into many sinful ways and into the valley of shadow of death and damnation. God is merciful that He has sent the missionaries of the cross from across the ocean bearing the great message of salvation that we of the Hermit Nation too have seen the light and heard the joyful news. And, we of the hermit of the Hermit, too, have now received the happy news . . . the happiest news the world has heard since its creation!"

And out of his traveling bag he brought forth several books and pamphlets, all Christian literature, some in Chinese, others translated into Korean from English. There were one Old Testament, one New

Testament and two Gospels of St. Matthew and St. John in Chinese, imported from China, for the Korean translation had not yet been completed. Among the pamphlets printed in Korean were the *Apostles' Creed,* the *Lord's Prayer,* the *Ten Commandments,* "*The Coming of Christianity into Korea,*" *The Pilgrims' Progress,*" "*The Story of a Rich Man,*" etc. And my Big Uncle asked everyone to read them and study them diligently and memorize the Ten Commandments, the Lord's Prayer, and the Apostles' Creed by heart for they contained the most essential points of Christian doctrine.

And then he told us how the Christian churches were built in Seoul and Pyeng Yang where the newly converted Korean Christians congregated for worship, how the mission schools were conducted and taught along the lines of modern educational system, and how the mission hospitals and dispensaries were being operated in the interest of those who were in need of medical care. And he spoke highly of the missionaries from Me-Gook (Beautiful Country or America) who carried the Bible in one hand and the medicine case in another in order to heal the sick in body as well as to save the sin-sick soul from spiritual agony and death. Strange though they looked at first, he said, but how kind and how understanding they were toward the people to whom they have been sent to serve and to save.

Then, sitting back with a broad smile on his face, he said, "Now, why do you suppose I am telling you about all these wonderful things that are being done out there? Because I want you to know that I am going to take you all out to Pyeng Yang in the coming spring. Wouldn't you like to go with me?" he asked, looking around to see how they liked it.

"O, to Pyeng Yang I will be glad to go with you!" answered my Middle Uncle, who was always good natured and sportsmanlike. And the rest of the family responded in the affirmative not quite as loudly, but eloquently and enthusiastically enough by showing happy smiles on their faces, including mine. Yes, everybody was happy that before long we would be going to Pyeng Yang, the second city in the land, and to new life and civilization, leaving behind the tiger-infested mountain country.

So from then on till the coming spring we made preparations for our exodus from Mansan to Pyeng Yang. Our houses and lands were to be disposed of by my Big Uncle himself. We needed at least eight oxen for our transportation purpose, and we had only three. There were two at the Big House and one at my house. My New Uncle had to go out and buy five more. By day, men folks cut down trees and my Middle Uncle made sleighs out of them. And the women folks did the washing, sewing and packing. And by night we sat around studying the Bible and reciting the Lord's Prayer, the Ten Commandments and the Apostles' Creed. Before the winter was over everybody knew them by heart, and we were exceedingly happy.

I could read both the Testaments printed in Chinese. It was then that I was grateful I had learned those characters which were so difficult when I first started to learn them. And how interesting were those Bible Stories to me! The story of the creation and of Noah and the ark, the story of Jacob and his twelve sons, their flight to Egypt and their exodus therefrom, and their long journey toward their Promised Land, and the life story of Jesus! They were so absorbingly interesting to me that I certainly did burn the midnight oil to read them. Memorizing my daily lessons had become a regular habit to me so that I used to know the first half of St. Matthew's Gospel by heart.

In the meantime, my Big Uncle, who was born a traveler and expounder of mysteries, now proved to be a self-appointed itinerary preacher with eloquence and conviction. His first visit, of course, was with Kim Gamyuk, our closest neighbor. He spent many days and nights with him at his house, and I am sure he was one of the first converts he made in that part of the country. I doubt very much whether he was equally successful with his political friends, Kim-Doong-goon and Kim Gamyuk of the town. Usually government officials and upper-class people everywhere, as was even at the time of Christ himself, are like the stony ground of Jesus' parable, hard to put in seed, to take root, or to grow anything on it.

My Middle Uncle had skillfully made open sleighs and also covered ones, the former to carry the household belongings and the latter to accommodate the womenfolks and the youngsters, drawn by oxen and escorted by the menfolk. Each ox pulled a train of two sleighs, one freight and one passenger. So my father took care of one train and my New Uncle also took care of one trainload of his own family and the belongings. The Big House family was divided into six trains, and the one my grandmother was on was placed near the middle of the long train conducted by my Big Uncle who rode on my horse, given to me by Kim Gamyuk's son, my neighborly friend. It was a young mare he gave me to ride on my journey, but not the colt which he had promised me. And, of course, while my Big Uncle rode on my horse, I rode in my grandmother's sleigh. We had stored up in the Big House all kinds of furs which my huntsman uncle brought home during those many years. So everybody wore fur caps, fur coats, fur wraps, fur overalls, fur gloves, and fur-lined shoes, and we kept ourselves nice and warm in the yet wintry weather on our journey out of the mountainous region.

One day in March, our exodus began. The Big House party started out early down the steep mountain trail, narrow and crooked, buried in knee-deep snow. The sun was just rising over the mountain when I saw from my house, the train of twelve sleighs drawn by six oxen gliding down the hillside across the river. Wasn't that a wonderful sight! If I were an American lad, I certainly would have thought they were Santa Clauses coming so soon again in the month of March in a big company like that, and thrilled to see what bulky loads they were bringing along with them!

I ran out to meet them across the river which was frozen over and smooth as a pane of glass. In the Exodus from Egypt, the Red Sea had split up to make way for the Israelites. Here in our exodus, the river had frozen over to make a smooth pathway for the sleigh ride.

So now altogether, we started out from my house on our long journey, parading down the road by the river, overlooking the village where I went to school. I was glad that I did not have to go to that school anymore, but still, leaving it behind me made me feel rather sorry. I thought of my house and the Big House where I spent my childhood days of many fond memories that I can still remember so distinctly. Before our leaving, my father and my uncles must have visited their father's grave once more and made some arrangements with the Kims to take care of it now that they were going far away.

Soon we arrived in the district town, where the

people lined up on either side of the street, and stared at us with wonder and bewilderment. The eight trains of sixteen sleighs in a line, drawn by eight oxen, must have been some sight and spectacle to the onlookers! The first stop we made was in front of Kim Doonggoon's house, while my Big Uncle was saying good-bye to his good old friend, who in turn bade us farewell and a happy journey.

We moved along after our lunch until sunset, when we arrived at an inn to put up for the night. Of course, my Big Uncle was there already waiting for us. Thus, we traveled again the second day. And on the third day, we stopped at the house of the parents of one of my cousins-in-law. All the time I was with my dear grandmother in her sleigh, she gave me some of the tasty broiled venison which she had brought along with her. She was so mindful of me that she did not forget me even when everybody else was all excited and in a state of confusion. She always thought of me first and last, wherever she was and whatever she was doing. Is it any wonder that I loved her so dearly?

From Mangsan to Pyeng Yang were some three hundred lis, or something like over a hundred miles, and it took us six or seven days to make the journey. Day after day, as we plowed through the snow-covered, narrow mountain roads, I noticed the mountains getting gradually lower and the valleys gradually wider until we came to a wide open level land at the end of our journey on a bright sunny day. We arrived in a village called Sho-woo-mul, or Cow's Well, of the district of Pyeng Yang, some six miles east of the city of Pyeng Yang.

So at last we had come to our promised land flowing with shining streams and glowing with red soil. This was a farming country and my folks were farmers, and they came here to till the soil for their living. This was good soil for farming, and as for them, "All's well when soil's well." And what a difference I saw here! No more mountains so high and rugged, no more tigers of which to be afraid. The only high ground I saw was a knoll just above the big spring to our right foreground which was destined to be the site of our new church to be built there in the near future. Out of some seventy houses in the village scattered around in a bow shape, only five of them were tile-roofed, including our own, and all the rest were thatch-roofed small dwellings.

Led by my Big Uncle, our caravan drove up to the front of our new house with the tail end of it still at the entrance of the village. And what a spectacle it must have been to the village folk here. For they all poured out to see the big show before their eyes. "O my, who are they?" someone wanted to know. "Where are they coming from?" asked another. And somebody who knew said, "Why, don't you know? That must be the Charr-Chosey's family coming out from Mangsan. And I heard they are the Tien-ju-hak-jangs," (an abusive term used for the Catholics and for the Christians in general). "O yea! So that's what they are, eh!" said his neighbor. "We never had any of those strangers in this village of ours yet. We'll wait and see!"

So that was the kind of reception we got from some of the people who regarded us as stranger of strangers on our first arrival there, and we were to wait and see also. Plenty of snow was still on the field here, too, but the streets and the yards were very wet and muddy in the melted snow, and so sticky that I carried the red clay mud under my feet at least one-tenth of my own weight when I climbed up the front porch of the new house of ours near the east end of the village.

It was a big house and was big enough for the Big House family alone, but not quite big enough for all the twenty-two members of the whole party to live there together. But, what else could we do but to make the best of what we already had? So, that night and all the following nights, all the womenfolk stayed together in the main building, and all the menfolk slept in the sarang, or guest house, and four of the eight oxen were placed in our neighbors' barns. How the old folks liked it I do not know, but I liked all the excitement and moving about. It was such fun!

6

The First Church in Pyeng Yang

On the first Sunday after we arrived in Sho-Woo-Mool, my Big Uncle took all the male members of the Charr household to the First Presbyterian Church on Sool-Mak-Gol, or Saloon Alley, in the city of Pyeng Yang for the first time. We got up that morning while it was still dark. After early breakfast, with our prayer books and hymn books (Chan-Song-Ga) in satchels slung over our shoulders and backs, we walked six miles toward the city. As we reached the east bank of Dai-Dong-Gang, the sun was rising behind the Moon-Soo-Bong hill-top which we had climbed only half an hour ago.

Behold, the Dai-Dong-Gang! It was the biggest and bluest river that I had ever seen in my life. "Oh, what a big river this is!" I said to my father.

"Yes, my son," he said. "It is one of the five greatest rivers in the country and is called Dai-Dong-Gang. But don't you know that it is the same identical river that flowed down by our old house in Mangsan? Only that was one of the two tributaries of this big river," he explained.

Oh, how interesting it was to me to know that because that river back in Mang-san was very dear to me, and now I had come to the same river which was much larger down here. And, for certain, I was destined to live by this famous river for many years to come, drinking from it the sweetest and tastiest water known in the land. It was the water that made the sons and daughters of Pyeng Yang, who drank out of this river, the strongest, smartest, and bravest people of the country, it was said.

A big river it was, indeed. At that time of the year, only the main channel closest to the west bank was full and deep enough for small ships to dock there. In rainy and flood season, when it was full from bank to bank up to the city gate, it was a mile wide. The river near my house back in Mangsan was shallow enough for me to wade across it or to use the stepping stones. But here it was so deep and wide, with no bridge over it, that people and animals alike were ferried over in small, flat-bottom boats, back and forth, from morning till night.

And behold the ancient wall of the ancient city standing parallel to the river on the opposite shore, with a big tower and its upturned gables like the wings of a flying eagle atop the Dai-dong gate, the main eastern entrance to the city. It was the first time in my life I had ever seen such a big stone wall some thirty to forty feet high, built on the steep bank and rocky cliff. It looked strong and very picturesque to me. But what was that for, I wondered. If we had walls like that around our houses back in Mangsan, we could certainly keep the tigers out, I thought.

As we were moving toward the water's edge over the half a mile of dry river bed of sand and gravel partly covered with snow, I looked around far and near, enjoying the famous scenery of the famed city. The great wall stretching north and south of the gate along the river continued on around the city for ten miles, including the outer wall, my father told me. How was it that he knew so much of Pyeng Yang already? He had been to the city with my Big Uncle the other day to escort Madame Kim, the wife of the

Secretary of State to her home near the Governor's palace and to pay a visit to Choi Chosey, the rich landowner friend of my uncle and one of the first Christians in the city. That's how he knew so many interesting things about the city.

Now we reached the water's edge where there was a landing place. Seeing that the ferry boat was tied up on the opposite shore, my Big Uncle called to the boatman to ferry us over. At this early hour of the day the boatman was not expecting any passengers. We were the only ones, but he was there and responding to my uncle's call, he rowed his boat over in a few minutes.

Greeting my uncle respectfully, the boatman said, "Ah, it is you, sir, traveling so early."

"Yes, young man," answered my uncle, "I am going to church at Sool-mak-gol with my brothers and our children. And I am sorry to make you work on Sunday like this. I would like very much to have you come with us to our church on Sundays and Wednesday evenings. You are working for my friend Choi Chosey, I know, and I am sure he will be glad to see you in the church with us all."

"I don't see, sir, how I could do that," he replied. "I am a poor fellow, and I can't afford to idle one moment of the day or night."

"Oh, please don't say that, young man," answered my uncle in a persuasive manner. "Going to church on Sunday is not idling at all. If only you knew that the Americans, who work only six days a week, are the richest people in the world, you wouldn't say that, I know. We are all poor, but perhaps we can work a little harder during the six days and observe the Sunday religiously and profitably." So my uncle preached Christianity to everybody he met and everywhere he went. And he was not alone in doing that, for I, too, and every Christian, did the same, and every Christian was a missionary to his fellow countrymen. Is it any wonder, then, that Christianity spread by leaps and bounds in Korea?

Landing on the opposite shore, my uncle led us up to the gateway to the city. Here no one had to tell me the name of the massive gate which we were about to enter when I saw the large name plate hanging up there on the face of the tower atop the gateway. Carved in three large Chinese characters, it said, "Dai-Dong-Mun," meaning "Great East Gate." The gate was left wide open and there was no guard posted there as it had been ever since the Japanese invasion in the sixteenth century, my uncle told me. The arched gateway was about ten feet high and twice as wide, wide enough for horsemen to ride four abreast. And the iron-clad gate, hinged on both sides of the dark gateway and swung back to the wall, looked very old and rusty. And, then, some forty feet further back, there was the inner gateway with the inner gate left open like the outer gate. Looking up, I saw the huge tower set firmly atop the gateways.

"What a gate!" I exclaimed and entered and behold, the city of Pyeng Yang! I was thrilled to realize that I was now actually in Pyeng Yang, the northern Metropolis, the ancient capital city of Kija, the king who reigned in the twelfth century before Christ, and the founder of the Korean civilization which was younger than that of the Chinese, but much older than that of the Japanese.

For the first time in my life I saw a walled city packed with houses on either side of the street inside the gate. They were small tile-roofed, single-storied houses with paper windows. In fact, they were the downtown stores and market places. At this early hour, there was hardly anybody out in the street except a few water carriers who went through the gate making the street and the gateway wet and muddy. The big and elegant looking house belonging to Elder Choi Chosey was near the gate to our left at the corner of Dai-Dong street and Saloon Alley. He was in the combination hotel and grain market business. He and his family lived in the rear, the hotel in front, and the shop outside on the sidewalk.

This being Sunday, the shop was not open when we arrived at his house, and when we knocked, no one answered. And my uncle said to us, "He is not up yet, I guess, because we got here too early. Well, I know what we can do right now. How would you like to visit the 'Yang-gwan' (or the missionary home district) out on the West side?"

"O, we'll be glad to," was the ready response, for everybody was eager to know what kind of a place was Yang-gwan and to see where the missionaries lived. So we set out toward Yang-gwan in a north-westerly direction.

Walking up the Dai-dong Street slowly, looking this way and that, the first persons we saw about were the Japanese merchants in their shops. Here, I saw the foreigners for the first time. I saw their steamboats, painted in black and white, tied up in the river. My father whispered to me saying those were the Wai-nom, or an abusive term applying to the Japanese, meaning Dwarfish Villains. They were small in size with cropped heads like the Buddhist monks, and bushy black eyebrows, wearing no trousers but gowns like women, which looked odd to me. They wore biforked socks and topless slippers, walking like ducks and sitting like school boys, kneeling down by the charcoal fire and trying to keep themselves warm. They were selling chinaware, kerosene and Japanese cookies and candies.

Now we came to the intersection of the main street, running north and south. Here I saw the Korean shops of all kinds on both sides of the street with stock ranging from bamboo fiber hats to pottery and cast iron rice pots. My attention was directed to a big paper shop with a large sign written on the doorway. "Ah, here's the shop where they sell paper, and I know where to buy it now," I said to myself. I had been in need of paper so badly back in Mangsan, and I loved paper more than anything else when I was small. Honestly, paper was more precious to me than candy. Every time my father or mother gave me some money to buy some candy, I bought paper with it instead.

Turning north now, we walked up the Main Street until we came to another intersection where the nationally known Pal-gak-jip, or the House of Eight Gables, a cafe famous for its ice-cold noodles, was located. Following the main street bent westward, we walked up a good distance and came to a point where the Main street turned north again leading to the governor's palace. Instead of following it, we walked straight ahead up the hilly narrow street, down a little ways, and through the small Shang-soo-gu gate and we were then out on the west side of the city.

Pointing at the opposite hillside, my uncle said, "Ah, there's the Yang-gwan! Do you see those big beautiful houses over there with glass windows dazzling in the morning sun?"

Yes, we saw them. They were in full view now as we were getting closer to those elegant looking big houses located far apart, some on the lower level, some on the top of the hill. Glass windows! That sounded odd to me. "Through the glass windows everybody can look into the house, can't they? And I would be afraid of thieves." I wondered and worried myself. "And another thing. Those houses on the hilltop looked too cold in winter time and too hot in summer time. All our houses are built deep down in the hollows. Now, isn't it strange?" I said to myself.

The first house we came closest to was the house of Ma-Moksa's. It was in the shape of Korean alphabet "K", or the inverted capital letter "L" surrounded by a stone wall covered with tiles. This was the very first missionary residence where the Rev. Samuel Moffitt stayed when he first came to Pyeng Yang and until he moved later into a new house built for him and his newly wed wife, formerly Miss Field, a little ways north of it. During those early days, there were three or four missionaries living together in that same old building. Dr. Wells, We-Mok-sa (Rev. Wittimore) and Han-Moksa (Rev. Hunter) were the other occupants. They all had come as single men at first, it seemed to me, whether they were married or single. Some time later, Mr. Wittimore was transferred to Sun-Chun, and Dr. Wells and Mr. Hunter moved into their newly-built homes nearby when their respective families arrived from America.

We just looked around through the open gateway and over the fence to see how the house looked and what the missionaries looked like. I was surprised to find out that I could not see anything through those many glass windows as I had thought I could! Around the back and above this building, we saw two other houses upon the hill. Bassi-Bu-in (Miss Margaret Best) occupied one to the east, and the Nee-Moksa

(Rev. and Mrs. Graham Lee) occupied the other. Miss Best, by the way, was from Park College, Parkville, Missouri, where I myself went to school many years later. At the time, Dr. William Baird and his family lived in the same house with Miss Best.

Mr. Lee, I believe, built all those missionary homes with the help of Korean carpenters. He was a great carpenter as well as a singing preacher. Several years later he built the great Central Presbyterian Church on the top of the Jang-dai-jai hill above the Main street in the heart of the city.

Those were the only missionary homes in existence when we visited them for the first time. Of course, we could not see anything through those glass windows from the outside, but the missionaries themselves might have seen us walking around in a group and peeping through the gates and over the fences. Didn't they think we looked funny, I wondered. Although we did not see any missionaries, we saw their homes, and we all agreed that they were like fairyland palaces looking so grand and elegant, peacefully quiet and comfortable, except that they looked too cold in winter from the winds on the hilltop and too hot in the summer because it was close to the sun, I thought.

Now we turned back to go to our Sunday School with Elder Choi Chosey and his family. Coming through the West Gate, down the West Gate Street, then turning north on Main Street, we returned to the home of the Christian businessman who was then up and waiting for us. My uncle introduced us to his old friend and his family. We were very pleased to meet and become acquainted with the first Christian-Koreans in Pyeng Yang.

When my uncle told the host of our early morning's sight-seeing trip out to the Yang-gwan district, he said, "That's fine. And you'll see more of these missionary homes on those hilltops all around as we expect more missionaries to arrive from Me-gook soon. Our church is growing fast day by day as more new converts are made, and we need more missionaries, both preachers and doctors, more churches and schools, and many Korean church workers and teachers to be trained for the service." He told us how deeply he was interested in studying the Bible and how interesting it was to know the missionaries who were so good and kind.

As a matter of fact, he had come in more close contact with the missionaries than many other Christians because he was one of the great businessmen who could help them in the business line quite a lot. Pyeng Yang businessmen had the reputation of being pretty slick and tricky with people in general and with strangers and foreigners in particular. No one could cheat him out of any business transaction. Now where did Nee Mok-sa get the lumber and other materials to build the missionary homes, church buildings, schools and dispensaries? From Mr. Choi, of course, who was the purchasing agent and a Christian businessman. He had helped to build the First Presbyterian Church only a block south of his home on the Saloon Alley facing the city wall.

Soon it was Sunday School time, and we went to the First Church for the first time. The church, a large tile-roofed building, together with two or three outer buildings, was enclosed by a high stone wall all around, covering spacious open spaces both inside and out. There were two gates, one on the east and another on the west side. The church building was in the shape of a capital letter "T", having three wings, the north wing of which was separated and reserved for ladies only with a curtain at least five feet high. This, too, was according to the custom of the country that men and women were not supposed to face each other, much less sit together side by side in public as we do in America. In fact, up to that date, the Korean ladies were still wearing their jang-ot (veil gown) or sak-ga-ji (hoop basket) out in the streets.

There was a small low platform built against the west wall so that it directly faced the east wing and the north and south wings on either side of it. A few American-made folding chairs were placed there with a lectern in front and a door back of them. Through this door, the missionaries would enter and find their seats on the platform which commanded full view of all three wings, including the ladies' section without any obstruction.

With the congregation sitting on the floor covered with reed mattings, cross-legged, the sitting capacity could be arranged at will as was the case in our Big House, time and again. The people could move over a little or squeeze in between whenever it was found necessary. That's how we could get along when new converts multiplied and new churches were not in sight. Each person brought his or her own Bible and hymn books to the church just as pupils going to school with their text books.

Here they came—men, women, young and old— eager to study the Bible and to learn to sing the Christian hymn. Soon a crowd gathered there and three missionaries came in through the side door. Everybody looked up to them. There were one lady and two men all dressed in black, the men's trouser legs so tight and the lady's skirt sweeping the floor. The lady wore a hat and the men removed theirs. Korean men wore their hats inside and out, and we were all

dressed in white. This was the first time in my life
I saw the American missionaries, and I began to notice the differences. They were tall and straight with
brown hair, blue eyes, prominent noses and light com-
plexions, and looked very strange to me at first, indeed. But their smiling faces fascinated me readily,
and before long it made me wonder if I had seen them
somewhere before. Yes, smiling faces look familiar
to me always.

As soon as they entered the church, however, they
first knelt down by their seats and said their prayer
before doing anything else. Rev. Graham Lee, or Nee
Moksa, who was a music leader, stood up, opening a
hymnal and said in Korean, "Let's sing hymn number
eight, 'Yesu sarang ha-sim-un' or 'Jesus Loves Me,
This I Know.' " That was the very first hymn we all
learned to sing, and how sweet and melodious it
sounded to me to hear it sung for the first time. We
sang it, or rather they sang it, over and over again
many times. My folks and I, being newcomers, simply
sat down open-mouthed, watching Nee Moksa and
the others sing. It sounded so good to me that I wished
I could sing it like the rest of them. I did learn to sing
soon after that and I used to go to the country churches
teaching others to sing the familiar hymns!

The singing lesson now being over, our Sunday
School was now divided up into Bible study groups
conducted by the missionaries and the advanced students who soon became Josa (Assistant Pastor) and
jahng-no (Elder). Kiel Sun-du, Kim Jong-sup, Bahng
Ki-chang and Choi Chosey were the leading Korean
Christians in Pyeng Yang. With Nee Moksa and
Wee Moksa teaching the old pupils, advanced students
teaching the newcomers and Bassi Buin (Miss Best)
teaching the ladies, the Bible study was very interest-

ing to say the least, so much so that the two hours of Bible study period went fast indeed.

At the conclusion of the Sunday School exercises, my uncle and Choi Chosey presented us to the missionaries, who shook hands with each of us and talked to us in perfect Korean. How interesting it was to me to hear them speak our own language much better than most of us could. All the time, while the others were talking to them, I was absorbed in observing the kind of clothes the two men had on, the shoes they wore, the white collars and neckties around their necks and the gold watch and chain they wore in their vest pockets which they pulled out once in awhile to see what time it was. From that day on I wished I could dress like that.

Promising to return to the church for the afternoon worship at two o'clock, everybody went home. Choi Chosey took us over to his home and treated us to the first city dinner which we had ever enjoyed. Of course, my Big Uncle had stopped there many times before, and his friendship with our host was of longstanding. It was through him that my uncle first heard of Christianity, and it was through him that my uncle bought the house and the farm in Showoo-mul, before he brought us out of Mangsan. During and after the dinner, I heard them talking about their church work, both here in the city and in Showoo-mul, and saying something about building a church in our village and bringing someone to be in charge of it, and about starting a Christian school like the ones they had in the city. They were some of the most devout Christians I had ever known in those early days of Christianity in Korea.

Soon we heard our church bell ringing, and our host told us it was time for us to go to church for our afternoon worship. Taking all morning in our Bible study and singing practice, our regular Sunday service was being held in the afternoon, and it had been the custom of all the Protestant churches of early days in Pyeng Yang all the time until I left home. Already a good crowd had gathered there when we went inside the gate. It was only the first bell, and I saw menfolks milling about in front of the sarang or outer house, which was the primary schoolhouse belonging to the church. Among them I noticed a Korean man who was all dressed up like a missionary from head to foot.

Every man still wore top-knots and every boy wore a pigtail, and so did I. But this was the first Korean man I had seen who had his hair cut, and instead of a black bamboo fiber hat, he wore a dark felt hat and blue serge suit. He wore the patent leather shoes in place of the straw sandals or the leather slippers, as did the others. Moreover, he wore a gold watch and chain in his vest pocket! I could not help looking at him a long, long time with wonder and admiration. Who was this man, I wanted to know. Later I learned that he was Mr. Choi Yong-wha, Dr. Wells' interpreter and assistant surgeon from Seoul. He went to the Bai-Jai School, a Methodist Mission School in Seoul, and learned to speak English. So he could speak English, too! What a lucky man was he, I thought. While Jack London was in Korea during the early days of the Russo-Japanese War, Choi went with him as his interpreter. I wished that I could speak English like him and wear a suit of clothes like him and a gold watch and chain.

At the pealing of the second bell, we were already inside the church, and I saw four or five missionaries come in together. Three of them were new to me—

one woman and two men. The lady was Mrs. Lee, I think. One of the two men was blond-haired and be-spectacled Dr. Wells, and the other was Ma Moksa (Rev. Samuel Moffitt) a slim, tall, handsome and young-looking man with light brown hair and mustache, blue eyes and a dimple at the point of his chin, and all smiles on his well-shaped and pink-cheeked face when he talked. And how well he could talk Korean!

There were twice as many people gathered for this service as there were at the Sunday School that morning. Soon the service began by singing the identical hymns which we learned to sing at the Sunday School, led by Nee Moksa who had a beautiful vibrant voice and was an experienced music leader. After a prayer, reading of Scripture, and singing another hymn, Ma Moksa preached an inspiring sermon in fluent Korean. Of course, I can remember neither the Scripture read nor the topic of his sermon now. Yet it must have been a sermon based on the same "Old, old story of Jesus and His love" that touched the hearts of everyone present there, including mine.

And all the time Ma Moksa was standing there preaching I watched him most intently, observing how he looked, how he was dressed, and how he preached, and dreaming if I could only be like him some day. If I could not be an American-born like him, at least I could dress like him and preach like him, I thought. Yes, I wished that I could go to Me-Gook some day and come back as a missionary to my native country!

7

The Dragon Lake

Upon our return home, we told the folks all the wonderful experiences we had had in the city, and my uncle promised to take the womenfolk to the city church the next time if they so desired. Of course, they said they wanted to visit the city, the church, and meet the missionaries and Korean Christians, espe-
* cially Elder Croi's family. Before the farming season began, they did take a trip or two, and were happy and satisfied with what they saw. But, of course, my two aged grandmothers could not make the trip. The only unfavorable comment they offered after meeting the American ladies was that their waistlines were so tight and slender like that of an ant or wasp, that they feared they might break in two!

In the village we were the only Christians, and having no church of our own here, we had to walk six miles to go to the church in the city, and back every Sunday, which was a little too much for us. When the farming season began, it was physically impossible, no matter how devout Christians we might be. So, it was decided that we should hold a Bible study and Sunday service in our own house by ourselves, only occasionally going to the city church. Soon, this new plan went into effect, and through singing hymns, offering prayers as printed in the books, and reading and discussing Bible scriptures on Sundays and Wednesday evenings we did pretty well. In fact, those twenty-two ardent members in a compact group would make a pretty good-sized congregation for any small church anywhere.

But the people of the village heard of our doings

and, evidently, talked about it in a hostile manner. For one day as I was out playing in our own yard, suddenly, a group of small boys of my size came throwing missiles at me from all directions, calling me "Tien-ju-hak-jang-y." And one of the missiles, which was a fist-sized dried red clay mud, harder than a rock itself, landed squarely on my mouth, piercing my upper lip against my front teeth. It knocked me down on the ground, bleeding and crying. I still carry that scar to this day!

At the sound of my cry, my Big Uncle came running out of the sarang, lifted me up and took me inside. My grandmother saw me in that condition and almost cried, too. My uncle applied some poultice on the wounded place and bound it up with a bandage and said to me tenderly, "It will be all right soon." And, opening up again the fifth chapter of Matthew's Gospel, he read to me thus: " 'Blessed are ye when men shall revile you, and persecute you, and shall say all manner of evil against you falsely, for my sake. Rejoice, and be exceedingly glad; for great is your reward in heaven: for so persecuted they the prophets which were before you . . . But I say unto you, that ye resist not evil: but whosoever shall smite thee on the right cheek, turn to him the other also.' So my boy, you are a Christian now. Rejoice and be exceedingly glad."

"Yes, sir," I said, still crying. "But how can I do that when they hurt me so badly and when they made me so mad?"

"It is hard, it is hard, I know," he said, "but think of Christ, what He did when men reviled Him, nay, when they crucified Him on the cross. He prayed for them for they did not know what they were doing."

Then, almost good-naturedly, he told everybody

gathered around him that there were going to be a lot of fellow Christians in the village before long. Indeed, pretty soon, two Christian leaders arrived in our village, Han Chosey, the eloquent, and Jung Chosey, the scholarly, to team up with Charr Chosey, the generous. The two of them were baptized by Mah-Moska, if I am not mistaken, but Han Chosey, the eloquent, was the oldest Christian although in age he was the youngest of the three. He was the most active and most capable member, having already been well-trained for Christian work. And, naturally, he was to be in charge of the local church to be established here in our village. The Rev. Samuel Moffitt himself was supervising the whole district of Pyeng Yang east of the river and to the north.

At the time when he, Han Chosey, was converted, the persecution of the Christians, first the Catholics, then the Protestants by royal decrees, was still the order of the day. Han Chosey was arrested and brought before the governor of Pyeng-an-do. The governor asked him if he were a Christian, and he said he was without a moment of hesitation. The governor asked him again if he believed in God, and he said he did. Then the governor roared, "Don't you know, ignorant and rebellious citizen, that it is a treasonable crime to embrace the foreign religion or to believe in foreign God forbidden by his majesty's decrees? The crime is punishable by death! But, however, if you will now point at your God and revile him in my presence, I will set you free. Will you do that and live, or die a traitor's death?"

Han Chosey stood up and said boldly, "If your Excellency will revile God, perhaps I would. But who would revile God, the Creator, whose children we all are, and by whose grace we all breathe and have our being? God in Heaven is looking down upon us, and sees what we are doing and listens to what we are saying here. And, whoever in the world had ever dared to curse God and not been punished for it? Your Excellency is my governor and is like my father to me. And I cannot and I would not revile your Excellency for anything whatsoever. God Almighty is our great Ruler and Father of us all. How then can I revile my God and your Excellency's God? And, if I did, should I not be punished for it severely rather than be rewarded for it by your Excellency?"

The governor was dumbfounded and tongue-tied, and could find no word to speak. No, he couldn't say "Yes", he couldn't say, "No." And after a pause of a few minutes, with paled face and choked voice, he motioned his officers to let the prisoner go free and in peace. So this modern Paul of Pyeng Yang went preaching the Gospel of the Nazarene unmolested for the first time!

In subsequent months, the governor often invited Han Chosey to his palace and had him tell the wonderful story of Christ, God, and of the mission of the messengers of the Gospel from Me-Gook. Since then, whenever a similar case of persecution by any district magistrates was brought to the attention of Han Chosey, who was now Han Josa, or Preacher Han, it was personally reported to the governor himself, and the case was immediately settled in favor of the accused and the matter was hushed up with his subordinates.

And the governor was rewarded for it soon in the medical services which were rendered to his wife by Dr. Wells, our missionary physician and surgeon. Mr. Choi Yang-Wha, who went with Dr. Wells as his interpreter and as his assistant surgeon, was honored by the governor. He was given the honorary title of Jusa for the fluent English he spoke and for the valuable services he rendered to him in behalf of his beautiful consort.

And "Charr Chosey the Generous" was the reputation which my Big Uncle gained here soon. A stranger though he was in this country place he had soon become the first citizen of the village, of the township and of the county. He was made Jip-kang, or the headman of the county. People flocked to his sarang (love and guest house were synonymous) from near and far, Christians and non-Christians alike.

Now, with the help of his co-workers, within a few years, ninety-nine percent of the population of this hamlet were brought to the Christian fold. A new church was built by the people themselves on the top of the knoll, above the big spring, replacing Jung Chosey's old tile house. And a school was built right next to the church in order to teach their children along lines patterned after the missionary schools that were being conducted in the city. Within the radius of fifty lis to the north, east and south came the new converts to our church on Sundays in the same way we went to the First Church in the city of Pyeng Yang. Every Sunday morning when I went to church, they were already there awaiting us, and I used to wonder why it was that the people who came from many miles away were the earliest arrivals! The people from the surrounding villages would arrive next, and the townspeople would be the last ones to come up to join them.

After the services were over, those who came from the distant villages, men, women, and children, found hospitalities at my Big Uncle's home Sunday after Sunday in the most kind and generous care of my Big

Aunt. She was a mother-in-law to the wives of her four sons now, and if anyone should doubt my statement concerning her, I would advise him to ask those daughters-in-law and be satisfied. They will tell him that she was even more motherly to them than their own mothers could have ever been. A mother-in-law was not any too popular even in old Korea, if one can understand what I mean. May God bless her soul! A more motherly, more generous, more kindly lady and more Christian-like woman, I have seldom seen.

The name "Sho-woo-mul", or Cow's Well, given to the big spring below our church, was a misnomer. In the first place, it was not a well at all; it was a spring, a big spouting spring . . . its water clear and cold in summertime and steaming warm in winter, pouring out of a rocky cavern under the large oak trees standing on the side of the hill. The women of the village, young and old alike, with black earthen jugs carried on the top of their heads, came here to draw the water from in front of the mouth of the spring. A small lake was formed about twenty feet below it that never froze all winter. Locally, it was called "Dragon Lake." The shining stream that flowed down from it had irrigated hundreds of acres of rice fields belonging to several communities along its downward journey. What an undignified name someone had given to so noble and beautiful a large spring such as this!

Seeing was deceiving to my Big Uncle when he came to see it for the first time. "Why, it is a jang-chun (or giant spring)!" he exclaimed. "And certainly it is not a cow's well. We need a more appropriate name for this jang-chun. Jang-chun it is, and why not call it that, calling the village Jang-chun-dong and our church Jang-chun Presbyterian Church?" All his friends agreed with him, and it had been called by that name ever since. It was so recorded in the annals of the district government office in the city of Pyeng Yang.

Now, it so happened that there was a severe drought in the county of New-li-bang, in the district of Pyeng Yang, which my uncle represented. It was the duty of the chief magistrate of the district to offer a ki-woo-je, or a prayer for rain, by the side of a lake or a river situated in the affected area. The idea was that, according to their superstitious belief, the dragon which was the king of the sea, had the control of all the water above and below the land, and that it must be propitiated for water from the skies by the representative of the people who needed rain for their scorching lands. And, it was thought that if the Dragon King himself could not be reached far out into the sea, at least a kinglet dragon, which was supposed to repose in the lakes and in the deep spots in the river, could be appeased, so that it would rise up to the skies and bring down the desired rain to earth.

It was the duty of my uncle to represent the people in his county, who were still non-Christians, in making known to the magistrate, asking for a ki-woo-je in behalf of the people in his jurisdiction who were clamoring for it. He was now a devout Christian himself, and no longer believed in such a thing. Yet, the big majority of the people whom he represented were still superstitious, and he could not very well refuse to do the duty which was required of him. So he simply told the magistrate what the people wanted, that was all.

When it came to the question of selecting a most appropriate place for the occasion, of course, the Dragon Lake at Jang-chun was chosen by the magistrate, its fame having been spread far and wide. The existence of such a big spring and the lake therefrom had never been known so well before, not until my uncle discovered and appreciated it after his coming here.

So, it was decided to hold the ki-woo-je ceremony here at Jang-chun right in front of our church, and preparations were made by the officials of the magistrate's office. We did not like the idea, but what could we do? Neither my uncle, nor the church people in the village, could do anything about it, just so that we, as Christians, were not required to participate in it in any manner. It was fun for me, though, to watch and see what they were doing. Really, it was the first time I had ever seen and witnessed a ki-woo-je, else I would have never known what it was like.

At the appointed hour, which was high noon of that day, the chief magistrate of the district of Pyeng Yang, in his blue and white official silk robe, headgear, breast plate and high boots arrived in his sa-in-kio, or four-man sedan chair, vanguarded and rearguarded by his retinue. The level ground on the west bank of the lake, shaded by tall trees, making a natural canopy, was carpeted by green grass, and made the perfect setting for the occasion prepared for the magistrate.

The spot in the center foreground, facing the lake, was covered with matting upon which an altar or a table was placed. As soon as the official party arranged the places on the ground according to their rank and file, an officer with a water pitcher in his hand walked out to the lake, filled it with water, walked back to the altar, and poured it into a shining silver cup which was placed there by another officer, and then retired to the rear. That done, the magistrate himself, now walked three steps forward and bowed down before the altar, facing the lake, with his palms joined in front of him and his forehead touching the matting. Of course, the east bank of the lake was cleared of people so that no one could see what he was doing directly in front of him. I was standing on the top of the hill to the west looking down from far off.

The officers who were lined up behind him now also bowed down. The magistrate, kneeling down most humbly, led a sort of chant "Cook-goong-bai-yoi," or something like that, and the others responded in unison. Then the magistrate began to read his written prayer from a parchment spread out before the altar. Because of the distance, I couldn't hear what was said, and even if I heard it, I could not have understood the meaning of it because all the official documents and ceremonials were written in pure Chinese characters. Whenever I heard them read these documents, they sounded like listening to a Chinese whose spoken language I never could understand.

The rather brief ceremony being over, the magistrate, accompanied by his retinue, departed the same way he had come. But there was no promising sign of any kind visible anywhere in the blazing skies, not a speck of black cloud could be seen in the wide horizon. In vain the poor people were looking for some supernatural phenomenon to appear forthwith before their eyes. We all suffered the drought, Christians and non-Christians alike, but the Christian population was skeptical about the kind of rain the dragon would bring from the heavens above. In fact, everybody knew that there was no dragon, not even the tiniest baby dragon, in the small body of water called Dragon Lake. It was only about four or five feet deep in the deepest part in the middle of it, and there were no fish bigger than two inches long, if a real big fish were thought to be a would-be dragon.

As for us Christians, we had gathered in our church on Sundays and weekday evenings praying for rain for weeks already. Our own prayer did not bring any rain forthwith either, for that matter. And there were some discussions among ourselves on the effectiveness of our prayer, and, undoubtedly, there was quite a bit of impatience shown by some members in our own household, too. And my uncle told them, "Wait on the Lord and be patient, my children. Our prayer will be answered sooner or later. He is our Almighty Father and wiser than all of us. And, you just can't ask him for every little thing and expect to get it immediately any more than you can from me. He can't be ordered around, you see. We've offered our prayers to our Heavenly Father for what we need, and when He sees fit to do so, He will surely grant us what we asked for, sooner or later."

It started to rain a few days later and continued for many days. And how happy were the people to see and taste the sweet rainfall that drenched the scorched earth! Soon the non-Christians began to speculate upon the merits of the ki-woo-je, believing their dragon had brought down the rain. The newly converted Christians, on the other hand, were persuaded to believe that it was the Christian God who had answered their prayer. That reminded me of the story of the contest between Elijah and Queen Jezebel's 580 priests of Baal, in the Old Testament, each trying to prove the powers of his own god, and, of course, Elijah's Jehovah came out victorious. Our case in Jang-chun was not quite as dramatic and as demonstrative as that though. The people themselves were brought out to see the great Light and to distinguish the true and only God from all the other gods of old superstitions. For, I think, it was about the last ki-woo-je ever offered in that part of the country since the coming of Christianity.

8

My Life's Ambition

"Your young men shall see visions."—*Joel* II: 28.

In the fall of our first anniversary here in Jang-chun, my father decided to move into the city in order to make a living there, but chiefly to send me to the missionary school in Yang-gwan district. My father bought a small thatch-roofed house just outside the Sang-soo-goo gate, not far from the Rev. Moffitt's house. And how happy I was to be in the city and to be right near the American missionaries. I thought I had already come pretty close to Me-Gook where I longed to be some day.

The very first thing I did as soon as we moved into the city was to stroll around the missionary homes, and look into those glass windows over the walls or peep through the barbed wire fences or the open gates. For I was so curious to see everything that was new to me. Maybe I was overdoing it to the extent that one of my eyes got bad. Still, that did not stop me from wandering around there day after day, hour after hour. I had not started going to school until a few days later. With one hand covering my bad eye, I started out again one morning, and as I was walking toward the Yang-gwan, I saw people moving in and out of a building on the hillside beyond Mah-Moksa's house and below the house which was occupied by Miss Best. My curiosity was aroused. I wanted to see what was going on in there. Slowly, step by step, I approached the place. Now I reached the gate which was wide open. There was nobody to stop me.

The building stood some fifty feet inside the gate. I walked in and slowly moved toward it. It was a single story building like all the Korean buildings were and there was a stairway leading up to the front porch. Looking up, I saw the front door left ajar after a man just walked in. I was not afraid to go in, but I did not care to just then. Maybe I acted like the country boy that I was, but I was not afraid of anything, not even a tiger in the Mangsan mountains. I just wanted to see from outside through the glass windows, for I found that this was one of those houses which had the glass windows without a curtain hanging on the inside.

So I started to look around. And as I turned the first corner I happened to see through the window a man in a white smock handling a bottle inside the window, and the man saw me at the same time that I saw him. A minute or two later, the man in white came out of the front door, down the steps, turned the corner and beckoning to me said, "Oh, boy, do you want to see the doctor?" He was a Korean, and I said, "Why, no, sir, I did not come to see the doctor. I was just looking around."

"But," he said, "I see you've got a bad eye. Come with me. The doctor will look at it and will give you some medicine for it. It wouldn't hurt you."

Saying thus, he led me by the hand into the building. I was not afraid. I was just curious about all this. On entering I saw Dr. Wells whom I recognized readily. Then I knew it was the Je-Joong-won or the Salvation Dispensary where Dr. Wells had charge. Then, too, I found what he was doing. He was a medical missionary and not a preaching missionary. That's why

I had never seen him taking much of a part in the church services, except in leading the church music, occasionally, when Nee-Moksa was away. So he was a physician and surgeon, taking care of those who were sick in body, working hard during the week, while others preached and taught on Sundays. And that's why he never cared much to learn to speak the Korean language like the others and had Mr. Choi Yong-wha as his interpreter. Dr. Wells, I understand, was a native of Portland, Oregon. *

Now when I saw him he was in a white smock, too, and with a knife in his hand standing by a man lying prone on a table. Was I scared of him then? Oh, no. Whatever he had in his hand, I was not afraid of him because I knew that a missionary wouldn't harm anybody. When my friend showed my bad eye to him, he looked into it, then he told him to take me into the next room and put some ointment into my eye. Didn't I see some of the cutest looking small bottles on the shelves there? I wished that I had some of those bottles to play with.

Now, this friend of mine was also Dr. Wells' assistant, besides Choi Yong-wha, and his name was Kim Ik-sam. Dr. Wells simply called him Sam. He had learned to be quite an expert in performing his duties as a pharmacist and in operating on minor surgical cases. Dr. Wells had this man with him every day in his work and called him every time he needed him. "Sam, do this; Sam, do that." So that he got into the habit of calling everybody Sam. "Man" in Korean is "saram," and he used to get saram and Sam mixed up, so that he used to say "this sam so and so, and that sam so and so."

Well, Mr. Sam Kim first washed my sore eye with a piece of cotton dipped in a liquid, which must have been Boric Acid solution, and then applied something like jelly, which I now know to be Boric Acid ointment, covered it up with a piece of gauze and bandaged it with a length of adhesive tape. This done, he gave me a small bottle filled with that liquid and a small round cardboard container filled with the ointment, directing me to take off the bandage the next morning, wash the eye with the liquid, put some of the ointment on and bandage it up again with a new piece of gauze which he also gave me. He told me to come back to see him on the third day so that he could look it over and see if my eye was getting along all right.

While Mr. Sam Kim was bandaging up my eye, I was startled by a man crying like a scared child in the operating room in front. It was that Korean patient whom I saw lying on the operating table when I came in. "Don't kill me, Yang-dai-in (American gentlemen)!" he yelled. I turned around and saw Dr. Wells straightening up himself and his knife dripping with blood, and his patient moaning like a gun-shot animal. Was I scared? Oh, no. Never! I was just curious to know what was going on there, that was all. And Dr. Wells was saying, "Ah, Sam, what's the matter with this sam? Did he think I was killing him? Ha, ha! I just saved him. It's all over now, and this sam is all right. Sam, tell this sam to go home now and come back the day after tomorrow so that I can look him over." When he was told to go, the man got up, put on his turban and walked out in a hurry.

On the third day I returned to the dispensary and I saw that same man presenting to Dr. Wells a big basket full of hong-gam, or fresh red persimmons, with grateful bows, thanking him for the successful operation which he had performed on him. Now, he was so thankful to him that he said he had wanted to bring him a bottle of good wine, but that his friends told him the missionaries did not drink, so he brought him the persimmons instead. He was not yet a Christian, but had heard of the skillful missionary surgeon. And Dr. Wells told him neither did he drink nor did he want to see anybody else drink. And smelling his breath he told the man that he must quit drinking, for drinking would surely kill him in a very short time. And he did quit drinking soon after that and became a devout Christian, I know, because I met him many times at the First Church on Sundays and Wednesday evenings months later.

Mr. Sam Kim welcomed me back to the same prescription room where he had treated my eye the last time. He removed the bandage from my eye, and after cleansing it in the Boric Acid solution, he said it looked all right to him, and asked me how I felt. I said I felt just fine, and I could see everything clearly as if nothing had ever happened. And I said to him, "Oh, it's wonderful to be a doctor, isn't it? I would like to be a doctor like you some day!"

"Oh, I'm no doctor, young man," he said. "I do what Dr. Wells tells me to do, that's all."

"But, Mister, you doctored my eye, all right," I said.

"Well," he said, smiling, "I'll show you to Dr. Wells and see what he says about your eye," and took me to the doctor in the other room. As soon as he looked into my eye Dr. Wells said, "Well, Sam, you certainly did a good job on this boy. His eyes are all right, both of them." *

"Thank you, doctor," said Mr. Sam Kim. "Do you know what this boy just called me? He called me a doctor, and he said he wants to be a doctor, too."

"Is that so?" he said, smiling at me. "Of course,

Sam is more than an ordinary doctor, now, and we need more men like him. And you would like to be a doctor, too, eh? That's fine. But it's too bad that there's no medical school near here yet for you to learn to be a doctor. Maybe some day soon we may have one, I hope." Both of them shook hands with me, and Mr. Kim told me to come to see him again whenever I needed his help in the future. I never had any occasion to do so since that day, yet I remember them very dearly to this day.

Indeed, I was inspired to be a doctor like Dr. Wells ever since that day. In fact, I wanted to be a doctor like him as well as a preacher like Ma-Moksa. I wanted to carry the Bible in one hand and a medicine case in the other as a home missionary to my own people in order to cure their sin-sick souls as well as their bodily ills like those two missionaries were doing.

Maybe I was too ambitious? Perhaps. Anyway, I wanted to be a doctor if I could not be both. Besides Dr. Wells, who was my model doctor, there were a lot of herbalist doctors in Pyeng Yang who had shops on either side of the Main Street and in the outlying district towns whom I also admired. The Chinese herb doctors in America were doing well, it seemed to me. The Koreans, naturally, had learned it from the Chinese and the Chinese inherited the medical art from their ancient king. Here's a rhyme which proves it to be a historical fact:

> "The old king Yum-de Sin-nong-see,
> Man's body and cow's head had he:
> All the herbs on earth tasted he,
> And became the father of apothecary."

I went home happy, and my parents were even hap-

pier than I was to see me come back with both eyes
bright as the daylight. I told them all about the doctor and the hospital, and how good they were and
how people got cured of all kinds of physical ailments
there. Then I told them that I wanted to become a
doctor like Dr. Wells and speak English like Choi
Yong-wha. My father said there was no doctor school
in the country that he knew of. To learn to be a doctor, he said, the only place to go was the place where
the doctor had come from, which was Me-gook, and
that he did not even know where it was located except
that he heard it was somewhere in the west, thousands
of miles across the seas. And he also said that the
first place to go to learn and know anything was school,
and that the new missionary school taught geography,
arithmetic, and many other new things that the old
fashioned schools had never taught.

So the next day my father took me to the missionary
school located by an orchard belonging to the new
house which was being built for Bai Moksa, or Dr.
William Baird, who was the head of the department
of education of the Presbyterian Church in Pyeng
Yang. Professor Park Ja-joong was then the teacher
of the primary school which had started not long before. He was a scholarly man, kindly and considerate,
and I liked him from that day till the day, a few years
later, I went away from Shoong-sil Middle School,
where he was also my teacher.

My father, in the meantime, was engaged in a small
business of his own to earn a living. As a newcomer
to the strange city, of course, he could not think of
going into a more intricate and dignified business in
which he had no experience. He was a dirt farmer,
and he knew the value of the dirt. So he went ped-
dling plaster dirt in the streets of Pyeng Yang. To

start out with, he bought a pony. He would go out to the "no man's land" by the bank of the Bo-tong-kang, on the west end of the city, dig up a load of the fine clay loamy dirt, and haul it to the city on the back of the pony. The business was quite good in the fall when the people needed the dirt to plaster up the walls, floors and fireplaces of their homes and stores, getting ready for the approaching winter. But when winter did come, which was a long one in that part of the country, his business season was closed.

So with the help of Elder Choi, my father bought up a quadrangular tile-roofed house located on the Sul-see-dang-gol, the street leading to the north gate, called Chil-sung-mun, or the Seven Star Gate, the gate-way to all points north. This was the street of in-numerable inns and hotels, and my father went into the hotel business here. In his hotel business I showed him the newly-acquired knowledge of modern educa-tion turned into practical use. I was my father's book-keeper and accountant. By adding up so much taken in, and subtracting so much paid out every day, and multiplying so much by so many days of the month, I was able to tell my father how he was doing in his business.

My father thought it wonderful that I could figure them out so easily with a pencil and a piece of paper instead of using a handful of sticks, or the abacus which himself and his ancestors employed. He was delighted, and I was quite proud of myself. I thought I was doing nicely with the arithmetic part of his business, but his business was not doing too well, according to the figures. For it was while we were living in this house that the Central Presbyterian Church was being erected on the Jang-dai-jai hilltop and that my father had an awful hard time raising the sum which he had pledged toward the church fund. It was only about sixty yen, if I am not mistaken. He paid it all up though in several installments.

Very well, indeed, I remember that Sunday when the dedicatory service was being held in that magnificent new church building on the highest point in the heart of the city. At the sweet sound of that big bell, donated by someone in the United States, whose name I have forgotten, that Sunday afternoon, people from far and wide came pouring into that new church of ours, constructed in the shape of the capital letter "L". Honestly, it was the biggest modern building of that kind I had ever seen in my life, that is, looking from the outside. One wing was reserved for the ladies only, with a big curtain hanging between the two wings, as were all the other churches, and I had never seen the interior of that "no man's land" sanctuary.

I saw the largest congregation of the missionaries sitting together on that high and spacious platform at that time. Indeed, they had come from far and wide, Methodists as well as Presbyterians. If I am not mistaken, they were Rev. Appenzeller of the Methodist Church, from Seoul; Dr. Jones from Chemulpo; Rev. James Gale and Rev. Horace Underwood, both Presbyterians, from Seoul, and others. Everybody was there that day. Of course, all the Charr family from Jang-chun were there, too. The new big church was packed that very first day of its opening, and continued so. Soon, smaller new branch churches sprung up in the different sections of the city and in the outlying districts in order to accommodate the rapidly growing congregation. Indeed, the churches and schools were cropping out of the soil like the mushrooms in the balmy springtime!

Two years later, we moved to Nee-mun-gol, next

to the wall and north of the Dai-dong-gate. At the north end of the street was located the Pyeng Yang army barracks. Of course, we used to have three thousand strong Korean soldiers garrisoned in Pyeng Yang in those good old days. On Saturdays, I used to go up to the parade ground, west of the barracks, to see the soldiers drill, to listen to their bugle calls and to see them parade around the big smooth field. My house was not far from there, and I was awakened by their reveille every morning. O, how I loved it! Col. Jung-gwan-do, the Commanding Officer of the regiment, who lived just a block south of my house, was my model soldier-general for my sketch drawings in my boyhood days. I saw him riding past my house on his sleek looking white horse uncountable times. He was in blue uniform with gold braid and epaulettes and in high boots, wearing a shining sword on his side, jingling as the horse went trotting along the street, escorted by a foot soldier following behind.

"Ah, that's what I want to be when I get big, a great soldier, a general," I used to say to myself. I used to have all the great ambitions to be and to do everything that looked grand and wonderful to me. I was a little great dreamer. So far, I wanted to be a great surgeon and physician like Dr. Wells, a soldier like Jung-gwan-do, a missionary like Ma-Mok-sa, to speak English like Choi Yong-wha, and to see the Land of the Golden Mountain once in my lifetime!

I was not the only one who wanted to learn to speak English like Mr. Choi. There were many young men, all older than I, including a soldier named Lee Gun-bai and the Rev. Lee's cook, named Jung Won-Myeng whom I met later in Hawaii, who were eager to learn English from him. So they had organized a club called

"Myen-hak-hoi," or "Hard Learning Club," and started evening classes right in my school room.

Those were the happy days for my people, young and old, Christian and non-Christian, at least for a few years. The country was declared independent, the king proclaimed himself as an emperor, promising reforms, and "Dok-nip-hyup-hoi" or the "Independence Club," was organized under the leadership of Dr. Sur Jai-pil who had returned from America. My father and Big Uncle were the members of the Pyeng Yang Chapter of that club along with hundreds of leading Christians who were the brains and backers of the organization.

Ahn Chang-ho, the young silver-tongued orator of Pyeng Yang and a great patriot, delivered a stirring oration at the Qai-ja-dyung Pavilion gathering, condemning the greedy, corrupt, and unscrupulous local and national government officials and demanding sweeping political and social reforms. He advocated a good government and encouragement of modern education, thus insuring progress and unity of the people and maintaining the newly acquired independence, so that the once Hermit Kingdom could become a modern nation, united and strong.

Indeed, everybody was happy, everything looked rosy, expectations were high, and enthusiasm overwhelming. Going at this rate, if left alone, the Independence Club might have accomplished some good for the nation as a whole. But that was not the case. It was not to be. Like any other reform movement which met the same fate before and since, this one, too, was nipped in the bud by the old political cliques that would not stand for the public criticism, nor for the popular demand for sweeping reforms. To them, reform meant signing away of all the power and pres-

tige which they were in the habit of enjoying heretofore. It meant giving up their very livelihood. So,
by insinuation they made it appear before the emperor that the Independence Club was but a hotbed
of treason and rebellion, and hired the thugs of the
peddlers guild, called "Boo-sang," to disperse the
club meetings with hobnail studded hickory clubs, and
jailed, murdered and exiled the leaders of the reform
movement. Ahn Kyrung-soo, of Seoul, was murdered
in prison, Dr. Sur Jai-pil was exiled back to the
United States, and Ahn Chang-ho escaped to America
also, where he organized a similar patriotic associa-
* tion among the Koreans newly arriving from Hawaii.

Thus another reform movement went down, but,
thank God, Christianity continued to grow at acceler-
ated speed. Following the erection of the Central
Presbyterian Church on Jang-dai-jai, the big beautiful
Methodist Church was built on Nam-san-jai, or the
South Hill, near the West Gate. I used to go to that
church occasionally on Sunday evenings and attended
the services there. That's why I had come to know
* Noble Mok-sa, Dr. Hall and Morris Mok-sa among
the Methodist missionaries, and I knew Mr. Kim
Deuk-soo and Kim Chang-sik Moksa very well. They
had a hospital and dispensary of their own and also
a primary school on the hillside there.

It was about this time that the Shoong-sil Middle
School was just built on Dal-gok-jai, facing the missionary homes to the north. It was a two-story structure, with glass windows all around and surrounded
by spacious grounds, where I used to play football
with the missionaries and my fellow students. The
building had four class rooms on the ground floor and
three upstairs, including the north room which was
used also as the assembly hall. When it opened its

doors for the first time, there were only four students. One of them was my cousin, the scholar cousin of mine who was destined to succeed his scholarly father, my Big Uncle. He was a self-educated man, all this time tutored by his father. Now, he was one of the four first students to enter this first modern school of learning and first to graduate from it four years later.

And at about the same time, my father decided to move back to the farm for, evidently, he found out that he was a better farmer than he was a business man. So we moved back to a small village called Goodong-chang, about a mile southwest of Jang-chun, where my father bought a small thatch-roofed house. I was glad to be back to the country because I loved the farm, too, and then I was now near to my grandmother's house and all my young cousins with whom I had grown up together from my childhood days. Then, too, I liked the small church and school in Jangchun where we all went. Really, it was more like coming back to my home town.

My dear grandmother passed away at the age of eighty-two in the fall of the following year. And remembering how kindly she had been to me and how much I loved her since my childhood days in the Big House in the Mangsan mountains, I shed tears of deepest grief and sorrow at her deathbed. She had loved me most, and I sorrowed her most.

On the day of her funeral, people came from far and near to form the line of procession nearly half a mile long on the way to her final resting place which my Big Uncle had found for her. Perhaps the place he had chosen for her burial was not at all picked at random as I come to think of it now. He might have selected that particular spot years ago, who knows? Maybe he did it just before letting my Middle Uncle build his house on the side of the hill by the river only about a mile south of the Big House and just about the same distance east of my house up along the long ridge of foothills running parallel to the river.

Some three hundred yards west of my Middle Uncle's house and about fifty yards above the river bank there was a cozy nook, facing south, secluded and sheltered by granite bed rocks on the two sides and pine trees in the back. What better site than this he or anybody else could have picked for my grandmother's grave? My uncle knew a good place when he saw one, and he had found this ideal site . . . a nice and quiet, snug and sunny spot for his mother's final resting place.

Mah-Moksa (Rev. Moffitt) himself performed the last rites in the presence of hundreds of the white-garbed throng of Korean Christians who had lined up by the side of the hill, overlooking the river and the grain fields beyond it, who with bowed heads, listened to the message of the life hereafter and of resurrection. The weather was glorious, the surroundings beautiful, and the service truly impressive and inspiring, the like of which the people, Christian or non-Christian, had never before witnessed here. I came away much comforted, knowing that our dear God, the Heavenly Father, will be with her to the end of the world until we shall meet again at Jesus' feet!

Those were the happiest days of my early boyhood, and thus I was enjoying the country life until one Sunday, a year later, my cousin from the city met me and my father at the church and told us that I was ready to enter the Shoong-sil Middle School that fall where he would be a member of the Junior class. He said he had bought a house near the school and he and his wife were going to make a home there. During his first two years in school, he was boarding at the home of one of his classmates. Now, he said, I could stay at his home and go to the same school with him. So I returned to the city and entered Shoongsil high school.

In his spare hours, my cousin worked for Sho-Moksa, or the Rev. Swallon, as his secretary, in preparing the Sunday School lesson leaflets that were being translated and ready to be printed on a small job press installed near the school building. Later, Dr. Baird had him for his secretary in connection with the school work. He was the best penman as well as one of the best students in the school and everyone admired his beautiful handwriting. I was one of the admirers, and I tried to copy him. Honestly, if he was the best penman in his own group, he told me, I was the best in my own set. I know I was not.

My school was the only two-story building that I had ever seen in the city except the old pavilions or towers over the city gateways. It was another one of those buildings with glass windows. From the second floor windows facing the missionary homes on the opposite hilltop, I could look over the whole neighborhood between the Sang-soo-goo gate and the Bo-tong-mun and the river beyond it. In the immediate foreground, there was the open athletic field where I used to play football, introduced by the missionaries. Mr. Hunter, the more than six-foot tall, husky missionary was the best kicker, I remember. Oh, how far and high he used to kick the ball, and how many times I ruined my patent leather slippers in trying to kick the ball as he did! Mr. Coontz, who had just come from America, was the athletic instructor that year. No regular football or baseball games, as yet, were played in those early days, however.

Geography was the most interesting subject to me at the mission high school, and my cousin himself taught the subject very interestingly, using the textbook called "Sa-Min-Pil-Dee," or "Everybody Should Know," compiled in Korean by Professor Homer B. Hulbert, the American Advisor to the emperor. From this book I had learned to know that there were four oceans and five continents, where the different countries were located, and the names of each country, city, town, and seaport. There was a large map, (was it
* a Rand McNally Map?) hanging on the wall in the assembly room which showed Korea situated at one end of the map and the United States at the opposite end. Pointing at a place on the map, my cousin said, "Now, this is San Francisco, the seaport town, the port of entry, where Mr. Ahn Chang-ho, Bang-Wha-joong, David Lee, Kim Gwan-yu, Jung-Deung-nup, and Nee Bgung-june had first landed when they went to Me-Gook last year."

Wasn't that interesting! "Ah, San Francisco! So that's the name and that's where it is," I said to myself. "And that's where Mr. Ahn Chang-ho went. I, too, wish I could get there someday," I dreamed,

9
The Wonderful Dream

It was on the Sunday morning of the 28th of February, 1904. The sunshine was bright, and it was made brighter by its reflection from the frozen snow on the ground. Though cold, free from the usual Siberian wind sweeping down from the north, the morning was calm and serene. At my cousin's home where I stayed, near the missionary homes and the missionary high school where I went, I was getting ready to go to my Sunday School. Then, all of a sudden, I heard the report of a volley of gunshots coming from the direction of the ancient city wall upon the hilltop, shattering the peace and quiet of the Sabbath morning.

"What was that? That sounded like gunshots! What's happening? Surely, there can be no tiger hunting inside the city of Pyeng Yang!" I said to myself, and I was scared. So were my cousin's wife with her little baby boy and my girl cousin, Faith, who, too, stayed here and went to the missionary high school for girls. My Scholar cousin had gone up to the Rev. Swallon's house on the hilltop to look after the Sunday School lesson leaflets he was working on with the missionary who was in charge of them, and we were all alone in the house.

Then there was a sudden quiet again, and the suspense was even more scaring, not knowing what was to follow. We locked all the doors in the house, kept ourselves quiet and offered our prayers to God in our hearts. It was the first time any gun was fired in this

ancient capital city since the Battle of Pyeng Yang in
the Sino-Japanese War exactly ten years before, and
only recently we had returned from our mountain refuge to which my father and his two brothers and their
families had fled from that war. I guessed then there
was another war and another battle was being fought
then and there. For only a couple of weeks before, I
had seen a Japanese delegation in the courtyard of the
Rev. Samuel Moffit's house, reporting the Japanese
victory over the Russians in the naval battle fought
at Chemulpo Harbor, on the Yellow Sea coast, and
shouting, "Banzai, Banzai!"

The awful suspense was ended after quite awhile.
It seemed like ages to me when I began to hear the
doors of our neighbors opening cautiously, and then
the squeaking sound of feet over the snow-covered
ground and the muffled voices of our neighbors
gathered in the street corner outside, asking each
other the same question, "What's happened?" No
one seemed to know the answer except that "the shots
came from the direction of the North Gate." Just
then, I heard my cousin's voice. I opened the door
and saw him with an American flag in his hand and
heard him tell the neighbors that a small band of
Russian Cossacks had approached the North Gate
and, after exchanging a few shots with the Japanese
guards posted on the wall, had withdrawn. He said
that he and "Sho-Moksa" (or the Rev. Swallon in
Korea), had witnessed the scene from the hilltop
missionary home close to the wall through a spyglass,
and that he was just coming from there. "The war is
on now," he said, "and the Japanese troops which
landed at Chemulpo are expected to be here any moment."

At that moment, I saw a man come running down

from the direction of the North Gate, all excited. He said he had seen a Russian scout, who had been hiding in a haystack, discovered by some Korean farmers outside the North Gate, and he had been captured by the Japanese and taken to the governor's palace for safekeeping until the arrival of the Japanese troops.

So the Russians had already come and the Japanese were soon to come. Then there would be a bloody land battle in the once peaceful land of the Hermit Kingdom, once again in modern times! "When two whales are fighting, the poor, innocent, little shrimp is caught between them," is a Korean proverb. My cousin had the American flag attached to a long bamboo pole and placed it in front of the house none too soon for the Japanese troops arrived two days later. One infantry division entered the South gate, via Seoul, and a cavalry regiment, via Chinnampo, on the west coast, entered the Bo-tong-Gate, the outer West Gate, inside of which we lived. From the top floor window of my school, I saw them marching in with their sabers shimmering in the sunlight, slung loosely by the sides of their mounts, and dragging the field guns behind them. They were to be billeted in our neighborhood on their way to Port Arthur in Manchuria.

After school was out, I sat by the north window of my school, facing the missionary homes on the opposite hilltop, and I dreamed a day dream. "Ah, there is America herself right over there," I said to myself. "High above the others, those houses seem like some fairyland palaces! How calm and peaceful they look! Just look at those windows dazzling in the golden glow of the setting sun. That's Goom-San, or the Land of the Golden Mountain. And we call it Me-Gook, or Beautiful Country. It must be a beautiful country, indeed, and a big, strong and rich country!

"Oh, how calm and undisturbed are the people inside those houses while there is a war going on all around us and we are scared; only their star-spangled flags waving gently against the cold blue sky. Though they are in a war-torn foreign land, they seem to be better secure here than we are in our native land so that we borrowed their flag and displayed it at our house for protection against any possible danger from
* the Japanese, our historical enemy!

"Oh, Me-Gook! Oh, the big Beautiful Country! Oh, the Land of the Golden Mountain! Oh, I wish I had been born there! I can't help that I wasn't born there, but I wish I could be there once in my lifetime and come back as a missionary like the Rev. Moffitt and a medical missionary like Dr. Wells, some day!

"Ah, the Golden Mountain! I imagine it must be a very big, high and beautiful mountain made of and covered with pure gold that shines brilliantly, like the morning star so bright, that can be seen and looked up to from every direction, far and wide.

"Ah, the Golden Mountain! Oh, how wonderful it must be, and how much more wonderful it would be to see it once in my lifetime! The land of promise of modern times, flowing with milk of wisdom and honey of freedom, they say it is, and I hope I have an opportunity to be there some day!" I dreamed.

10

Go to America, My Boy

Came September, and back to the school I went. I
started in the second year course. I was glad to be
back in school after having gone through a period of
hopelessness and uncertainty of it as entertained by
my father who was very ill. Now I was in school for
one thing, although the chances of my going to America
remained as remote as ever. Actually, I never had
the slightest idea of my really going to America,
realizing that there was no one in my family or in my
uncle's family who was able to finance the trip. Maybe
it was for that reason that my desire to attain that
almost impossible goal was the more strong in me.

My father knew it, and he dreamed my dreams, too.
He told my Big Uncle why he had tried to make some
money from the money exchange business during the
Russo-Japanese War and lost all he had, so my Big
Uncle also knew that I badly wanted to go to America.
Now, could he help? He was not a rich uncle of mine.
Nobody was rich in the Charr family, but if he was
not rich in silver and gold, certainly, he was rich in
source of information and sound advice. He said to
my father, "Yes, I understand you perfectly, my dear
brother. However, your boy is not the only one who
has that ambition nowadays. My boy, Chung-surk
has the same idea, too. Well, I'll find a way for you.
There ought to be a way." Indeed, when there is a
will, there must be a way.

And he did find a way. One day, on October 12 to

be precise, (though by the Lunar calendar) yes, on the same fateful day, in 1492, Christopher Columbus discovered America, my uncle discovered a way to America for me. What a wonderful coincidence as to both the date and the event that had taken place!

It was during the lunch hour at my cousin's home that I saw my Big Uncle come in, together with my youngest cousin, Chungsurk. Without much ado, my uncle, with radiant smiles, said to me, "Easurk, my boy, how would you like to go to Me-gook?"

"To Me-gook, sir?" I responded, automatically, but without fully understanding the meaning of what he was saying. It was all so sudden that I could not believe my ears. At the mention of the word "Me-gook," my ears perked up and my eyes brightened. My lips were parted, but so trembling with surprise was I that I could not utter another word!

"Yes, my boy, wouldn't you like to go to Me-gook by way of Hawaii? You always wanted to go to Me-gook, I know. Your father told me so. So wished your cousin here, too, and he is going with you," he said, all excited, eyeing my cousin who was all smiles on his round boyish face. "But my father, will he . . . does he . . ."

"Oh, yes, my boy, your father knows all about it. He is very glad to see you go to America as you always wished," he said.

Then he explained that there was the Hawaii immigration open for Korean labor that was needed in the sugar plantations there, and hundreds and thousands of Koreans, young and old, were going by the shiploads. Two shiploads of them had already gone during the past twelve months, and the third shipload was getting ready to leave in the next two weeks. A friend of his, named Kim Jong-ok, who had gone there with the first shipload, had just returned to take back with him his wife and friends on the next ship bound for Honolulu.

With great enthusiasm my uncle told us what he had heard from his friend, all the good things about Hawaii, the land of perpetual summer, the land of mango, guava, bananas and bread fruit grown unattended by human toil, and if it was not for the pineapples and the sugar-cane that needed cultivation and harvesting, there would be no need of the bending of the backs or sweating of the brows for man's subsistence. All that one had to do was to lie down under the bread tree and cocoanut palm, and eat, drink and be merry in the cool of the shade and of the ocean breeze and he would not want for anything. No wonder it was poetically called "The Paradise Island!"

"But, of course," he said, "everybody can't do that except the natives there. For if it wasn't for the sugar-cane, which is the king crop there, there wouldn't be any immigration of labor, nor would there be any such opportunity open for you to go there on your way to San Francisco, which is only a week's journey from there."

Also, he said that his friend said that it was interesting to learn that the island, or a group of islands, which is an American territory, was a melting pot of all the five colored races represented there. Besides the natives and a few Americans themselves, there were the Portuguese, Porto Ricans, Filipinos, Chinese, Koreans and Japanese who were going there in great numbers. And work over there was not hard at all, he said his friend told him. The work which lasted only six days a week was more like "taking a nap under a pear tree," or "as easy as eating cake lying down." Men, women and boys all work so that I myself fitted in so nicely,

earning monthly wages in American gold dollars which was equivalent to the annual salary of the governor
* of Pyeng-an-do, believe it or not.

And the living conditions over there were excellent, too, he said. White painted bungalows were given free along with water, fuel, light and furniture. They gave church buildings to each camp of each group or nationality for religious services, and even their preachers' salaries were paid for by the plantation owners. They enjoyed the freedom of religion and free institutions. They were free to go out in their native costumes or in American dress just as they wished. And schools were open for their children free of tuition, and night schools were organized among the people themselves to enable the adults who desired to learn the English language.

"Yes, sir, I wanted to learn English by night in order to go to school in America when I get there, and I am going to work hard in order to make plenty of money to go to America with," I said.

"That's it. That's the idea, my boy," said my uncle. "And, now look. I've got two passports here for you two boys. They are issued by the Foreign Office of His Majesty's Imperial Government of Korea." On mine, though, he had added a few years to my age in order to make me look more like the able-bodied
* laborer that I should be.

My scholar cousin Nee-surk, his wife and my cousin, Faith, were also there listening to what was said of the wonderful place to which we were going which sounded like a fairy tale. My passport was about the last vestige of the independent Korean government which prescribed me as a citizen of the then independent Korea and for my safe conduct as such in my sojourn to the Republic of the United States of America.

I am proud of the fact that I came away as a free Korean. I still possess my passport, well-kept and preserved to this date.

"Now," said my uncle, "go to Professor Park and tell him that you are going to Hawaii on your way to America and that you are now going home with us in order to take leave of your parents." When I told my teacher I was going to Me-gook, by way of Hawaii, he was greatly surprised, and said that I was the youngest person going to America so far as he knew, at least from his school and from that part of the country. Wishing me a safe journey and all the success in the world for me, he said that he might not live to see me return from such a long journey abroad. And true to his own prediction, he passed away soon after I had landed in America.

That afternoon, accompanied by my uncle and cousin, I went home happily excited. My father was happy to see me happy although my mother was a little sad. He asked me questions and I answered him and told him what I had heard and done before I left the city. And he told me he was happy that my uncle had found a way for me to go to America. Because he said, "My son, I want to tell you now that it was to enable me to send you to America that I had gone into that money exchange business. You told me many times you wanted to go abroad for your medical studies and I wanted to send you to America, the greatest country in the world to learn everything first hand, they say. You see, I've never had a chance to go to school when I was a boy like you, and consequently in all my life I have been illiterate and ignorant in all things, even in the old-fashioned learning. You have already *
started on the road to modern learning, and now you are going to America which I know is the best country

in the world. The others come to take and destroy. America alone comes to give and save, to help and cure, to teach and preach the great Gospel of peace and salvation.

"You are my first born son, and my hope is in you and in America. Wishing to go to America has been your dream, I know, and wishing to send you to Me-gook has been my dream during these many years since we came to Pyeng Yang. I am a sick man who can't help you. But, now. God be blessed! He shows the way. Your opportunity has come at last. Your Big Uncle came over the other day with that happy news that made me very happy, indeed. And, now are you happy to go to America, the land of your dreams?" he asked me.

"Yes, father," I said, "I'm happy, indeed, to go to America, but you are very sick and I can't leave you like this."

"Oh, don't you worry about me, son. I am happy now, and I'll be all right pretty soon. Your future is my prayer, and in your future I live. Besides, your brother, Ray-surk will take your place while you are away," he said.

So saying, he smiled a very contented and joyous smile. And likewise everybody else was happy . . . my mother, grandmother and my brother. Then he asked me what I was studying in the school and what was the most interesting thing I had to tell him about. And I told him that geography was the most interesting subject to me, and that I had learned the direction in which America was situated and how to get there. When I told him America was situated in the westerly direction, and to go west was to go in an easterly direction, he laughed heartily like a little boy. That was the first time in a long while we had heard him laugh like that and everyone joined him. Well, he certainly thought I was telling him a good joke. He said he had never heard such a paradoxical thing like that before.

"You are trying to make me laugh, aren't you, son?" he said. "To go west is to go east, you said, ha, ha! You can't mean that, son. For you can't say that to go to the city of Pyeng Yang, which is west of here, is to go east, can you? If you do, wouldn't you be going away from instead of going toward the city? Anybody can see that, don't you think so?"

"Well, father, really, there are many ways to go to the city," I said. "The city being very close to us from here, however, it would be the shortest way to go west. But they say you can arrive at the same point by going straight in the opposite direction, too. Therefore, to go to Me-gook is to go west as well as to go east. The American missionaries came westward to the Orient because it was a shorter distance that way. They could have come eastward as well. So I am going to follow their route back toward Me-gook. That much is not so hard for me to understand, father, provided that the earth is round. But where the fixed point of East and West is, I simply can't understand myself. For as I understand it, Hawaii is west of Me-gook, Japan is west of Hawaii, and Korea is west of Japan, yet our country is called, 'The Eastern Country' instead of 'The Western Country,' and Me-gook, which is way back east of us, is called 'The Great Western Country' instead of 'The Great Eastern Country.' It seems to me that every country is either east or west of every other country on earth which would prove to show that the earth is round, all right, though. But, if the earth is round and it rotates about the sun once every day so that it is going round and round all

the time, then where is the East and where is the
West? I can't understand that, father."

"We can't understand a lot of things, son," said
my father. "One thing I understand though, is that
all the new things that come from Me-gook seem to
be just the opposite from the old ways. For instance,
we open our doors out; they . . . the missionaries
. . . open theirs in. We men wear hats inside as well
as outside; they take theirs off inside. We put our
hair up in topknots; they keep theirs down, cut short.
Their wives wear the topknots instead. We dress in
white; they, in black. Our trousers are roomy, theirs
tight; we sit down on the floor; they sit up in chairs.
'Gentlemen first' with us; 'ladies first' with them. We
men and women segregate; they congregate always.
Did you notice them? Yes, all things are opposite.
It's no wonder they have come East westward!"

"Isn't that the truth?" I agreed with him. "Yet I
like them. Strange though they seem, I like their ways
of thinking and their ways of doing things. Theirs
are the scientific ways, they say. They must have come
East in the westerly direction, all right, as they say
they did, because I know they always tell us the truth."

"No doubt about that, son," he said. "They are
wonderful people, I know, and they have come from
a wonderful country far advanced in modern civilization, and you are now going there to learn those strange
but wonderful things. As for whichever way you may
go there, in an easterly or westerly direction, I don't
care. All that I care is that you get there!" he said,
stroking my jet-black long hair. All the while my
mother, sitting between myself and my little brother
and holding our hands, listened. So did my grandmother, who passed away a few years later.

October 14, 1904, was the memorable day, the day

I left home for America. Early that morning my cousin, Chung-surk, came over to my house to take me with him to my Big Uncle, who was to accompany us to the city and to Chinnampo where we were to embark for America. With a small bundle of my * clothes slung over my back, I bade goodbye to all my dear ones and started out. Just before I stepped out of my home, my father, with tears in his eyes, pulled out a small stringful of old coins . . . twenty-five Korean pennies with square holes in the middle . . . and put it into my hand and said, "Son, this is all I have left and I am giving it to you. Make good use of it, and may God be with you always. Goodbye now; I hope to see you return soon!" My mother sobbed while still clutching my hand in hers. I took the coins but said nothing, not understanding the full significance of it nor realizing the extent of the love and affection attached to it. Perhaps, I was too young to fathom the very deep interest that my father took in me and in my future as I do now. The Korean proverb is that, "To understand fully the affections of one's parent is when he becomes a parent himself."

When we reached the Big House, they were all waiting for us. There was every member of the Charr family, with the exception of my home folk, gathered there, and the relatives of the bride of my cousin Chung-surk. They were all smiling, I thought, except the two mothers of my cousin's couple, who looked rather sad, and my cousin's wife who was actually weeping because she was not going with her husband this time. My uncle thought it advisable that her husband should go alone first to prepare a place and send for her later.

At length my uncle stood up and said, "Like the old saying, 'Though you may see your friends off a thousand miles, you will come to one parting'; suppose we bid them farewell and let them go now, realizing that the sooner they depart, the sooner they'll return. I am going to take them back to the city today, then to Chinnampo where they will board a steamer bound for Hawaii. I will be back in a few days to tell you all about it," he told his family, and then led us off. Saying goodbye to each other, some with smiles and some in tears, we left the Big House and the village of Jang-chun.

Back in the city that afternoon, the first thing I did was to get a haircut. I had long, straight, raven-black hair over two feet long, braided down on my back, touching my ankles, and the end tied in a bow with maroon-colored Chinese silk ribbon. A haircut was the first requisite on my way to America. My uncle returned from the city office of the "Hawaii Development Company" or the Hawaii Immigration Agency, with two Koreans who were to journey to Hawaii with us, and one of them was my barber. Using a pair of scissors found in the sewing basket belonging to my cousin's wife, he chopped off my hair as if he were chopping down a tree with a dull pocket knife. Oh, what a horrible-looking haircut I found I had when I looked into the mirror! I was so ashamed of it that I had to cover up my head with an old cap given to me by Preacher Han's son, and pulled it way down to my ears.

Having heard of my going to America by way of Hawaii, all my friends came to see me and congratulate me during that afternoon and evening. Indeed, they were surprised to know that I was the first one among them to embark for America as they all dreamed of doing, so I was envied by all. I was secretly proud of myself and thought to myself, "So I beat you all to it, eh, fellows?"

Of course, I didn't forget to say goodbye to the Reverend Moffitt who baptised me and who was the first American who came to Pyeng Yang. When I went over to his home that evening and told him I was on my way to America, he said, "Oh, how nice, Easurk! I'm glad, and I wish you all the success from your trip." Then he asked me what I intended to learn in America. When I told him that I intended to learn to be a doctor and return as a medical missionary from America, he was delighted and said, "That's just fine. We need more doctors, especially Korean doctors for the Korean people. May God bless you and keep you until your return as a Christian doctor." Then he continued on, "I'm going to write you a letter of introduction, to whom it may concern, which might be of help to you as a stranger in a strange land, and a strange land it will be to you indeed, my friend. You will find some will be good, I assure you, but some others will not be as good as you might expect them to be, so be careful, won't you, my young friend? Please remember that, and go to a church everywhere you go where you will find Christians who will lead you right. And please don't forget to pray to God for His guidance, as you will be far away from your home and your loved ones. Now goodbye and good luck to you, as we say in Me-gook, till we meet again soon," he said, and shook my hands so gently and affectionately.

Early the next morning, my friends Kiel-Jin-hyung, Jang Hay-soon, Paik Shinchil, Nee Kijong, and others, on their way to school, came in to say goodbye. The first two named followed me to the United States several years later and have returned home since. On that bright, sunny morning of October 15, 1904, bidding goodbye to my dear cousin Nee-surk and his wife and cousin, Faith, and accompanied by my Big Uncle, my cousin Chung-surk, and the two fellow-travelers, I left the ancient city of Pyeng Yang, where I had first seen the light of the New World through the missionaries, and I was on my way to the land of my dreams.

Out of the Botong gate and across the Botong River we traveled on foot some twenty-miles that day and stopped at an inn for the night, nursing my sore feet, and just before the sunset the next day, we reached Chinnampo on the Yellow Sea coast. What a pleasant surprise was waiting there for me! There I met a few familiar faces that I used to see back in Pyeng Yang. One of them was a next door neighbor, a young man named Oh, whom I used to know. Two other young men, Kim and Choi, the former with his wife, a cousin of Oh's, who were formerly cooks at the missionary homes and two others, Shinn and Kim. All lived in my neighborhood. Of course, they all knew my uncle, too. Weren't they glad to see me and wasn't I glad to see them! Forgetting all my aching feet and legs, I was glad now that I had come instead of returning home when my feet and legs began to get so very sore. We were to be fellow-travelers and sojourners together in the days and months ahead and perhaps even for years to come, and we were happy together, talking about good old Pyeng Yang behind us and about the future prospects ahead of us in the New World toward which we were about to journey together.

My uncle was glad to find us among good company to travel with and he was greatly pleased and satisfied. Our boat was not there as yet, and we had to wait quite a few days at the lodging place at the expense of the Hawaii Development Company of which we were welcomed guests. That being the case, on the following morning, my uncle, who had stopped at a hotel in town, came in and said to my cousin and me, "Well, boys, I've come to say goodbye to you now. I'm told that your boat won't be leaving for quite a while yet, and I cannot tarry here too long for I have an important business matter to attend to back in Pyeng Yang. Besides, you are among good company, so I can set my mind at rest. I'm very sorry that I won't be able to see you off, but I've got to leave for the city at once. I want you to write me as often as you can, telling me how you are getting along and how things are with you. Easurk, I want you to write to your father also, as he will be so anxious to hear from you. And boys, pray to God for His guidance and read the Bible for His words of comfort and instruction. I am going to pray for you always. Now, goodbye, and have a safe voyage. May God be with you on your journey and until your return home someday soon!"

And he said, "Goodbye, boys, goodbye, till we meet again!"

"Goodbye, father," said my cousin, and "Goodbye, sir, Big Uncle," I said.

11

On the Paradise Island

A week later, our boat arrived in Chinnampo, and we set sail on a fine sunshiny morning. The boat was called Ohayo Maru, a small Japanese steamer plying between here and Yokohama. Its passengers were made up entirely of the Korean emigrants bound for Hawaii numbering a score or so persons, including two women and a small boy. However, my uncle's friend, Kim Jong-ok, could not sail with us as was expected. He was to follow us to Honolulu on the next shipload which was destined to be the last one before the Hawaii immigration terminated altogether. My cousin's wife would be coming on that boat, too.

It was the first time I was ever on a ship and for the first time I saw the Yellow Sea. As soon as the ship was out in the open sea it began to rock and roll, and I was already getting a dizzy spell. By nightfall, the ship was rounding the Jang-san-got Point, the promontory famous for innumerable shipwrecks. The boat was now rolling violently, tossing around all the movable things in it from side to side. I was one of them. It made me very sick, indeed, and it made everybody else sick except one man who was with his wife and a boy. He and his family were placed right next to us on one side and the Kim couple on the other side in the same section so that we, my cousin and I, were sandwiched in between them. Hahn was his name, and he was a fine Christian man who was related to Mr. Ahn Changho, the patriot. He certainly was a great help to us all. The rocking boat made me so sick that I thought I was going to die! But, gradually the storm subsided as we passed over the danger point. It was my first experience on a boat out in the stormy sea, and I was bound to have plenty more of it, I feared.

We arrived at Chemulpo, the Port of Seoul, nearly at noon the next day. Here, some more emigrant pas- *
sengers were picked up, and we proceeded to Pusan, the last seaport to visit before leaving my native land. More than two hundred people got on our boat here at Pusan. They were the natives of this southeastern province of Kyung-sang-do, the seat of the ancient Silla civilization and the most populous of all the eight original provinces. The number of the emigrants alone tell the story. The Korean emigrants now totaled some 350 on the boat, including several women and children.

Finally bidding farewell to our native country, we set sail for Kobe, Japan, across the Korean Strait, which was just about a day's journey, and brushing by the Tsushima Islands, belonging to Japan, the home of the Shimadori wrestlers, we reached the pine-covered shores of the island kingdom. Passing through the channelports of Shimonoseki and Moji, we stopped at Kobe in the late afternoon of the following day to pick up the first batch of Japanese emigrants. At dusk we continued on through the night and arrived at Yokohama early the next morning. Here we were transferred to a giant four-stacker American steamer called Mongolia, the sistership of Manchuria. The ship was so large that there was no pier to dock it close to the shore, so the ship was anchored off a mile or so out in the Tokyo Bay. Sampans, or small skiffs, were employed to transfer all the passengers, including the bulk of the Japanese emigrants that were picked up here. It took them half a day to get the ship ready for sail. Now, the emigrants of the two nationalities totalled something like 900 . . . some 350 Koreans and 550 Japanese. At last, with a thundering blast of whistle from the big ship we were off again on our last leg of the journey to Honolulu.

At long last, on the morning of the fourteenth day, (I think it was), on the Pacific Ocean, we sighted the Diamond Head looming ahead in the distance. That's where Honolulu was situated, I was told. "Ah, so that's my stepping stone to San Francisco," I said to myself. And as the ship came close to the harbor I saw my stepping stone appearing bigger and bigger and clearer until I found it to be a pretty big-sized rocky cliff standing out to the sea when our ship docked at the pier close to the shore.

And what a delightful little place was the Honolulu town, like a gem of the ocean, basking in the warmth of the bright sun! By the calendar it was winter. But by the climate it was summer. It would be snowing then in Korea. Here from the deck, I saw the people moving about in shirt sleeves and panama hats, and the natives diving into the ocean bottom after the small coins tossed by the passengers from the upper deck. Truly, this was the wonderland, the land of perpetual summer and the land of perfect peace, I thought, and was glad.

And what a cosmopolitan land it was! Men of all shades and sizes were there, too. Back in the old country I had seen only four different foreign nationalities . . . the Chinese, the Japanese, the French (priest), and the American. Here, in addition to these four, I saw the Negro who was as black as charcoal, and the Malayan as brown as the charcoal-toasted chestnut. And what giants those policemen and steve-

dores of the native Kanaka were! Only in fairy tales
had I heard of men so big and so stout. Then and
there, I began to see and understand what I had read
about in the books.

It was just about noon-hour when we were landed
and brought to a large building right by the pier. It
must have been the headquarters of the Hawaii Development Company which had brought us here. The
first thing we found there was our lunch . . . our
lunch in red and white which was prepared on a long
table with benches on either side of it in a spacious
room, nice and clean and cool. Yes, that red salmon
and white rice tasted mighty good to me, I should
say. That was the first time in my life, like in almost
everything else, I tasted that red fish that was so good
that day.

As soon as our repast was over, a roll call was in
order. It was reported "All present and accounted
for," which proved that we arrived there safe and
sound without any untoward happenings on the ship.
That done, we were now divided up into several groups
to be sent to the several different plantations in the
different islands. Some of them had the preference,
and others had none. Most of them were sent by boat
to the biggest island called Hawaii which was some
distance from Honolulu. Myself, my cousin and most
of my original company from Pyeng Yang were most
fortunate to be sent together to the Ewa Plantation
on the island of Oahu, the same island on which Honolulu is located. It was only a few miles west of there.
Others got on small boats to go to the other islands,
some big, some small. But we got on the train bound
for Ewa.

It was the first time in my life I had ever been on a
train. Back home, with my father, I had helped build

a railway bed for the Japanese, but had never even seen a train until that day. How fast that train traveled! It was flying, I thought. It went so fast that the telegraph poles on the side of the railroad looked to me like they were leaning half way down to the ground. And looking out through the windows, I saw the luxuriant growth of vegetation all along the way. Everything was in green and red in wintertime. Oh, I forgot. There was no winter there, that's right. There was nothing but days of perpetual summer and nights of cooling ocean breezes. The scenery was beautiful; the climate delightful. All my listeners agreed with me when I said, "Oh, isn't this like the Paradise on earth! And wasn't the Garden of Eden said to be something like this?"

The train stopped entirely too soon for me. We had come to the Ewa station. From the station I saw the great big sugar mill of the plantation a short distance to the northeast with the sky-high smoke stacks sticking up. Here we were transferred from the passenger train to the train of flat cars which was waiting for us. It belonged to the plantation proper, and those flat cars were used for hauling sugar cane from the fields to the mill and for transporting the workers to and from the more distant fields. Now we were bound for the Korean camp just a little ways east of the mill.

The whole plantation was divided into three separate camps: the Korean camp on the east side; the Chinese camp, some distance north of it; and the Japanese on the west side—all centered around the mill and the administration buildings adjoining the superintendent's residence and the plantation store. On the ship, *Mongolia,* the Chinese cooks were quartered in the rear, the Japanese in the front, and we

Koreans were in the middle part of the steerage, which was coincidentally an exact duplicate of the geographic positions of their respective countries on the map. Here the order had been jumbled slightly. Somehow or other this trio of races of people were found together wherever they went.

It took us but a few minutes to get to our camp which was found right by the railroad tracks and bound by the cane fields on two sides. I saw the rows of the whitewashed cabins in the camp. Reflected in the later afternoon sun, they looked pretty good to me from the distance. Now when the train stopped, and just as we were alighting from the cars and wondering just which way to turn, looking this way and that, I saw a man, in light brown mounted on a white horse, racing toward us from the direction of the mill which we had just passed. Coming closer, the horseman, waving his hat, greeting us in Korean, saying, "You are welcome, my fellow-countrymen! I just went to the depot to meet you, but I was a little too late. I'm very sorry!"

Weren't we happy to hear a fellow-countryman greeting us in our native tongue in a faraway strange land! And, wasn't I glad to see a fellow-townsman who called me by name most unexpectedly! Of course he knew me and I knew him. He was none other than Boss Jung of the Korean camp here and he had come from Pyeng Yang, too. Several others of my company knew him also. And I knew an interesting story about him, too.

He was one of those ambitious young men who wanted to learn to speak English with the idea that he was coming to America some day. So he had come to the Hard Learning Club in Pyeng Yang one evening and told Choi Yong-wha, the English teacher, that he was going to learn English from him. And Choi was said to have said to him that it would be impossible for him to speak English because his lips were too thick. As a matter of fact, his lips were not at all any thicker than anybody else's. It is a fact, too, that everybody seems to have that trouble when trying to learn a foreign language at first.

Well, Jung was not discouraged by Choi's joking remark. On the contrary, he had determined more than ever to learn to speak English some day better than Choi did himself. So he did. He had gone to an American gold mining camp in the north and working as a flunky to the American engineers there, he had learned to speak English well enough to be the Korean interpreter and supervisor of the Korean settlement here. He had come to Hawaii on the first shipload,
* I believe.

Now Boss Jung led us into the camp where we were welcomed by our fellow-countrymen who had arrived there one or two shiploads before us. They were glad so see us for they were few in number and were feeling rather lonesome. And, we, as newcomers, were even more glad to see our fellow-beings sojourning in a strange land thousands of miles away from home. Then, too, we felt that we were strangers of strangers and that they could help us out in many ways, as we found everything so strange.

Of the many strange things which I had seen and heard there, the strangest that I had come across was that I had two Sundays in one week, or in two successive days. The day we arrived there happened to be Sunday, as sure as we were there and had our red and white lunch in Honolulu. But, we were told it was not Sunday; it was only Saturday. We were all puzzled. We could not all be wrong or forgotten the days or weeks while crossing the ocean. It took us exactly two weeks, if I am not mistaken. Now we were told it was not Sunday; it was only Saturday. I did not know what to think, or how to account for that one day we had gained. Then, all of a sudden, a bright idea came out of my head and I said, "I know, I know now. We gained a day because our ship traveled so fast!"

Of course nobody in our company knew anything about the international date line set up somewhere in the Pacific. At least I did not see any line when we crossed it. Well, at any rate, to gain a day was better than to lose one, I thought. Besides, observing two Sundays in a week was better than only one. Moreover, we had missed Sunday service that day if it were Sunday, and had missed many Sundays already for nearly a month, and I thought we were fortunate to have that extra Sunday to make up for all the Sundays that we had missed.

So, on the morning following, we were gathered in the lobby of Boss Jung's cabin in the heart of the camp, for as yet there was no regular church building in existence, nor a preacher present. So Boss Jung himself preached a sermon. He was an all around man there; he was everything; he did everything. He was the interpreter, camp boss, social leader, preacher, language teacher, mail carrier, and what-not. All in Sunday attire, some in white or brown suits, most still in Korean costume, we men, women, and children were happy to observe our first Sunday service together in a strange land where we had come to stay and to make a living.

Now, after a couple days of rest and preparation, I went out to work for the first time. I was sent to a place where they were making a new field out of the wasteland full of bramble brushwood. Oh, yes, I had gone out there on a train early that morning, and I thought it was lots of fun to ride to the place of work. A mansize pickaxe was given to me with which to work. I was to cut down the brushwood and to dig up the roots with it. That pickaxe was so big and heavy, and my hands so small and tender, that pretty soon both of my palms blistered and began to bleed.

To be sure, I was too small for that kind of work, and my hands were never used to any rough "stuff" like that. The only things that I was accustomed to were pen and paper, and nothing else. Although my father was a farmer, I had never done any farm work back in the old country. My father had intended me to be a scholar, and a scholar's hands should be as soft as silk and fingers as pointed as a brush pen. Athletics were never known until the missionaries came with the modern idea of physical training. All forms of physical exertion were not dignified, nor befitting a scholarly person to indulge in, according to the old Korean conception.

My foreman of that first day was a Korean young man named Yun (who lives in Los Angeles now) and who happened to be my next room neighbor and a close friend of Boss Jung himself. And he, too, was a Pyeng Yangite, if that means anything. Well, he bandaged up my hands with his own handkerchief, and gave a "water boy" job to finish up that day's work to me. The next day, I was transferred to another field doing "ho-ri ho-ri" work, or discarding the old leaves off the sugar cane that leaned down on the ground. The work itself was not quite as heavy as with a pickaxe. If it had not been for the dreaded centipedes that crawled around under almost every cane and in between the leaves that scared me every time I saw one, and which bit me many times, or the hairlike bristles on the dry leaves that, when brushed against them, stuck to my skin and my clothes, it would not have been so bad. Well, good or bad, there was no choice in the matter. Besides, it was only my stepping stone to America, and I did not mind it so very much at first. They were all in a day's work, I thought.

So I worked every day, and before I realized, I had come to the end of the first month and my first payday. At the paymaster's window I proudly presented my "bango," or Japanese term for number, stamped on a small brass disc. I received a tiny brown pay envelope containing eight ($8.00) dollars in coin . . . one five-dollar gold piece and three silver dollars . . . for the sixteen days I worked. Oh boy! Oh joy! It was the first time in my life I had earned money! And American silver and gold at that! And, it was the first time in my life I had ever seen GOLD, and now I owned it!

Was I happy! And I felt like a man, too, for I was paid as was my cousin and everybody else, at the rate of fifteen dollars a month, or an average of fifty cents a day. Working ten hours a day, I made five cents an hour which wasn't much when figured backwards like that. With that earning capacity, I figured I could not get rich very quick over there, which was not my purpose for being there. As I said before, it was only my stepping stone to America, and I had determined to work every day and save every nickel I earned with that idea in my mind . . . to be able to go to San Francisco as soon as possible.

Ours was the smallest camp, so far as our own population was concerned. There were six by six rows of cabins in the whole camp, and we occupied only three rows on the east end. The rest was partly occupied by some Portuguese and Puerto Ricans. Those Puerto Ricans were the happiest people I had ever seen. (They were of the Negro origin.) They were directly opposite from my cabin, and I could not help watching them sing and dance day and night all the time when they were not working. And that was the first time I had ever seen men and women swinging around in each other's arms. That looked awfully strange to me, of course, as my folks back home had never done such things . . . not even husband and wife together. Social customs of different people were different, I observed.

Those Hawaiian bananas, fully ripe on the trees when picked, were one of the finest fruits in the world. They tasted very good, indeed. I used to buy them from the Bak-kay, or the Chinese, who also sold vegetables to our cook. The Chinese had come there many years ago and settled as truck gardeners. The term Bak-kay, meaning "White Devel," was originated by the Chinese themselves; and now others called the Chinamen Bak-kay, thinking that was another name for them.

Speaking of Esperanto, or a universal language, here in the plantations was spoken an international language, a mixture or amalgam of tongues of all the races and nationalities represented there. Not understanding English myself, when I first heard them talk so rapidly I thought they all spoke English so well and so fluently. But, soon I discovered it was not altogether English, and it was the old story of the Tower of Babel repeated.

Now, some of the sugar cane fields were ready for harvest . . . to be cut and gathered and hauled to the mill there, to be made into the snow white granulated sugar. The cutting was called "cutchi cutchi," or the Japanese pronunciation for the word to "cut." Well, the cutting was about the hardest work that there was out in the fields, requiring long and muscular arms to wield the big topping knife, called machete, which is half knife and half clipper with upturned hook at the point that both cut and pulled. It is used in all the tropical countries, and it was more like the Chinese broad sword. No wonder the Chinese were the expert sugar cane cutters there.

Of course, I could not do that kind of work. At least I was not asked to do just that. The job which they gave me to do was to gather up those that were already cut and carry them out to the flat cars that were waiting on the tracks. This job was called "Hop-bye," or carrying. The way to do it was to tie up an armful of the cane into a bundle with a gunny sack and carry it over the shoulder or on the back, take it up to the flat car and dump it there. Some fields were so wide and so long that to carry a load from one end of the field to the other was hard work, indeed. Besides, when the needle-like bristles falling off the dry leaves pricked my sweating skin with stinging pain and the cloud of dust choked my throat in the steaming hot sun, and my foreman, who was either a native or Portuguese, urged me along hollering "biki," or hurry, hurry, it was made still harder.

In the meantime, my cousin had sent for his wife, and she had just arrived with the last shipload, accompanied by Kim Jong-ok and his wife and friends. It was the very last ship to leave Korea, as the Oriental immigration to Hawaii had just been terminated with that very ship. (The Koreans in Hawaii totalled some 6,747, and out of that number, some 2,000 came over to the Mainland.) She brought me a letter from my Big Uncle saying that my father was very sick, worse than before I left home, and that he wanted to know how soon I was leaving for America. I was very sad, indeed, that my father's condition had become worse instead of better, and that I didn't know how soon, if ever, I was to reach my destination, under the circumstances. Just then, my cousin came over to me and said that his father, my Big Uncle, was just as anxious as my father to have me sent to America as soon as possible. He had sent fifteen dollars in care of my cousin's wife, and asked him to buy me passage to San Francisco immediately.

It was really a great sacrifice and effort on his part to arrange that sum of money back in my old country. Fifteen dollars meant more than thirty yen and thirty yen meant more than three hundred ryang, which was quite a fortune. Still, that sum was not quite enough to buy me even a steerage ticket on a steamer to the Mainland. I had to have thirty-one dollars . . . thirty dollars for the ticket itself, and one dollar of commission for the agent who did the buying.

My cousin said to me, "This sum which my father sent is not quite enough, I know, but making up the balance myself, I will buy you a ticket so you will go on to America first. I will manage to follow you as soon as possible."

"Oh, thank you," I said, "but how can I go alone without you? I must wait until you are ready to go with me. Back in the native country I might be able to travel alone, perhaps, but to the faraway-strange land, how could I travel all by myself?"

"Oh, you shouldn't worry about that," he replied, "since you will have somebody over there who will look after you when you get there, I'm sure. Mr. Ahn Chang-ho, the great Korean patriot, and Mr. Kim Sung-moo, my wife's brother, who went there two years ago, will take good care of you. On your way to San Francisco, you will have your traveling companions whom you know so very well, so you shouldn't be lonesome aboard the ship. Your friends, Mr. Oh and Mr. Shinn and three ladies and a little girl, all from Pyeng Yang, who are already in Honolulu, are going with you on the next steamer sailing next week. Now, wouldn't that suit you all right?"

The following day, a friend of mine named Yun, took me out to Honolulu and bought me a dark coat and a pair of white duck pants, thinking that would be about the ideal suit to wear in San Francisco. Another friend, named Hong, bought me a new pair of shoes. Now I was all dressed up from head to foot with gifts from my friends.

At last I was all set to sail for America, and had come to Honolulu to wait for my Dreamland Express to San Francisco which was due in three days. It was at a Japanese hotel where my friends, the ladies and I stopped. Even in those early days there were more Japanese in Honolulu and in all the islands than any other race or nationality, and they were operating hotels and all sorts of small businesses. There I discovered that the Orientals go with other Orientals, whether or not they like each other, their appearance, their tastes, their backgrounds, and their living standards being very much alike.

Now, the day of my departure arrived, as did the big ship, early that morning. The ship was called Manchuria, the sister ship of Mongolia, on which I had arrived some six months before. That six months' time had seemed so long while I was on the

plantation. Now it seemed like it was only yesterday, and I felt sorry that I was going to leave her
. . . the Paradise Island . . . with whom I had fallen
in love at first sight. If the "Paradise Island" was
a poetic name given her by the American admirer, I
learned that the Chinese name for her was "Dahn
Hiang-san," or "Sandalwood Fragrant Mountain."
Although I disliked the plantation work, I loved the
Aloha land, dearly.

12

The Land of My Dreams

Aboard "Manchuria," the sister ship of "Mongolia," the large American steamer with American crew and Chinese cooks, there were quite a few steerage passengers, mostly Japanese and a few Koreans, as well as the first class passengers who were Americans. The Koreans consisted of three women and a little girl and three men, including myself. Young Mrs. Lee with her mother-in-law was going to meet her husband in San Francisco, and Mrs. Lim with her little daughter was bound for Los Angeles to join her husband there. My two friends were D. Y. Shinn and D. Y. Oh, the two fellow-townsmen of mine who had been my fellow-travelers ever since I left home.

It took seven days to reach the Mainland from Honolulu. Actually, it had been more than six months from home. A long journey! On the morning of June 26, 1905, the steamer plowed through the Golden Gate strait, the "gateway to America," into the San Francisco Bay, and docked at a pier in the harbor. We were ushered in by a bright, sunshiny morning, and what a grand and glorious feeling I experienced, and oh how happy I was at that moment! God be praised that at last I had now come to the land of my dreams, a promised land flowing with milk of wisdom and honey of freedom!

Viewing San Francisco from where I was standing on the deck of the ship, I noticed a remarkable likeness in topography between this city and my native city of Pyeng Yang. It reminded me of my first visit to Pyeng Yang, when I viewed it from the east bank of Dai-dong River. For instance, the twin hills atop the city in the background . . . the Russian Hill to the north was comparable to the Jang-dai-jai hill, and on this Russian Hill stood the Central Presby-terian Church; and the Nob Hill to the south re-sembled the Nam-san-jai Hill, and on Nob Hill stood the Methodist Church. Then, too, the Telegraph Hill in the foreground looked much like the Nien-gwang-dyung and the Dai-don-mun pavilions perched atop the high ancient city wall along the west bank of the river.

The likeness of the two cities did not stop there. I discovered later that the natural layout of San Francisco was very much like the city of Pyeng Yang, while the Twin Peaks in the distance had the appear-ance of Sam Gwang-san, where there was an Ameri-can cemetery. Both cities were located between two waters . . . one between an ocean and a bay, and the other between two rivers. In fact, both were pen-insulas . . . the isthmus of one was at the north end of the city and that of the other at the south end.

Here, at last, I had come to the city of my dreams, and finding its appearance so much like that of my native home town made me feel "at home" and happy indeed! Thus, while I was enjoying the nat-ural scenery and experiencing the realization of the thrills of my lifetime dreams, a white uniformed man appeared suddenly on the deck. He was the medical inspector from the Immigration Service, I learned. He had all the steerage passengers lined up on the deck in two separate groups. The Japanese, being numerous, were lined up in two long lines facing each other, men in one line and women in another.

My company of Koreans, being so few in number, were lined up in a corner. Not knowing what it was all about, I was all eyes, wondering what was going to happen next. I noticed everyone, including my friend, Oh, had a scared look on his face. It was a well-known fact among the immigrants that the medical inspector at a port of entry was regarded as the person one dreaded most to meet. He held the key to America. He may let you land or may send you back home. Because one had entered the Golden Gate did not necessarily mean that he was in America. He or she must pass the physical examination conducted by this all-important medical inspector before being allowed to land.

Now I saw the inspector coming toward our group. Evidently he was going to look us over first, I thought. The old saying back home is, "Well, if it's a beating you are to get, sooner the better to get it over with." My pal, Oh, who was standing next to me, whispered that I should pull down my coat sleeves as he was doing. He was trying to cover up the pus marks of the itches on his hands and wrists which he had contracted from the sugar plantation, and which I had contracted from him. As he frightened me, I heeded his warning and followed his example, thinking that I could get by with that. Being optimistic in nature, I had never thought of the seriousness of the matter until he called it to my attention. If discovered and proved serious, he whispered to me, we may be sent back to Honolulu or even back to Korea. What a great disappointment it would be to me or to him if that should be the case! To have arrived at the "gateway to America" and then turned back would be a terrible thing indeed. That was something I had never dreamed of. If such a thing should happen to us, it would certainly break our hearts. Moreover what a terrible disappointment it would be to our dear ones back in Hawaii and back home!

While thus worrying myself in anticipation of all sorts of forebodings which would inevitably follow if I should fail to pass the inspection, the inspector gave me the surprise of my life. Greeting us with a smiling face and in our native tongue, he said, "Han-gook chin-goo-dul isim-niga?" or, "Are you my Korean friends?"

In surprised voices and with happy smiles, we all said together, "Yey," or "Yes, sir."

"Ah, dai-dan-y ban-gap sum-ni-da," or "I am very glad to see you all," he said and told us that he was Dr. Drew, formerly a medical missionary sent to Mok-po, in South Korea. God is great; God be praised! A missionary at home bade me farewell and a former missionary here received me so kindly. And, I wanted to go back to Korea as a medical missionary myself!

Now, smiling with friendly greetings, he shook hands with each and every one of us down the line, making it appear more like a reception line than an inspection line. When he came to my friend and me, he noticed the itches on our hands and informed us very kindly that we had the itches, but he assured us it was nothing serious and advised us to get some sulphuric ointment from a drug store and apply it on our hands as soon as we were landed.

Was I happy! He certainly made us happy. The reception, rather the inspection, being over, he told us that the Korean hotel proprietor named "Whang" was waiting for us down below and that we were free to go down to meet him. In parting, he said, "I'll be seeing you at your hotel some day soon, I hope. If I'm not too busy, I'll be coming over for a nice bowl of Korean noodles in kimchi (pickle), of which I'm very fond."

Whew! What a sensational relief! We certainly were all very happy. Those poor Japanese standing on the other side of the deck, witnessing the scene, must have wished they, too, were Koreans that day, I thought.

So now we were safely landed, and sure enough the Korean hotel man was waiting for us at the foot of the gangway. It certainly was good to see a fellow-countryman in a faraway land, who was ready to receive us and to lead us away. My friend, Ahn Chang-ho, the Korean patriot, was not on hand to meet me just then, but I was glad to have a fellow-Korean welcome me to his hotel, which was located on Filbert Street in the North Beach section, near Columbus Park.

It was the latter part of the month of June, and I thought I was most appropriately attired in black coat and white duck pants. However, the hotel man did not agree with me when he said that I might be stoned to death if I should venture out into the streets in white duck pants. I thought it odd that the summer pants in summertime should offend any-one so much that I should be stoned in a civilized country like this. Being a stranger in a strange land though, I thought I must be careful and cautious, if not actually being scared of anything like that.

Across the Embarcadero, the hotel man took us to a street-car which was drawn by a team of horses or mules, I cannot remember which now. This was the first street-car on which I ever rode. The car was pulled uphill by the quadrupeds to the intersection of Broadway and Columbus Avenue, where we transferred to the electric car running north. We got off at Filbert Street and soon arrived safely at the Korean hotel, and I was not molested on account of my white duck pants.

The hotel was a two-story house located in a residential district, which was nice and quiet throughout the day. Only occasionally the silence was broken by the cart wheels rolling over the cobblestone pavement and by the loud cries of the fruit vendors announcing their wares, "Dime a dozen bananas!" (Back in Hawaii it had cost us a nickel for a whole bunch of bananas!) It was some time later that I learned to know those peddlers were Italians . . . as they are to this day; and that the section was inhabited largely by the Italian settlers.

In the hotel room that night, I wrote to my father, to my uncle, and to my cousin in Hawaii, telling them joyously and proudly that I had arrived safely and landed in San Francisco, the big beautiful city by the Golden Gate, in the promised land of my dreams flowing with milk of wisdom and honey of freedom.

Taking heed to the advice given to me by the hotel man, I stayed indoors every day for a whole week. Indeed, I was afraid to go out in my white pants, lest someone might stone me. Then, too, I found out it was so cold here in the month of June that I actually shivered inside the house. No wonder nobody wore summer pants here in the summertime. Looking out through the windows, I saw people out in the street wearing dark, heavy clothes in daytime and overcoats at night. I had neither black pants nor overcoat to wear, nor had I any money left in my pocket to buy anything. No, I could not spare even a dime to buy a dozen bananas from the vendors when I was feeling lonesome and hungry sometimes. Like the old saying back home, I was "looking like a borrowed bag of oats placed in a corner," and "acting like a country hen lost on the palace grounds," not knowing what to do or which way to turn.

Our Sunday service was held in the lobby of the hotel on the afternoon of my first Sunday in America. To this service came a few Korean young men who were here before me, some merchants selling Korean ginseng to the Chinese, and others who were "school boys," working in American homes for room and board and going to school during school hours. Two of them were from my neighborhood in Pyeng Yang, one of whom was an old schoolmate of mine named Kim Kwan-yu, who lives now in Los Angeles, and the other was a former classmate of my scholar cousin and the elder son of Elder Pang of the Central Presbyterian Church. Together with the group of newcomers from Hawaii, it was a good size congregation. I sat between Kim and my old pal, Oh, facing the window.

Of course, Brother Pang himself conducted the service, singing, praying, and preaching in Korean. It was impressive to me, firstly, because it was the very first time I attended Sunday service on the American soil, and secondly, because I was happy in meeting my old acquaintances and fellow-countrymen there, singing, praying and preaching in our native tongue in the land from whence the missionaries had come and taught us how to sing and pray and preach.

Then what a strange thing happened to us that

day in Christian America! It was just when we all stood up and were singing the closing hymn, a well-aimed missile, a fist-sized rock, like a bombshell, banged through the front window, barely missing Brother Pang and me who were just inside the window!

Stunned and startled as we were, we stopped the service right there and then, and Mr. Whang, the proprietor, stepped outside to investigate. He did not see anything or anybody outside, he told us when he came back. He simply said, "I am sorry that this happened. This is the first time such a thing has happened here for this is usually a nice and quiet neighborhood, I know. I guess it must have been a passerby ruffian or a Sunday drunkard who did it."

I noticed everyone had a troubled look on his face, but no one said anything for they were too stunned, especially the newcomers. I said to myself, "How strange! The same thing happened to me when I first moved into a strange village back in Korea because I was a Christian but they were not. And now I've just arrived in my dream city of Christian America, the land of the missionaries, I am stoned while singing a Christian hymn in Korean translation but to the same identical American tune on Sunday! Or was it because someone saw me in white pants come into this house?" I said to Brother Pang, who later attended Occidental College and became the first pastor of the Korean Church in Los Angeles, "Oh, how can such a thing like this happen here in America? I am surprised! You've been here for four years now and you ought to know. Do they do terrible things like this often? I thought all the Americans were Christians as the missionaries are!"

"Of course," he replied in a rather tremulous

voice, "Christians they all profess to be and everything is called a Christian institution here, yet you
can't take them too literally. To be sure, there are
true Christians, many of them, who are law abiding,
kind and generous hearted, and who sent out the
missionaries to the foreign lands. But there are
others who are not really Christians in the truest
sense of the words, who break all the Ten Commandments and more on Sabbath Day as any other
day on the calendar. There are some bad people
here, too, don't you see? You can't expect every
American to be like the missionaries are. That's why
some of the missionaries back in Korea did not want
us to come here because they were afraid we might
be spoiled under some bad influence while we are
here. So, don't be discouraged. You will soon find
a school-boy job and go to school to learn all the
good things that America can offer, for that's what
we are here for, isn't it?"

"You are right, Brother Pang, and I am glad to
hear you say so," I said.

Undoubtedly the real cause of that incident was
the anti-Oriental labor sentiment that had just begun
to express itself in California. It was but a small *
sample of the long agitation which lasted more than
two decades, and at one time it almost created an
international crisis between Japan and the United
States, and the so-called "Gentlemen's Agreement"
averted that crisis. The influx of the Oriental labor
into the Pacific Coast region was vehemently resented
by the native labor element that felt itself being in-
truded upon.

Similar and more serious incidents began to occur
more and more frequently. Personal insults were
offered the Oriental, calling him "Jap," or "Scaby,"

meaning a scab, a dirty fellow who does the same work for lower wages than do others; missiles were thrown at him in the streets; mob violence threatened; school segregation proposed; services denied him at barber shops and restaurants; segregation in small town theatres; refusal of admission to places of amusement; and various other indignities and discriminatory treatment occurred.

In a Southern California town a year or so later, a house where the first Korean laborers moved into was threatened with a mob violence by the labor element of the town, but by the timely assistance rendered by the church people of the town the threatened violence was stopped. In another town, in 1914, there was another mob violence threatened against the Koreans. Mr. David Lee, pastor of the Korean church in San Francisco and president of the Korean National Association, made an appeal to the Secretary of State in Washington, Hon. William Jennings Bryan, asking for his intercession, and he responded promptly in stopping that mob violence.

Finally, however, despite the strong protests made by the Christian churches, educators, employer groups, and even by the Federal Government, that long anti-Oriental agitation culminated in the passing of the Alien Land Law in California and in several other states along the Pacific Coast, barring the Orientals from buying agricultural lands and closing the Oriental immigration by Federal law in 1924. The Chinese Exclusion Law was concluded, during President Arthur's administration and again in 1893 during President Cleveland's administration.

(Thirty years later, on April 24, 1950, the State District Court of Appeals of California, using the charter of the United Nations, declared California's

Alien Land Law, adopted in 1920 against the Japanese and other Asiatic nationals, as unenforceable. Justice Wilson's decision stated that the United Nations charter guarantees respect for human rights and fundamental freedom without regard for color, race or religion, and that the Alien Land Law was unenforceable because it discriminates against the Japanese and because its restrictions are untenable and indefensible. The ruling was the result of a suit taken to the court by a Japanese who had purchased the land which the state attempted to take away from him.)

13

First Days in America

By this time, all my fellow travelers from Honolulu, including my pal, Oh, had left for Southern California; some to Los Angeles, and others to Riverside where Mr. Ahn Changho, the Korean patriot himself was picking oranges for his living, and at the same time helping to find employment for his fellow-countrymen newly arriving from Hawaii from week to week, from month to month. He was a very kindly man, always helping others in every way possible.

A week later, another steamer arrived from Honolulu, bringing a few more Koreans from Hawaii. One of them was Mrs. Jong-Oak Kim, the lady in Honolulu with whom we had gone to the Salvation Army hall one evening just before leaving for San Francisco. She stopped at our hotel for a few hours on her way to the Southland, and it was through her that I heard the sad news from my home. As the old Korean saying goes, "Frost on top of snow," my first days of rather gloomy experiences in the New World were now greatly aggravated by the news that my father had passed away!

"Yes, my dear boy," said Mrs. Kim, "I am very sorry to break the bad news to you, but your cousin asked me to let you know that your father passed away over some three months ago now."

"Ah, my father's dead!" I mumbled, hot tears raining down my cheeks, and covering up my face with my hands, I went up to my bed to bury my face and grief in my pillow. And there I cried like a child that I was. I cried my heart out for it seemed to me then the end of the world had come upon me. The feeling of despair and desolation overcame me. Now that my dear father, who loved me and wished me success and had sent me to America, was gone and I would never see him again in this life, I thought I had nothing more to live for. It was he who had sent me here to learn to be a doctor, and it was he whom I had intended to restore to health as my first patient as soon as I became a medical missionary back in my native land. But now, when I had just arrived here and stranded, not knowing what to do or which way to turn, my father had already passed away, and I thought of my poor helpless mother and little brother left alone!

A few days later, my dear friend, Mr. Ahn Chang-ho arrived on the noon train from Riverside. This was the first time I had met him since he went away from Pyeng Yang more than five years ago. He was about the same age as my scholar cousin, tall and handsome looking, broad forehead and a serene coun-tenance. A more perfect gentleman and scholar, a greater patriot and more eloquent orator than he among my own people I've never yet seen. He loved and honored others, young and old, honestly and sincerely, and his fellow-countrymen everywhere, at home and abroad, loved and followed him. Truly he was the greatest leader of my people in modern times that I know of.

As soon as he arrived at my hotel and after a brief interview with the proprietor, he came up to see me sitting up in my bed. His cordial greetings, accom-panied by his friendly smiles, lifted me bodily out of my bed. "Hello, my young friend, I'm glad to see you here in America!" He greeted me as he approached me with open arms. Oh, how glad I was to see him and talk with him! And he said, "I'll be here awhile and I'll see to it that you will get a good start. And, I think you need more decent looking clothes because you are going to school here, and I am going to find a 'school boy' job for you."

Mr. Ahn was in the United States to organize the Koreans, who were arriving continually from Hawaii, into a fraternal association for mutual helpfulness and for self-government as newcomers into a strange land. Later, following the so-called "Five Point Treaty" of 1905 and the "Seven Point Treaty" of 1907, signing away to Japan the control of Korea's foreign affairs and police power at the point of the sword, the organization was changed into a patriotic
* society called "The Korean National Association."

It will be recalled that in 1907, a certain man named Stevens was shot to death by a Korean patriot in San Francisco. He was supposed to be an advisor to the emperor of Korea and paid by the Korean government. He was on his way to Washington on a secret mission entrusted by the emperor, but being bribed by the Japanese, he began to betray Korea's interests in favor of Japan's activities in Korea as
* soon as he arrived in America. Three years later, in 1910, Japan finally annexed Korea into the Japanese empire as a province and remained so until the Japanese were driven out by the Allied Powers, in August, 1945.

Mr. Ahn bought me a brand new three-piece suit of clothes the next day as he had promised. He told me he had borrowed ten dollars from a friend of his named Lee Keo-dam and with that money had bought the suit at a store near Chinatown. It was a nice looking suit and fit me fine. It made me feel nice and warm, and Mr. Ahn made me so happy and comfortable that I soon forgot all my broodings and sorrows.

One morning he took me to an employment agency, looking for a "school boy" job for me. He had been a "school boy" himself and his young wife a "school girl" when they first came to America. Since then he had been out hunting that job for someone else like myself. Whenever he could not find a suitable place through the employment agencies, he used to go around from door to door in a residential section in search of one. He would ring the door bell, and when the lady of the house came to the door, he would say, "HAVE YOU GOT A SCHOOL-BOY JOB, MADAM?" He said it in such a slow motion way, trying to make each word distinct, that the women would smile and try to answer him in the same manner.

Well, he found a job for me at a Japanese employment agency that morning. I can still remember the name of the street where I was offered the first "school boy" job, but couldn't keep it. It was on Fell Street, near Market Street. He took me to a big three-story building there. After a brief interview, the lady of the house told me to return the following morning to report for work. Mr. Ahn was rather busy with other things the next morning and he asked me if I could go alone and find the place all right. I said that I would try, and started out by myself.

I started out by taking the cable car at the corner of Mason Street and getting off at the end of the line at Market. It was when I was changing the car here that I think I became confused. I had the name and address of the place written on a slip of paper in my hand, and I was told to show it to the street-car conductor who would direct me to it. I either forgot to do that, or I was over-confident that I could locate the place without any assistance.

I got off some distance down on Market Street and walked a block south and started looking for that same building that looked just "so-and-so." How could I know I was on the wrong side of Market Street to find Fell Street, which was north of Mar-ket, or how could I know there were street signs placed at every corner that told the names of the streets, if I knew how to read?

After spending nearly an hour trying to locate the house which was not there, I felt so tired and dis-gusted that I decided to give up the hunt and return to my hotel. I was afraid to ride the streetcar alone again, so I walked all the way back to the hotel. Mr. Ahn was surprised to see me, and when I told him about my unsuccessful trip of the morning, he smiled and said, "Don't you worry, Easurk, I'll find another job for you. It's no use going back to that place now, for somebody else would be there by now, I'm afraid."

The next day, he found another "school boy" job for me. It was at a boarding house located on the south slope of the Nob Hill. Here, the woman told me I could sleep in my room at the back of the kitchen that night, for I was interviewed just after the dinner was finished, but I did not feel like stay-ing in the strange house that night all alone. I asked Mr. Ahn to tell her that I would be back in the morn-ing to start my work. Then she said that I must be there at six o'clock to build the fire in the kitchen stove for her. I said, "Yes, Ma'm" and returned to the hotel with Mr. Ahn.

How glad I was to see and talk to my fellow-countrymen who gathered there in the evenings to tell each other of their various experiences of the day, which were so very interesting to me that I sat up until late that night. When I got up in the morning and pulled up the window shade, I saw the sun was high in the sky. It was about eight o'clock! I knew I was too late to report for work, but thinking the woman might excuse me for the first day, I hurriedly put on my clothes and hastened over to that boarding house and knocked on the kitchen door. Yes, I found the place all right this time, unfortunately, for one can't imagine the sort of reception I got there that morning.

The woman was angry. She grew furious when she saw me come at that hour of the day to build her cooking stove fire and she yelled at me at the top of her voice, saying, "What do you want?" And I said, "Yes, ma'm," for that was all the English language I knew. "What? You come to build a fire now?" she asked. And I said, "Yes, ma'm," and she said, "I tell you, no. You are fired!" slamming the kitchen door in my face. I said, "Yes, ma'm," and turned to go. Really, I could not speak English as she did, but I think I understood what she said. From then on until I was in college, to say "Yes, ma'm" to a lady was all that was necessary in this land of "ladies first" everywhere and in everything, contrary to the "gentlemen first" in the Orient.

What else could I do but return to the good old hotel and report to Mr. Ahn what had happened to my second "school boy" job. When I told him my story, all he said to me was, "Well, don't you worry, my friend, I'll find you a better place than that right now," and we started out for the third time. Just as the old saying back in the old country that "If the first try failed, and if the second try also failed, the third try might be successful," I was successful in locating a "school boy" job this time.

The first place was not even to be found; the second place fired me even before I started to work; but at the third place the woman was so nice that she did not fire me even when I built the first fire in the oven. I learned the house work there and stayed as long as I wished. It was on Post Street near Van Ness Avenue where finally I found this job at two dollars a week, building cook stove fires in the mornings and evenings, helping the mother of a young man and a little girl to prepare breakfast and dinner, and to wash and clean the house on Saturdays. I had a room down in the basement.

During the rest of the day, I was supposed to be in school. However, this being the summer vacation time, taking my school lunch with me I walked to the Korean hotel every day and stayed there until it was time to go back to work. I stayed on this job for about three weeks until I quit. Yes, I did resign; I was not fired this time. I gave up the "school boy" job to look for a better paying regular job. This is a changing world!

At the hotel I saw people continually arriving from Hawaii and leaving for the East, North, and South in pursuit of real moneymaking employment. There was an agency looking for railroad workers for the San Pedro, Los Angeles and Salt Lake Line. Also, there was a big demand for hop and fruit pickers in the Sacramento and San Joaquin Valleys and in Southern California. From the discussions I heard,

I learned that the fruit pickers were well paid but that the work was only seasonal, whereas the railroad work was good and steady. One could work all the year around on the railroad and save between two hundred and three hundred dollars a year, easily. "Ah, two or three hundred dollars a year!" I exclaimed to myself. "That's a lot better than what I'm making now, only two dollars a week. I think I am going to work on the railroad and make some big money to go to school when the school opens in the fall."

Soon after Mr. Ahn left for Riverside, I had quit my school boy job and was ready to go to work on the railroad with a group of men who were going to Salt Lake City and thereabouts. But, luckily, Mr. Kim Sung-moo from Sacramento changed my mind for me, and I became a fruit picker in California instead. Mr. Kim was my cousin's brother-in-law and my scholar counsin's classmate at Shoong-sil Academy in Pyeng Yang before leaving for America along with several other older sets of students some five years previously. This group of earlier arrivals in this country was destined to become the nucleus of the Korean settlement in America and the leaders among their fellow-countrymen newly arriving from Hawaii, Mr. Ahn in the south, Mr. Kim in the north, and later David Lee in San Francisco.

So to Sacramento I went with Mr. Kim on the morrow. The capital city of the state was not so big and modern looking then as it is today. The bridge across the river was only a simple wooden structure, and the streets, especially in the Oriental section, were dusty country roads. The summer's heat was terrific, making me think it was hotter here than it was in Hawaii. Maybe it was not quite that hot, but

I felt it so because I had just come from San Francisco.

On the third day, Mr. Kim found a job for me in
a Korean camp in Vacaville, some distance back toward San Francisco. I went alone but I arrived there
safely and was met by a young man who was in
charge of the camp there. Boss Jung, they called
him, spoke English fluently. What a coincidence! I
had a Boss Jung in Hawaii, too, you will remember.
He had learned English at Bai-Jai mission school in
Seoul, Korea. There were four other men, including
the Shinns, an elderly man with a wife and a small
boy. The lady was the camp cook.

It was paradise to me, I thought, as compered to
the cane field work in Hawaii. Picking prunes,
peaches, and pears was easier, and cleaner work, and
the pay was more than double the Hawaiian pay,
being one dollar and fifteen cents a day. The fruit
season was soon over, however, in the middle of August. Then came the grape season and all roads led
to Fresno, the capital of the San Joaquin Valley
grape empire.

At Malaga we picked raisins at two cents a tray
for two weeks, and at Fresno we picked wine grapes
at three cents a box. The wine grape picking was
hard work, and I was soaked in sweat and my hands
were dripping red in blood and the grape juice. Hot
were the days and cold were the nights, sleeping in
the barns or under the fig trees. Working from
dawn to dusk, I made from three to four dollars a
day and saved enough money to pay my hotel bill in
San Francisco and to repay the ten dollars which I
owed to Mr. Ahn, who in turn owed it to his friend
for my first suit of Sunday clothes which I ever wore.

As soon as the grape season was over, the Shinn

family and I left for Riverside where the orange season would come next in about ten weeks, a little before the Christmas season. I was glad to be in Riverside where there were many old friends of mine who went before me, including my pal, Oh, and Mr. Ahn Chang-ho himself, his wife and her uncle, N. Kim, the camp boss and the best known Korean in Riverside.

Here in the sunny Southland, surrounded by orange groves and mingling with my old friends, I found myself to be quite happy and contented. The people of the town, especially the church people, were so very friendly to us Koreans. On the very first evening of my arrival at the Korean camp, I met some of the night school teachers from the Presbyterian Church who were teaching my people English in the assembly room of the main red building, 1532 Pachappa Avenue, I remember, where they held Sunday services. I can still remember some of the teachers' names—a Miss White, a beautiful blonde young lady; Mr. and Mrs. Irvine; and Miss Patterson, who was principal of the Irving School. And how kindly was the Rev. Alexander Aiken, who gave us immeasurable assistance and advice. Many of my people who went to his church every Sunday morning will remember.

Here in the camp of brick-red cottages on Pachappa Avenue, just south of East Fourteenth Street and east of the S. P. and Santa Fe railway tracks, interspersed with gum trees and pepper trees, I first learned to speak English at the night school. The camp was populated by Mexicans, Negroes, Japanese, and now Koreans. I was one of the overgrown kindergarten pupils learning to read the First Reader. "I see mama. I see a ball. I see an apple," and so forth. So I started to learn English at night school and, until the orange season began just before Christmas time, I spent most of my time in studying English from the readers, and I thought I was doing very well.

So, one day I went to a down town shoe store to buy me a new pair of Sunday shoes. This was the first pair of shoes I ever bought for myself. When the clerk asked me what size shoes I wore, I said, "Half past five, mister."

Smiling, the clerk said, "You mean you wear the size five and a half, don't you? We say 'half past five' when we speak of time only, you see."

"Thank you, mister," I said. "You will make a very good teacher at the night school in our camp."

"Oh, do you think so? I wish I could do that some day," he replied. Soon we became well acquainted after that, although I cannot recall his name now. I did some house work for him and we went to the Presbyterian church together.

I picked oranges from before Christmas until the following spring. It was during this time that I received a letter from my cousin in Hawaii, saying that he was leaving Honolulu and was due to arrive in San Francisco some time in April and was coming to live with me in Riverside. I was anxiously waiting for him and his wife when I heard the startling news of the great earthquake and fire in San Francisco on April 18, 1906, that was flashed across the country from coast to coast.

Naturally, I was greatly alarmed and worried, for fear my cousin had been caught in the fire if he had already arrived there then. Alas, yes, he had just arrived the day after the earthquake, which was followed by the great fire the next day, he told me in a telegram. Fortunately, however, under the kindly care of Dr. Drew of the Immigration Service, he and his wife were well taken care of in a church in Oakland, just across the bay. Dr. Drew was the former medical missionary to South Korea who had been so kind to me and my fellow passengers when we arrived there some ten months before that.

Down in the sunny Southland in those balmy spring days in Riverside, I was happy now that my cousin and his wife were with me again. They liked the place, the climate, the work, and the living conditions here as I did and the others, too. No wonder it had soon become the first largest Korean settlement in America, at least during the orange season of each year for a number of years. Subsequently, smaller Korean communities or camps sprung up in the nearby towns of Redlands, Upland, and Claremont, which were offsprings of the main settlement which was in Riverside; that is, before many of them began to move into the cities as operators of small shops, restaurants, and grocery stores in Los Angeles and San Francisco and in some eastern cities as they are found today.

This was my third year in America. I had come to America to get an American education, but as yet, I had never been "near the threshold of a schoolhouse," as the saying goes in Korea. True, three years ago, with the help of Mr. Ahn Chang-ho, I was a "school boy," in name at least. I had been a working man ever since, and was side-tracked from my objective by the lure of gold. I tried to pick gold off the orange trees and the grape vines.

Another orange season had come to an end, and I was about to move on to another place, following the crowd, when my Cousin Chungsurk stopped me.

He said I had better start going to school right there and then. He reasoned with me that it was of no use for me to try to make money to go to school later when really I was not saving any money at all. In fact, what little I had earned from my intermittent seasonal labor I had spent on my railway fares and during my off-work days and weeks. He told me to go to school in Riverside while he would take care of everything else for me.

So, for the first time in my three years in America I went to school, to the Irving School located at the east end of Fourteenth Street, a couple of blocks away from the Korean camp. Miss Patterson, one of our night school teachers, was the gracious principal of this grade school. There were already two Korean children in the school, a boy and a girl.

I was placed in the Third Grade to begin with. There I managed somehow to trail along with other pupils in three Rs. The main difficulty was that the built-in seats and desks were too small for me. I had a hard time squeezing myself in and out of my seat. But in about three weeks, I was lucky to be promoted to the Fifth Grade, and in another four weeks I was promoted to the Sixth Grade which was the top grade in the school and where the seats and desks were much larger, and my classmates were of my size. So I enjoyed my first school life in America until the school closed for the summer.

During that summer I picked peaches in Ontario and grapes in Cucamonga. And in the fall, I was in the Longfellow School at the west end of Fourteenth Street in Riverside. I was in the Seventh Grade there for a few weeks before I was invited to come to Salt Lake City by Mr. Kim, my cousin's brother-in-law, and go to school there. I went to Washington

School, back of the Mormon Temple, where stands today the State Capitol of Utah. I was then in the Eighth Grade.

Things began to change rapidly when I had been in school but for a few weeks in Salt Lake City. This was the year of the Financial Panic in the United States, in 1908, during the last days of President Theodore Roosevelt's administration and after William Howard Taft was elected President of the United States.

I knew what a panic was like though. Nearly one hundred Korean railway workers lost their jobs and poured into the city to huddle into two old buildings near my dormitory, located directly opposite the Tabernacle. They were packed in like sardines and lived like war refugees throughout the bleak winter months. They were all very poor folk, and we all suffered together. Obviously they had not saved up all that three hundred dollars a year working on the railroad, or else they did not work that long. All they had to eat was rice and soup. Perhaps they were lucky to have even that much. That soup was not any too tasty, to tell the truth. I ate it myself, so I know.

Professor Homer B. Hulbert, the author of "The History of Korea," and of "The Passing of Korea," was visiting with the Koreans in America at this time, and I had the rare privilege of meeting him in Salt Lake City for the first time. I met him again for the second time at Park College several years later, when he delivered an address on Korea.

The long winter of the panic in Salt Lake City painfully passed at last, and the spring of sunshine and hope was ushered in. The railroad workers went back to work, and like the rest of my fellow students,

I quit school and went to work again. Following a
group, I went up to the sugar beet fields in the southern part of Idaho, to a place called Whitney, a few
miles east of Preston, where there was a general mer-
chandise store and a few farm houses scattered
about. The native inhabitants were mostly Mor-
mons, I understood, who appeared to be somewhat
shy but substantially honest people, I thought.

In the sugar beet fields I worked only a short time
before I went back to California. Somehow or other,
I never could get along with the sugar industry,
either here or in Hawaii. In the midst of the "thin-
ning" season, I quit the work and back to California
I went to find Mr. Ahn Chang-ho had returned to
Korea and that Mr. Kim Sun-moo had followed him
and so did my old pal, Oh. From then on, I fell back
into the rut again. Now, equipped with somewhat
better English, I ventured into the "white collar
jobs," such as bus boy and waiter jobs in many of
the hotels and cafes, and meandered back and forth
over a dozen resorts up and down the State of California, to the north in summer and to the south in
winter. Starting out as a dishwasher at Hotel Glen-
wood in Riverside, I had become an expert hotel bus
boy. Along with several young Koreans, I was a bus
boy at Hotel Green and Hotel Maryland in Pasadena, Hotel Virginia in Long Beach, Hotel Lanker-
shim in Los Angeles, Hotel Arrowhead in Hot
Springs, Hotel Arlington and Hotel Potter in Santa
Barbara, Hotel Del Coronado at Coronado Beach,
Tahoe Tavern and Hotel Talac at Lake Tahoe. I
was a lobby boy one summer at Stratford Inn at Del
Mar, where I saw Mary Pickford once. The wealthy

Americans scattered their gold at those resorts, and I tried to earn a dollar a day to save it for five years, in vain.

14

"Go East, Young Man"

Like the children of Israel who had wandered aim-
lessly in the wilderness for forty years in sight of
their Promised Land, until Moses came, I rambled
about without any definite course or purpose for eight
long years, up to the summer of 1913, except for
about a year while I was in school. I was then a type-
setter for the Korean newspaper called "The New
Korea," an organ of the Korean National Association, which exists to this date, published then in San
Francisco. I was called to this position a year before from a summer hotel at Lake Tahoe where I
was a bus boy. So I was learning a Korean trade in
America, widening the knowledge in my native language, and doing my share of patriotic work among
my own people for their interest and toward the independence movement of my native country which
was bleeding under the Japanese imperialism. Thus,
my primary purpose in coming to America to get an
American education and to become a medical missionary back to my native country was entirely forgotten and neglected. Of course, I had intended to
go to an Eastern school some day, but my Moses
had not yet appeared to show me the way. Indeed,
nobody did, until that fateful day in August, 1913,
when I met the late Dr. George Shannon McCune
at the Korean headquarters in San Francisco.

Dr. McCune of Sunchun, Korea, my ancestral
home district, had just arrived in the States on his

first furlough. Since I had left my home a short
time before he went to Korea as a missionary and
teacher, I had never met him before. Yet, I met him
that day more gladly than others whom I had known
from my boyhood days in Pyeng Yang, except for
Dr. Moffitt whom I had met once in Riverside. As
soon as Dr. McCune found out who I was and what
I was doing, he said to me, "Ah, I am very glad to
tell you that there is just the right place for you that
I know of. Young man, go East to Park College,
my own Alma Mater!"

Dr. George Shannon McCune was visiting the Korean headquarters and the publishing establishment
located on Perry Street near Fourth and Howard
Streets, in San Francisco. He was one of the pioneer
missionaries who had gone to Korea. He lived there,
preached there, and taught there, serving our Lord
and His people there, spiritually, educationally, mor-
ally, and socially. It was no wonder that he would
visit the Korean sojourners in America. He was better known in Korea simply as "-Une Moksa" or the
"Reverend-Une," abbreviating his name to make it
sound like a Korean name which is usually spelled
"Yun." In fact, he was more than a Korean at heart
and in deed, even more than his adopted name.

So this faithful servant of our Lord, the late Dr.
McCune, who suffered much persecution in His great
cause and in His glorious name, was the man who
advised me to go to Park College, in Parkville, Missouri. He was stopping at the home of the Rev. Dr.
Lapsley McAfee in Berkeley, just across the bay.
Dr. McAfee was a brother of Mrs. McCune, and
they were the son and daughter of the founder of
Park College, Dr. John A. McAfee. I was directed
by Dr. McCune to come over there the next day to

get up-to-date information concerning Park College
from his brother-in-law who would know more about
it, and for a letter of recommendation which he himself would write to Park College before the actual
day of opening enrollment.

At the home of Dr. McAfee the next day, I
learned that the college was going to open on the second Tuesday in September, so that I would have
ample time to wind up my affairs here and visit my
cousin living in Pasadena before leaving for the
East. Dr. McCune obtained from Dr. McAfee an
application form which he had received from Park
and asked me to fill it out and sign my name to it
alongside of his own, endorsing my application. Actually though, I was not going to enroll in the college
itself, but in the Academy which was a part of the
college. This was exactly the kind of school I had
been looking for all those many years in vain until
that fateful day. Now I found it through Dr. Mc-
Cune!

I was then so excited about it all, without being
fully informed of every angle, that I asked, saying,
"But, Dr. McCune, please tell me more about Park
College and what I am to do. You see, I haven't
any money to pay the tuition and for room and board
to go to school there. What shall I do?"

"I know you haven't the money," he said, "and
that's why I want you to go to Park. Park College
is for students exactly like you. I was like you when
I went there many years ago. You don't have to have
money to go to Park. If you had, you would be advised to go to school elsewhere. You see, Park has
never refused a deserving student on account of a
lack of money! Of course, it is not that Park is so
very rich that it refuses to accept money from stu-

dents. In fact, the school is being supported by dona-
tions, large and small, from Christian friends everywhere, from all over the world. There is the 'Self-
help Department' there, enabling the students to
work for their education, room, and board. You see,
at Park, every student, boy or girl, works. He or
she works half a day and goes to classes another half
day. You are a typesetter and printer here now.
Maybe you will be given the same kind of work
there in the College Press. Wouldn't that be all
right with you? Besides, you will be the first Korean
student to go to Park, and you will be welcomed, I'm
sure."

"That will be just fine, Dr. McCune. I will go
without any worries then," I said to him. Of course,
we carried on this conversation both in Korean and
English. Although he had lived in Korea only seven
years, he spoke Korean very much better than I
spoke English. He learned to speak there, but I did
not. Maybe he was more diligent and intelligent than
I. Before parting, he told me he would mail that
afternoon his letter of recommendation to Dr. A. L.
Wolfe, the Acting President of Park College. "Well,
good luck to you. I will follow you soon and will be
glad to see you in Parkville," he said, shaking my
hand most affectionately.

Need I say that he was the man for whom I had
been praying all those many years to come and show
me the way? He had come at last, and I was getting ready to go to just the kind of school I was
looking for. Indeed, if it had not been for him, I
would have been the aimless wanderer that I had
been all my life. Who knows? With all my grateful
heart I simply said, just before I left him, "Thank
you very much, Dr. McCune, for everything, and I'll

always remember you for this. Good-bye, sir. I'll be very happy to see you at Park very soon."

At the Ferry Building the next day, I bade farewell to my bosom friend, Kang Chang-hai, and left for the Southland. In Pasadena I was glad to be at my cousin's home once again. He and his wife were happy to know that at last I was going to a Christian school where Dr. McCune himself was graduated before going to Korea as a missionary. During my five days' stay there, they treated me wonderfully. My cousin was a devout orthodox Presbyterian, and his wife was an excellent cook, so I was well-nourished, both spiritually and physically, on the eve of my distant journey half way across the continent. My cousin promised me, at our parting, that he would help me out financially while I was at Park, which he did considerably.

Toward Parkville, Missouri, I set out on a fine September day. I boarded an east-bound Santa Fe train going to Kansas City. What a large country I saw from the train! Through the fertile fields and prairie lands, over the high mountains and across the big rivers, the fast running train wheels rolled along for three days and two nights. The State of California alone is twice the size of Korea. The State of Kansas is about the equal size of my native country of some eighty-five thousand square miles. I traveled through six states until I finally arrived at Kansas City, Missouri, which was only the half-way mark across the great land of the Golden Mountain.

EEC's mother in Korea (date unknown). Courtesy of
Philip Y. Charr.

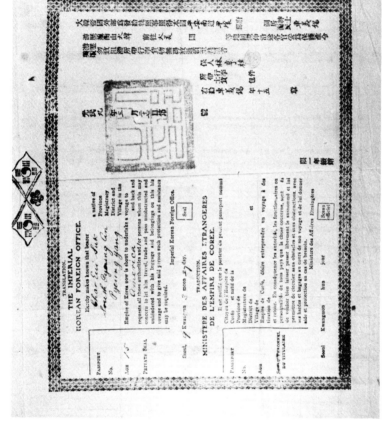

EEC's passport, 1904. Courtesy of Philip Y. Charr.

Honorable Discharge from the Army of the United States

2483   258

TO ALL WHOM IT MAY CONCERN:

This is to Certify, That _Easurk E. Charr #2577684_

Private First Class Medical Department

_U.S. Army_____, as a TESTIMONIAL OF HONEST AND FAITHFUL

SERVICE, is hereby HONORABLY DISCHARGED from the military service of the

UNITED STATES by reason of Authority Telegram A.G.O. November 15,1918.

Said _Easurk E. Charr_____ was born

in _Kanggyay, Pyungando_, in the State of _Korea_

When enlisted he was _34_ years of age and by occupation a _Student_

He had _brown_ eyes, _black_ hair, _yellow_ complexion, and

was _5_ feet _4_ inches in height.

Given under my hand at _Base Hosp. Camp A.A. Humphreys, Va_ this

_28th_ day of _December_, one thousand nine hundred and _eighteen_

Major Medical Corps
Commanding.

Form No. 525, A. G. O.
Ed. Aug. 20-17—500,000.
* Insert grade and company and regiment or corps or department; e. g., "Corporal, Company A, 1st Infantry;" "Sergeant, Quartermaster Corps;" "Sergeant, First Class, Medical Department."
† Insert "Regular Army," "National Army," "National Guard," "Regular Army Reserve," or "Enlisted Reserve Corps," as the case may be.
‡ If discharged prior to expiration of service, give number, date, and source of order or description of authority therefor.   3—3144

EEC's honorable discharge from the U.S. army, 1918. Courtesy of Anna Charr Kim.

ENLISTMENT RECORD.

Name: .... Grade: _Private 1st Class_

Enlisted ...., 191_ , at ....

Serving in .... enlistment period at date of discharge.

Prior service: * .... None

Noncommissioned officer: .... None

Marksmanship, gunner qualification or rating: † .... None

Horsemanship: .... None

Battles, engagements, skirmishes, expeditions: .... None

Knowledge of any vocation: .... None

Wounds received in service: .... None

Physical condition when discharged: .... Good

Typhoid prophylaxis completed .... May 3, 1918

Paratyphoid prophylaxis completed .... May 3, 1918

Married or single: .... Single

Character: _Excellent_

Remarks: ....

Signature of soldier: _Easurk Emsen Charr_

Entitled to travel pay to
Pomona, California
$35.21
Dec. 28 18

....
Captain, Sanitary Corps
Commanding _Det. Med. Dept._

EEC's enlistment record, 1918. Courtesy of Anna Charr Kim.

EEC (second from right, back row) as a member of the League of the Friends of Korea at Park College, 1920. Courtesy of the Park College Photographic History Collection, Park College Library.

EEC (right) with George Paik (second from left) and two unidentified professors from Park College, 1922. Courtesy of Philip Y. Charr.

Evelyn Kim before her marriage to EEC, 1926. Courtesy of Philip Y. Charr.

Evelyn Kim's family in Korea during the Japanese colonial period (date and names unknown). Courtesy of Philip Y. Charr.

The Charrs' wedding on the campus of the University of Chicago, 1928. Courtesy of Anna Charr Kim.

EEC in San Francisco with his three children: (from left) Anna, Flora, and Philip, 1936. Courtesy of Anna Charr Kim.

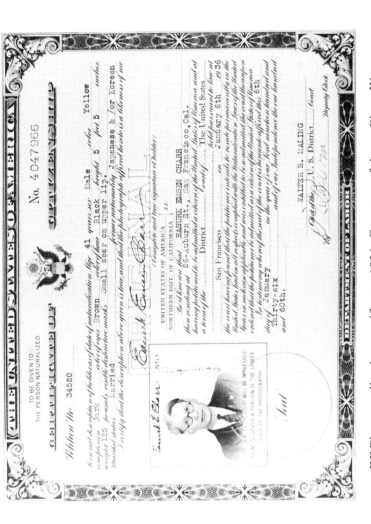

EEC's naturalization certificate, 1936. Courtesy of Anna Charr Kim.

EEC in his late fifties in front of the Soil Conservation Service building in Portland, Oregon, where he
worked during the 1940s. Courtesy of Philip Y. Charr.

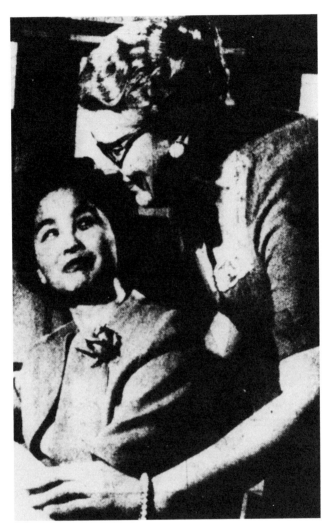

Evelyn Charr informs her employer, Evelyn Gibson, that she is eligible to become a citizen, which she did four years later. This photo apeared in the *Portland Oregonian* on June 3, 1954. Courtesy of the Oregon Historical Society (#OrHi90092).

15

Park College

Park College in Parkville, Missouri, has been the dearest spot on the map of the United States to me ever since that mid-September day in 1913. Only nine miles from Kansas City across the river by the Burlington train in a northwesterly direction, I arrived at the small Parkville station, situated on the north bank of the great Missouri River flowing swiftly by, with a large Adams Express sign displayed as were the Wells Fargo signs in the farther western railway stations in those days. Looking up from the open windows of the train to the beautiful hillside campus in the background, I saw the ivy-covered college buildings—the old McCormick Chapel, just back of the station house, the old Copley Hall, the Alumni Hall, the tall Mackay Hall with its clock tower standing inspiringly on the upper terrace overlooking the woods to its left, where now stand the new Thompson Commons and the Herr House, and the Scott's Observatory on the hill-top above, and the peaceful village of Parkville to the right in the distance below. A truly scenic spot and an ideal location for the unique Christian institutions — the little Golden Mountain itself, I thought, and was happy!

Still more beautiful than the outward appearance of the campus was the genuine Christian character and atmosphere reflected by its students and teachers. This I readily discovered upon my arrival that day. As soon as I got off the train, I saw two students

come running toward me with broad smiles on their
faces and with four open hands, saying, "Hello,
there, we are glad to see you come!" And the bigger
one of the two said, "You are Easurk Emsen Charr
from San Francisco, I believe." When I replied that
I was, he said, "I heard you were coming. Give me
that suitcase of yours. I'll carry it for you and we'll
take you to Dr. Wolfe who is waiting to see you in
his office at the Mackay Hall up there," pointing to
the tall brownstone building with a bell tower, basking in the September sunshine upon the upper terrace. "By the way, will it be all right with you if I
call you by your middle name 'Emsen' rather than
your first name which is harder for me to say," asked
the bigger one.

"Why, that will be O.K. wth me, er-er-," I was
saying.

"Charlie — Charlie White is my name. Just call
me 'Charlie.' And let me introduce my friend, Herb,
Herbert Wolfe, Dr. Wolfe's son," he said. My close
friends call me "Emsen" ever since.

These two young men were members of the Fourth
Year class of the Academy, getting ready to enter
the college proper the following year, while I was to
be classified as the First Year. They were so very
friendly to me from the very moment when my feet
touched the campus grounds that it made me feel at
home. Here I was on a Christian college campus,
which made all the difference in the world. I had
never been to any other college or university campus
before then, but here I could readily see and feel that
this was a unique Christian school of higher learning
where the spirit of true and genuine Christian influence permeated the campus. There was neither East
nor West here, as I had quite often experienced in

life before and have since my college days. These
students were trained and lived while they were here,
and upon completion of their education they went out
into the world to teach and preach to others what
they had learned within the warm brown walls of
this world-renowned Park College, the unique Christian institution.

Dr. Wolfe was waiting for me in his office on the
second floor of Mackay Hall, the main building on
the campus where, besides the administrative offices,
all the classes of both the College and Academy were
held in those days. It was just two days before the
school opened, and he was expecting me. He, too,
without any introduction recognized me, and shaking
my hands, he said, "Easurk Emsen Charr, Dr. Mc-
Cune's boy, I believe. You are the first Korean student to come to Park, and I am very glad to see you
and to have you with us. Dr. McCune told me all *
about you in his letter which I received a few days
ago. Expecting you to arrive on the morning train,
I had posted these boys to meet you."

Being timid then as I always have been, all that I
had to say to him was, "Yes, sir. Thank you, sir. I
am glad to have come."

From his files he drew out my application which I
had filled out at Dr. McAfee's home in Berkeley, and
showing it to me, he said, smiling, "You write very
nicely and you speak English very well, too. And
your winsome smiles that I see! You will do. You'll
get along all right here, I'm sure. Now, run along
with the boys who will take you over to the Woodward Hall and see Mr. Nichols who will find a room
for you there. Later on they will also show you the
dining room where the students who remained on the
campus during the summer dine together. Well,

they'll tell you and show you everything there is for you to know."

As we turned to go out of his office, Dr. Wolfe called me back, saying, "Just a minute, young man. You said in the application you were a compositor and printer."

"Yes, sir, I was," I said, "but that's in Korean language, sir."

"Of course, I understand," he said, "but I don't suppose that would make any difference. You understand English well enough to do that in English just as well, I think. We need a young man like you in the printing office right away. Suppose I put you to work there. Would you like that?"

"Yes, sir! Thank you, sir!" I replied.

"Well, then Charlie will take you over to the Labor Hall in the morning to see Mr. Tuggle who is our Work Superintendent there. I'll call him up and tell him to assign you to Mr. Knapp who is in charge of the College Press. You can go now. Come back to see me two days from now on the Registration Day."

Now, taking turns carrying my suitcase, and walking north along the winding cinder path on the upper terrace and across the viaduct, we reached Woodward Hall, the Academy boys' dormitory standing among the tall oak trees. This building, as well as all the other buildings on the campus, was built of lime stones quarried from the wooded hills nearby and by the former students themselves, I was told. After meeting Mrs. Nichols, the dormitory matron, and placing my suitcase in a room assigned to me, my friends took me down to the dining room at the old Snyder Hall girls' dormitory. (It has long since been replaced by the new Copley-Thaw men's dormitory built during the First World War, but was used as the girls' dormitory again since World War II.) Here in the lobby, I met Mrs. Love, the gracious matron, and a group of students who had gathered there to partake of the noonday meal. There were two Chinese students, who were brothers and had come from China. Ting-Fu Tsiang was one of them who had just graduated from the Academy that spring and was getting ready to go to an Eastern college. He is now Dr. Tsiang, a former Chinese Ambassador to Russia and now the Nationalist Chinese government delegate to the United Nations.

Soon the tingling of the bell in the hands of Mrs. Love announced that lunch was now being served. Charlie and I went to a table together; of course, Herb went home to lunch. At the sound of another bell, everyone sat down with bowed heads, with the exception of someone who remained standing to say the grace, before starting with the food which was expertly prepared and served by the girl students. I found it certainly like a big, fine Christian family that lived together and worked together happily, in a genuine Christian atmosphere.

Henceforth, I lived as an American, not only on food, but in life and soul. I am proud to tell the world that not only as an ordinary American, but I lived here and was trained as a Christian American. Here at Park, as in many other Christian schools and colleges in America, Christian democracy prevailed, from the very foundation of society — education — Christian in spirit and democratic in method. With Christian spirit inculcated in the heads, hearts, and hands of every citizen from infancy up, our democracy, as I learned from Park, will work more efficiently and universally. For here at the tables sat

the college seniors and the Academy first years, East-
erners and Westerners, New Yorkers and Ozarkites,
Europeans and Asiatics; some from the farm and
backwoods, and others from the town and city homes.
They all worked hard; they all dressed plainly; they
all acted and behaved as Christian men and women.
Naturally, there was no trace of snobbery or sour
tone present here as was prevalent in some other
places. Why should there be any question of social
or industrial democracy in this country if the Park
College spirit and educational system be adopted universally and is applied and practiced to the advantage of all concerned?

Early the next morning after breakfast, I was directed by Mr. Tuggle, the work superintendent, to
report to Mr. Knapp in the printing office for work.
This I did. Mr. Knapp, an elegant-looking gentleman with an affable personality, received me kindly
and conversed with me more than an hour on various
subjects. He told me of a Hollington Tong, a former Chinese student who used to work in the printing office and had become a high official in the Nationalist government of China. He is now the Chinese ambassador in Washington.

When we came to the subject of printing, he said
to me, "So you are a printer, I've heard from Dr.
Wolfe. He called me up and told me he was sending
you down this morning. I'm glad to have you here,
for I need you. How long have you been in the
trade?"

"Well, sir, I was a type-setter for a Korean weekly
in San Francisco for a little over a year," I said.
"But I don't know anything about it in English. I
am willing to learn everything, sir. Will you please
teach me and show me how it is done?"

"Why, certainly," said Mr. Knapp. "I'll teach you everything there is for you to know and show you a trick or two of our trade, including the 'type lice' demonstration." And out of the capital and lower cases he showed me the different styles of type, from the old English to the Cheltenham Italic, and the various sizes and fonts of type, from nonpareil to great primer, and from the Em quads to the slug and pica. Then, in the rear of the front room he showed me a job press and a medium size cylinder press. In the next room he showed me a brand new paper cutter, a proof galley, a folding machine, a perforator, two mailers, a stapling machine, and the stock room where the paper was stored. The linotype machine was not there then. It was installed a few years later.

So, I was broken into the printing trade and remained in it, on and off, until my graduation from the college ten years later. Starting out as a typesetter, I became an all-around printer there. I was fortunate enough to have some part in the handling of the hundreds of thousands of copies of printed matter that went out from Park College while I was there. The weekly Parkville Church Bulletin was my especial assignment. The Park College Record, a weekly letter to its friends, was the chief item that kept everyone on the force busy. There some half-dozen students, both men and women, worked all the time. The Park College Catalogue and its supplementary pictorial bulletins, the Alumniad, the Stylus, a student weekly, and various other bulletins and programs for both the college and the student organizations were printed there.

I was enrolled and classified as a First Year in the Academy and assigned to the Snyder Hall for my meals for the first term. Now I was all provided for in the four essentials as a Park student — I had a place to live, a place to eat, a place to work, and a course of studies to pursue. The course consisted of English, Latin, History, and Algebra. Of the four subjects, English was the most difficult for me, despite the complimentary remark made to me by Dr. Wolfe in his office on the day of my arrival. English was hard for me as a distinct subject in itself, and it was doubly hard for me as a common medium used in studying all the other subjects. Especially was this true in my translation of Latin into English so that it made sense.

Park College was founded upon prayers by the Reverend John A. McAfee on the land donated by Col. George S. Park in 1875. "Fides et Labor" is the Park College Motto. Both the town and the college were named after Col. Park following the Civil War. It is claimed to be non-sectarian, yet Park is Presbyterian in that its chief supporters and
* friends are Presbyterians. No matter what denomination with which it may be identified, the religious life in the college was inspiring to me as to a host of others who were there before and after me. The students had come from Christian homes mostly, and together they formed a big Christian family, and here the Christian educators from the President of the college down to housemothers of the dormitories devoted their lives in the interest of the religious life of the students.

A student's religious life on the campus started early in the morning. Park College regulations required every student to be present at the Breakfast table for the brief morning service. So, on the first day of school, I was up at six and went to my dining room at six-thirty, where the daily morning service was held just before breakfast was served. There were altogether six separate dining rooms in those days and these were: the Snyder, the Nickel, the Zion, the Gillette near the printing office, the Sunset, and the Chestnut. The Gillette and the Zion, being the smallest girls' dormitories, were soon discontinued as dining halls, so I never had the pleasure of taking my meals at either of those two places.

I worked in the forenoon and went to my classes in the afternoon. Just before the classwork began, following the lunch hour, there was held the daily half-hour devotional service in the old McCormick chapel. Professor Kerr, of the Department of Bible, was the Chaplain, and every student was required to attend sermons and addresses to the student body. Visiting church leaders and missionaries from abroad were heard frequently, a great number of them being Park's own alumni. One of them was Dr. McCune himself, who spoke to us on his work in Korea, "the unique mission field."

At Park, there was no school on Mondays, but on Saturdays instead. The reason for that was to prevent the students from studying their Monday lessons on Sunday, as is done at almost every other school, thus keeping the Sabbath holy all day from dawn until night. I thought this was an ideal arrangement for I did not have to worry about my lessons from Saturday afteroon until the following Monday.

Two evenings each week were allotted to the students for their club meetings and social activities — Saturdays for the boys and Mondays for the girls. There were three men's and three women's literary clubs in the college and two boys' clubs and two girls' clubs in the Academy. They all went in pairs; that is, one boys' club associated with one girls' club to form a brother and sister club. The three college club halls were located on the top floor of Mackay Hall. The clubs were called Lowell (men's) and Lucerne, Parchevard and Caliopean, Orion and Aurora. The Academy clubs were named Philolexian and Philomathian, Andrion and Leontican; the former's hall was in the Labor Hall building and the latter's in the Alumni Hall.

Their fraternal loyalty and devotion to each other were admirably strong, and that spirit was quite evident when rival clubs were locked in a contest of some sort, whether forensic or athletic. It was all for the purpose of training, of course, and it served the purpose very well, but it was not anything like the fraternities and sororities in some other schools in the country.

After the first few weeks on the campus, I was invited to join the Academy Literary Clubs. Yes, I was invited by both clubs, the Philolexian and the Andrion. I could not join both at the same time, so I joined the former, of which my friend, Charlie White, was a member and first-term president. I was invited by all three college clubs to join them when I entered the college several years later; and again, I had to choose one out of three, and of course my choice was the Lowell Club. In my senior year in college, I was made its president for the middle term. I enjoyed very much the fellowship with the members of the Lowell-Lucerne clubs all the four years I was with them, and I still hum the dear old familiar song in the tune of "Sweet Genevieve" that I used to sing with them:

"O, Lowell Club, dear Lowell Club!
The years may come, the years may go:

But still the hand of memory weaves
Those dear old days in Lowell Club!"

Just at this time there was a Student Volunteer
Convention being held in Kansas City during the
Christmas-New Year holidays of 1913-14. Many of
the faculty members and many of the student body
of Park College attended the convention, and I was
one of them. Dr. and Mrs. Wolfe invited me to go
with them to the opening session. Right in the convention hall they found a very fine young Christian
couple who invited me to stay with them in their
beautiful apartment while I was attending the convention. Wasn't that grand of them! I have forgotten their name, I am sorry to say, but I shall always
remember them dearly. May God bless them whoever they were and wherever they may be now! They
gave me their own bedroom so I could sleep comfortably while they slept on a couch in their living
room, and treated me to a chicken dinner on Sunday!
The happy and enthusiastic throng of the student
delegates from all over the country, together with
thousands of others, filled the great Convention hall
to listen to the inspiring messages of "Evangeliza-
tion of the world in this generation" brought by the
leaders of the great movement, John R. Mott, Robert E. Speer, Sherwood Eddy, and others. I heard
them all and also heard the Hon. William Jennings
Bryan, then Secretary of State, who spoke at the
opening session of the convention. Of course, I could
not understand every word they said, but still I under-

stood what they were talking about all right and I
felt what everybody else there felt.

I found those speakers almost too eloquent for me
and their messages too urgent for me to wait until I
had become a doctor to be a missionary back in
Korea! I had just started my first year in Academy,
so it was really a long way to go from there. Yet,
tempus fugit, and how time did fly at Park! Time
flies when one is busy, and busy was the campus life,
to be sure. Before I realized it, the summer of 1914
had come, and along with several others, I stayed on
the campus, working in the college printing office.

It was a memorable summer, too, not only because
it was the first summer I spent there, but also because
it was the summer of the outbreak of the First World
War in Europe. Too well I remember that day in
July, while we were waiting to hear our lunch bell in
front of the dining room at the Nickel Dormitory,
when we read in the Kansas City Star the startling
news of Austria's declaration of war against Serbia,
which brought about the great conflict between the
Central Powers and the Allies.

How times changed! Only seven months before
that I had heard the urgent call for the Student Vol-
unteers to the flag of the Prince of Peace in order to
preach the Gospel of Peace in all the world in this
generation. Now, I heard them calling to arms all
the able-bodied men in many lands, eventually including the United States, in order to prosecute the war
against the autocratic governments of Germany and
Austria.

Soon another year of school had started, and again
I was assigned to the Snyder Hall for my meals for
the first term. There were four terms in the year so
far as the dining room assignments were concerned,

but the studies themselves were divided into two
semesters. Miss Harrison taught the Academy Latin
and History then, and was my teacher for the first
two years. She has since become the professor of
Education in the college. Professor Doterer taught
Algebra.

Somehow or another, they thought I was an artist,
and they made me a perennial artist for the clubs
which I had joined, and they made me the artist for
the college annual called the "Narva" when I was a
Junior in college several years later. I wished,
though, that there was a fine arts course offered at
Park College then, as there is one now, as I have
always appreciated greatly the artistic things.

During the Christmas holidays of that year, along
with a score of other students whose homes were too
far away to go to, I stayed on the campus as usual.
The only dining room open then was the Chestnut
Hall, which was the closest to my dormitory. Elderly
and kindly Mrs. Forsythe was the matron of this
girls' dormitory at the time, and I was invited to sit
at her own table many times. (This was before Mrs.
Schall came to take her place later.) Of all the different dormitories, I was privileged to dine here
more often than at the other place while I was at
Park.

Well, on one Sunday at the end of the holidays I
was staying in my room with a slight cold in my head
when Mrs. Nichols called me, saying that I was
wanted on the phone. It was about the noon hour
and the church service was just about over. When I
answered the phone, I recognized the kindly voice of
Mrs. Wolfe. "Oh, is it you, Emsen? Why, I looked
all over for you in the church, but I could not find

you there. I heard from one of the Woodward boys that you were not well. I am very sorry."

"Oh, I am all right, thank you," I replied. "I guess I have had too much sleigh-riding out in the snow with the Brown boys last night, that's all, Mrs. Wolfe."

"Well, then, I would like to have you come over to our home for dinner. This is your birthday, I know."

"My birthday today?" I said surprisedly. "Why, yes, indeed. That's right. This IS my birthday! I had forgotten all about it. How thoughtful of you to remember it! Certainly, I'll come right over, Mrs. Wolfe."

I did go over to her home for my birthday dinner that day. However, it was neither the first nor the last birthday or Sunday dinner to which I was invited. Innumerable times I have been there since that day. Each time one or more students besides myself, preferably, shall I say, some students from abroad or those who intended to go abroad as missionaries or to go into ministry, were there.

At one of those visits Mrs. Wolfe asked me if I had known a Miss Best, her best friend, who had gone to Pyeng Yang, my native city. She said Miss Best was a teacher at Park before going to Korea as a missionary. I said I ought to know her if I knew just whom she meant. What I meant was, as I have mentioned already on one of these pages once before, that the names of the Presbyterian missionaries in Korea were changed or modified to make them sound like Korean names, and I told her that I could not think of anyone called "Miss Best" in Pyeng Yang. Then she showed me a photograph of the lady in question, asking me if I could recognize who she was and if I had ever seen her.

"Why, of course, I know this lady," I said. "It's Baissie Bu-in or Madame Bai, who taught the women's Sunday School class at the First Presbyterian Church on the Saloon Alley when I first went to church with my folks. She lived for a while until the Hunters moved into the house on the top of the hill just this side of Rev. Graham Lee's and just beyond and above the Salvation Dispensary where my sore eye was treated once by Dr. Wells. I know the lady all right, Mrs. Wolfe, but I did not know she had come from Parkville. I remember, too, that she later lived with Dr. Baird's family until I went away from Pyeng Yang. You might be interested to know that Dr. Baird was called 'Bai Moksa' or 'Rev. Bai,' and I always thought they were related to each other in having the same family name. Of course, I knew she was a single lady, and naturally I thought she was a sister or a cousin of Dr. Baird's who was the superintendent of Shoongsil Academy of which I was a student."

Park sent many missionaries abroad, and many missionaries' children came to Park from abroad. Several of them were my classmates and schoolmates while I was there. Mary and Esther Swallon, Katherine and Lois Blair, Albert and Lillian Ross from Korea; the Hermans and McCandlisses from China; the Taylor sisters from Siam; the Browns from the Philippines; the Peekes and Altermans from Japan. My scholar cousin used to be Rev. Swallon's secretary in Pyeng Yang and Miss Ross, who was my classmate, had come from Sunchun, the same district where Dr. McCune worked with Rev. Ross, her father.

16
With Uncle Sam's Army

When I was in my third year in the Academy, because of poor health, I returned to California a few
weeks before the school closed for the summer. This
was in 1916. I stayed in California the following
year, going to high school in Claremont. While I
was there I did the janitor work at the Presbyterian
Church in Upland on Saturdays. It was the Rev.
Robert Stone's church, to which the Korean colony
of the town went. Mrs. William Boyd Stewart, a
very dear friend of my fellow-countrymen in California, taught the Korean Sunday School class there,
and I was made an interpreter for them. Miss Janet
Stone was my classmate for two years until we graduated together from Park College several years later.

It was while I stayed in Claremont, following the
declaration of war on Germany and Austria by the
Government of the United States, on April 6, 1917,
that I registered at Pomona for the Selective Service.
In the fall of that year, I returned to Park and continued my studies until I was drafted into the United
States Army on April 15, 1918.

Several other students were being drafted into the
military service at the same time as I. They were
mostly college men but there were two other Academy students besides myself — Sam King to the
Navy and Sheldon Cook to the Army. There was
quite a bit of excitement on the campus over our go-

ing to war. All the others being American citizens, they took it as a matter of course.

However, when it came to my case, they all wondered why it was that I had to go to war, for they all knew I was not a citizen. As a matter of fact, I did not have to go to war unless I wanted to. I did go because I wanted to. In the questionnaire which was sent to me, my draft board in Pomona asked me if I would refuse to be drafted because I was not a citizen. I answered, "No," because I had always wanted to be a soldier since my boyhood days when every day I saw Col. Jung Gwan-do riding by my house on his white horse in my native city of Pyeng Yang.

Perhaps that was merely a boyish fancy, but now I was inspired by President Wilson's war message to Congress, on April 2, 1917, when he said, "We are glad . . . to fight thus for the ultimate peace of the world for the liberation of its peoples, including the German people; for the rights of nations great and small and the privileges of men everywhere to choose their way of life and obedience. The world must be safe for democracy!"

Of course, I remember then that I used to interpret the Bible "too literally," as someone had advised me not to do, condemning the warring Christian nations. I was now convinced that "As long as there is a human race on this earth, there shall be wars," as I had often heard people say. How discouraging, but how true!

So far as I was concerned I had volunteered into the military service of the United States. And since there was the Medical Corps in the United States Army and as I had intended to study medicine, I wrote to the Surgeon General's office in Washington, saying that I preferred to be sent to the Army Medical Corps. My request was promptly granted. Was I happy! After passing the physical examination given at Platte City, seat of the Platte County in which Parkville was located, I was directed to the Medical Officers Training Camp at Fort Oglethorpe, Georgia.

When I wrote to my cousin in California about my joining the Army Medical Corps, he said it was a mighty fine thing to do. Who wouldn't fight for Uncle Sam who is fighting for the rights of nations great and small? For Korea is included in that, too, isn't it? "And I should think you can study medicine, as you always wished, while you are in the medical corps," he wrote to me.

On the morning of April 15, 1918, bidding farewell to Dr. and Mrs. Wolfe and all my friends, including George Paik and two other newly arrived Korean students, I was entrained for my army camp in the Dixie-land. Believe it or not, I was really thrilled that I was now an American soldier and that I was going to war alongside the Yankees. I had that grand and glorious feeling — the same sort of feeling which I had entertained on the morning of my landing in San Francisco more than ten years before that.

When lunch time came, our train was past Kansas City, and at the sound of "First call for dinner" shouted by a colored waiter, I went into the dining car and sat down at a table. Soon a colored waiter appeared and asked me for my order. When I presented to him my meal ticket which was issued to me by the Draft Board, he looked at it and then looking into my eyes, said, "Ahh, boss, I see you's a soldier! Congratulations! Dis here ticket is good for a sixty five cents' worth of dinna! I'll bring you all dat you can eat for dat!" When he came back with a trayful of good things to eat, he said, "Well, boss, where are you bound for?" When I told him I was bound for Georgia, he opened his mouth ever so wide and said, "Georgia! Ah, Georgia! Dat's my home state, good old Georgia! Dar's where I long to be! Good luck to you, boss — I mean soldier, boss, ha, ha, ha."

I did not reach Georgia on the same day. I had to change my train at Louisville, Kentucky. Arriving there at night, I slept on a bench in the station waiting room, waiting for my next train which was to arrive early the next morning. My next stop was at Chattanooga, Tennessee. By the time I reached my destination at Fort Oglethorpe, I had eaten up all my three tickets' worth of meals, and I arrived in the camp just in time for my first meal of "army beans."

It was a "detention camp," as they called it, a receiving center for all medical personnel of that section of the country. Physicians and surgeons were gathered there for officers' training, and the rookies like myself were there for rudimentary drilling and fatigue duties. For the most part it was a temporary stopping place for the newly enlisted and drafted men who were soon to be detached to different camps for more or less permanent duties. Thousands of them were already there in uniform and hundreds of new men were arriving daily and hourly from all directions.

Soon after our lunch, a batch of new arrivals were ordered to the Quartermaster's warehouse for our uniforms and everything else which soldiers needed. I was one of them. Out of the mountainous piles of supplies there, they issued to me a uniform with a hat, a pair of leggings, and two pairs of shoes — one dress and one campaign, two suits of underwear, three pairs of socks, two shirts, two blankets, and a mess kit and a belt, all dumped into a barracks bag made of blue denim and gathered at the top by a stout white cotton cord. Back in my tent when I was all dressed up in uniform, I looked and felt like a real American soldier. And wasn't I proud of myself! Really and truly I was. Now, my ambition number two was accomplished. My ambition number one, of course, was my coming to America.

On my second day in camp, I was put on K. P. duty. While I was busy working in the kitchen after the noonday meal, an officer — a captain in charge of the mess hall — came along and looking down on me, said, "You cook?"

Evidently, he was looking for a cook, and badly. Shaking my head and smiling, I answered, "No, sir, I'm no cook."

And he said, "Wouldn't you try?"

I replied, "No, thank you. I'm afraid I might spoil your dinner if I tried. You see, sir, I don't know how to cook. I was just a school boy."

Then, without further ado, the officer walked away. I thought he thought I was a Chinese and that every Chinese was a good cook.

On a Sunday, accompanied by several comrades, I walked over to the Chattanooga and Chickamauga Military Park and saw some of the relics of the Civil War there. I was at Oglethorpe only about ten days before I was detached to Camp A. A. Humphreys, Virginia. One morning after breakfast, some forty or more men, including myself, were ordered to pack up to leave instantly, but telling us not a word of our destination. Some of us thought we were going to another camp more or less permanent, and others conjectured that we were probably bound for France! How eager were some of the men to go to France! Anyway I was glad to leave because I was already getting tired of doing nothing worthwhile there as a soldier.

On the afternoon of that same day, we arrived by train at Acotinc Station, some ten miles south of Alexandria, Virginia. From there we walked down to the old camp at Fort Belvoir, passing through the main Army Engineers' camp called A. A. Humphreys. They had just started building a base hospital and men's living quarters near that camp, but for the present we were to station at Camp Belvoir until the new buildings were completed.

Camp Belvoir was quite a scenic spot. Situated in the woods on the west bank of the Potomac River, it was only five miles south of Mount Vernon. I heard it was a part of the old Fairfax estate which George Washington himself had surveyed and had his home at Mount Vernon. The camp contained five rows of three long barracks each. Of course, there were also some outer buildings, such as the guard house, the stables, and so forth. Whether the camp had been out of use until now, or had been vacated recently for us, I did not know, but when we arrived, everything was in order and in operation already. Major Moore, the commanding officer, was there. After a few days he left and Major Doer took his place. Captain Linden was also there, with Sergeant Johnson, and the mess hall was open with plenty of cooks, so that no one asked me if I could cook.

Day after day, new men arrived from the North and West, but mostly from New York. I was assigned to the Dispensary, helping the pharmacists in filling prescriptions and handing out cathartic compound pills and castor oil to my comrades. There were three pharmacists with whom I worked — Cullinane, a gray-haired and mild-mannered Irish gentleman from Boston; Gunvodahl, also gray-haired and a cigar-chewing Norwegian gentleman from Detroit; and a young Italian from New York, named Marciline, I think, who did not stay long enough for me to remember his name correctly. Lieutenant Shea, who was in charge of the Dispensary, and Lieutenant Timmons, in charge of the operating room next door, were gentlemen and scholars in army uniform.

When I wrote to my mother in Korea about my work in the army dispensary, she replied, "That's a good idea, son. In Korea the 'druggist-doctors' are in great need, and they make more money than do the physicians and surgeons."

Major Doer, the commandant, was a very fine man, indeed. He used to call me into his office and we sat down and talked together. He told me his story and I told him mine. He said he was interested to meet a Korean student; in fact, I was the first Korean he had ever met. So far as I know, I think I was about the only Oriental in uniform in that part of the country. Major Doer was a Pennsylvania State College graduate and was a practicing doctor before he entered military service. He had been married a few years before and had a wife and small boy back home. He was then six feet tall, a handsome man of about thirty-two years. I knew him so well from my first day there and for some eight months after that I can still picture him before my eyes. A few weeks after my arrival, he was promoted to Lieutenant Colonel.

There were men from all walks of life, as is the case in every army camp in time of war, and it generally takes quite some time to find one's own group in such a situation. In my case though, it did not take much time, nor any effort. For one thing, the camp was small and its entire personnel was less than one hundred. Well, I found three men of my group. One was Benjamin Saxon Bywater from New Orleans, whom I had met at Fort Oglethorpe when I first arrived there and who came here on the same train with me. He said to me that he was very glad we were going to the same place together. He was a stenographer and was in the military service before the war. He had become Major Doer's secretary with the rank of Sergeant right from the start. Soon after we arrived at Camp Belvoir, we found two bright looking young men both from Saginaw, Michigan. Clyde Caris and John Kruger were their names. They, too, were stenographers and were assigned to the staff office of Captain Robert Linden. Soon they became non-coms; first, corporals, then sergeants later. I was made Private First Class when they were made sergeants.

All three of my new friends were fine Christians and expert pianists. In the evenings we used to go down to the "Y" building, situated beautifully on the water's edge at the confluence of the Potomac River and a stream where the Army Engineers practiced in building and unbuilding pontoon bridges. We went to the "Y" to play and to listen to music, to read books, to see the movies, or to enjoy the entertainments presented there during the week days. On Sundays, we had brief religious services conducted by the "Y" men or by the visiting Army Chaplains. I was a lover of good books and I found that reading good books was the best entertainment I ever found. From the book shelves there, I got hold of a copy of "Ben Hur" which was donated and signed by Kathleen Norris, the well-known novelist of San Francisco.

Once every two weeks, on my week-end furloughs, I used to go up to Washington, which was only twenty-five miles up the Potomac River. On these trips I passed by Mount Vernon beautifully located on a knoll on the west bank of the river. There was a motor boat running between Newport News and Washington on Saturdays and Sundays. Sergeant Bywater and I went to Washington together occasionally and to a Chinese cafe for chop suey or chow mein. I used to stay over night in Washington at an old church near the John Marshall's Place north of Pennsylvania Avenue. There were a couple of dozen cots prepared in a spacious ante-room in order to accommodate visiting doughboys at the moderate charge of twenty-five cents a night.

The very friendly woman caretaker there told me that this same church had given valuable service during the Civil War days, when it was used as a hospital ward for the wounded soldiers who were brought in from the battlefields of Bull Run and Shennandoah. That showed it was quite a historic church with a proud record behind it. The place was indeed nice and cool and was inviting to anyone in a city which is usually hot in the summer. No wonder the place was always full to the brim. I was lucky, however, to find an empty cot every time I went there.

Washington was a beautiful city. The first thing I saw from the Potomac was the Washington Monument, that big shining white marble shaft soaring

more than five hundred feet into the sky. Then to
the west of it, some distance away, just on that side
of the great George Washington bridge, stood the
Lincoln Memorial overlooking the Potomac and the
State of Virginia. The Market Street in San Francisco was the largest in the country, I had thought
while I lived there, but here in Washington I found
the Pennsylvania Avenue to be the largest and the
most beautiful I had ever seen — so clean, so wide,
so straight — from the steps of the Capitol down to
the Treasury Building and the White House. I
walked past the White House several times, admiring the beauty of the official residence of President
Wilson who was my commander-in-chief.

On my subsequent visits to Washington, I went
inside the Smithsonian Institute on B Street, better
known as Constitution Street. On Capitol Hill I visited the Capitol, where the official guide showed me
the Rotunda, the Hall of Fame, and the Chamber of
the House of Representatives. Beautiful and interesting were these places which I had the privilege of
seeing and admiring. I was so proud of myself to
have seen the National Capitol, and, in order to
show my friends and my home folks that I had been
there, I sent dozens of beautifully decorated picture
cards which I bought from the guide at the entrance
of the Capitol.

Walking down Louisiana Avenue in a northeast-
erly direction, I went to the Union Station where I
saw crowds of people, soldiers and civilians, stream-
ing in and out of the trains there. Out in the streets,
there were even more crowds. Indeed, there were
plenty of uniformed men in Washington in those
days. Not only were there American soldiers, sailors
and officers, but also quite a few of them from our

Allied nations, and I had to salute every officer that I passed on the sidewalk. I thought it was a great honor and privilege to salute so many officers of so many nationalities, because I was proud of myself as a soldier in American uniform — that I was an American soldier.

One day as I was walking up Pennsylvania Avenue, I heard a small boy making a funny remark as he passed by me. He said to his father, "Oh, daddy, did you see that Chinese soldier?"

Back in the camp one morning Sergeant Johnson stepped into our Dispensary with a happy grin on his face and said to me, "Well, Private First Class Charr, I've got a bit of good news for you. That is, if you are interested! They want you up at the headquarters. You said you lived in this country over ten years, went to a college, and now you're in the United States Army. I suppose you'd like to be an American citizen, wouldn't you?"

"Wouldn't I want to be an American citizen!" I exclaimed. It was all so sudden that I could not believe my ears. "Sure, I do," I said, "but can this be true? For I know Orientals are never eligible for citizenship."

"But now it's different," continued Sergeant Johnson. "There is a special regulation being made now to naturalize everybody who is in the United States military service, I hear. Do you see the crowd waiting for you outside? What are you waiting for? Go with them, quick."

"All right, Sergeant, I'll go with them if you say so," I said, and I put on my hat and followed the cosmopolitan group up to the headquarters of Camp A. A. Humphreys. Inside the office I saw a dozen or so uniformed men behind the desks, asking each man what his nationality was and then looking up the printed list to see if his nationality were listed there. I was one of the last ones interviewed. When my turn came, I told my interviewer that my nationality was "Korean." He looked up and down the list alphabetically and otherwise several times, and then shaking his head said to me, "I am sorry, but the Korean nationality is not listed here. Neither the Chinese nor the Japanese nationalities are listed here among the eligibles. Some Filipinos are listed here though. You are neither one of them, are you?"

"No, I am not, but will you please tell me what's all the excitement about the new naturalization regulations," I said. "For I knew all the time that the Orientals were never eligible to American citizenship, but the European and some other nationalities were always eligible before. Well, now, just what does this special regulation say?" I asked. And the man said he did not know very much about the new law, but he thought it said ANYONE who was now in the armed forces of the United States was entitled to American citizenship.

"Are you sure it says 'anyone'?" I asked him.

"That's right," he answered, "I'm quite sure of that. I haven't got a copy of the regulation here with me, but I am sure that it starts out every paragraph with that word 'anyone'."

"Hm, 'anyone' it says, but it appears that I am not the one," I sighed. "Strange, isn't it?"

"It does seem strange, all right, and I can't explain it myself. You see, I'm no constitutional lawyer either to explain it to you or to argue with you on that point," he said. "I'll go and try to find out for you if you'll just wait for me a moment," he said and left me.

The other men near me all looked at me — some smiling, some laughing, some staring, and others shaking their heads — meaning just what, I did not know. After a while my interviewer returned with a gloomy look on his face and said to me that he didn't get any light on the subject from anyone, for no one there seemed to know anything more about it than to take the names of the men according to the nationalities listed on the printed form as eligible for citizenship. That was all. He said to me, "I am sorry, but there isn't anything else I can do for you."

Was I sad, or was I mad? Was my face red? Maybe I was all of that. Really, I was sad and disappointed because I had expected so much and did not gain anything, but I was not ready to fight for the thing which I had desired so much. I was too young to be bothered about anything like that just then. Besides, I had always known the existing law that did not include the Orientals among the eligibles, so I was not wholly unprepared to cushion the shock.

As soon as Sergeant Johnson saw me back in the camp, he asked me if I was going to be granted citizenship like the rest, and when I told him the sad story he, too, was disappointed and said, "You don't say! I'm very sorry to hear that. Why, I thought the new regulation would include you. So the man told you the law says 'anyone but you.' That's not fair. I just can't believe that to be true. What's the special regulation for? I would like to know. If 'anyone' is deserving special consideration, it ought to be you, I'll say. There must be some mistake somewhere. Don't you let that get you down for I'm sure it will be straightened out for you later."

In the meantime, my friend, Sergeant Ben Bywater, went back to the office and reported to the Colonel

the news of the day. Colonel Doer himself was interested in my case and wished to talk with me. Ben
came over to me and whispered into my ear, saying,
"The Colonel wants to see you in his office right
away, Comrade Charr."

Saluting Colonel Doer, I said, "Sir, did you send
for me?"

"Oh, yes, Private First Class Charr. Sit down
here. I want to talk with you."

I sat down in a chair as directed near his desk
which was piled with sheaves of his official papers.
Relinquishing his official task for a moment, he said
to me, "I am shocked to hear the bad news the Sergeant just brought in regarding your naturalization
matter. Of course, I don't know the particulars about
the new regulation nor the application of it, but I
thought certainly it would include you in any case.
Now, please tell me just what they told you up there."

"Well, sir, the man who interviewed me asked me
what nationality I was. 'Korean,' I told him. Then
he looked up a printed list of nationalities several
columns long and said he could not find mine among
the eligibles there. Neither the Chinese nor the Japanese nationalities were listed there, he told me," I
said.

"So, what did you do next?" the Colonel asked
me again.

"So, I started asking him some questions," I replied. "I turned inquisitive. I was curious to know
what it was all about that had disillusioned me tem-
porarily. I asked him just what the new regulation
said. He told me he did not have a copy of the new
regulation with him, but he said he was sure that
every paragraph starts out with the word '*Anyone
who is in so and so branch of the armed forces of*

the United States should be granted citizenship at once.' And when I said, 'You mean *ANYONE* but *ME?*' he said that was just about the case and there was nobody up there who knew anything more about it beyond that. That's all, sir."

"I see," said the Colonel, smiling. "If I understand it right, your interviewer had his instructions to go by, by the list of eligible nationalities provided him in a printed form. And if that's the case, I think it proves my theory formulated from your information that the new regulation is made, evidently, in the interest of those who were always eligible, perhaps, with the minor changes simplifying the process of making citizens of aliens who are now in the armed forces of the United States. That is, granting citizenship AT ONCE without going through the usual procedure which takes many years and months. And, if that's the situation, I am sorry to conclude that it would leave you out, wouldn't it?"

Then he went on to say further in this manner:

"I am sorry to say that the lawmakers in our Congress did not go far enough in making the special regulation to include you. Maybe they didn't know you were in the Army, too," he said smiling. "Well, any common law is made just like that, you see. They don't cover every specific case. They are made for general application, and are often very ambiguous, too. And that's where the lawyers come in with the different interpretations, trying to make the provisions of the laws suit their own specific cases.

"But, still I am sincerely hoping for something more concrete to turn up in your favor in the future. For I am fully in sympathy with you, like everybody else in this camp and in every other camp of the armed forces of this country who are your comrades

in arms. Who knows that there won't be a great veterans' organization formed after the war is over, one
that's similar to the Grand Army of the Republic,
with lofty ideals of patriotism and comradeship?
When that comes true, as I am sure it will, your
dreams as well as mine will also be realized. Be
patient and be of good cheer, therefore, Private First
Class Charr, for surely you will be rewarded with
citizenship rights for your service freely given to this
government, and if the government should forget
you, your comrades of the veterans' organization will
help you get it!"

I thanked him for his kindness and words of wisdom and I came away from his office infinitely hap-
pier than even those who were already assured of
their American citizenship. I felt as though mine,
too, was as good as promised to be given forthwith.
To me, hoping to get some good things to come was
a thousand times better than getting them readily
and forgetting them easily. I think he was indeed a
man of keen judgment and wonderful foresight. In
the light of my experience since that day, I found his
interpretation of the special naturalization regulation
absolutely correct. As to his foresight, his predic-
tions concerning a future veterans' organization and
its helpfulness to me personally as a veteran proved
to be marvelously accurate. If he were not a prophet,
certainly his utterances were prophetic. The American Legion was organized in Paris the following
year, and in later years, myself as a member of that
great organization, my dreams as well as his dreams
came true, just as he had said they would.

It was during those hot days of July that I heard
and read about the new German offensive in northern
France where our men were either defending their

positions heroically or countter-attacking the enemy lines bravely. Here at our hospital we were fighting, day and night, with all sorts of cases of ailments and diseases brought in for treatment and care. Occasionally we were given first-aid instructions and stretcher or litter-bearing drills out on the parade grounds right by the river, and later on we were given physical examinations, presumably for overseas service. We all thought, naturally, that we were being prepared to sail for France for overseas duty. But we were mistaken. For just then our new Base Hospital building was completed upon the hill, close to Camp A. A. Humphreys, and we were transferred to our new quarters there, leaving Camp Belvoir behind.

The new Base Hospital was situated in the woods some half mile south of the engineers' camp. It was an enormous single story wooden building all in one piece, with several wings spreading out to the north and south. The main entrance was at the west end of the building where the offices of the commanding officer, the waiting and reception room and the Dispensary were located side by side. Those corridors seemed miles long and the separate wards miles apart. The hospital was sandwiched in between the officers' quarters on the west and the men's barracks on the east, each separated from it by a roadway leading up to the main camp.

At first I thought the building was unnecessarily large, but before long it was full, and overflowed with the influenza patients. That awful epidemic of "flu" that swept over the nation also swept over the engineers' camp. Patients were brought in by the tens daily. More doctors and women nurses were needed in order to take care of these cases more adequately, and special cases had to be transferred to the Walter Reed Hospital in Washington. Those were really terrifying days when that horrible plague held full sway over the lives of hundreds of men who were fighting desperately with this invisible enemy instead of the Kaiser's hordes with whom they were being trained to contend. In spite of all the skillful ministration and expert nursing and care, I saw the exodus of the covered corpses parading down the long corridors toward the morgue, hourly and daily. It was a terrible thing to witness the scenes when the parents and brothers and sisters came weeping and grieving over their loved ones dying and dead, afflicted with that epidemic. The reception room was right next to our Dispensary, and I could not help witnessing the heartbreaking scenes day in and day out.

At the height of the "flu" epidemic, everybody in the hospital personnel had a scared look on his face. Each wondered, if not actually worried, if he wouldn't be the next victim of this contagious malady that seemed to attack the most healthy and robust looking persons more than others. The personnel of the hospital staff was kept miraculously intact until one day our commanding officer, Colonel Doer himself, was stricken with that "flu" and died of it within a few days! Besides the attending medical officer, no one else but his young wife and small boy were allowed to see him in his sick bed at his own living quarters just in front of the Dispensary.

Colonel Doer was no more, yet, I still remember him most deeply.

Such was the fierce battleground here at the Base Hospital at Camp A. A. Humphreys. Day and night we were so busy fighting this insidious and deadly enemy right here at the home front that we did not get to go across the "Big Pond." Naturally, many of us who were so anxious to see real action in the front lines in France were greatly disappointed. But, we had to be contented with our routine duty right here at the same spot until the war was over! Ours was the battle line, it seemed to us, even more formidable than the vaunted Hindenburg Line in France. Our battle raged all through the winter, through the Armistice Day and clear up to the end of the year. The Germans signed the armistice, but the "flu" would not.

It was about this time our comrades over there were winning the battle of their own as we were fighting ours at the hospital. In the Marne, in the Meuse-Argonne, in the Belliew Wood and at Chateau Thierry, the American forces were going over the top and smashing through the old Hindenburg Line. Following President Wilson's declaration of his famous "Fourteen Points," containing the principle of self-determination of each nation, great and small, all mankind was inspired, including the peoples of the Central Powers themselves, who had been enslaved and sacrificed by their warlords during the four years of devastating war. They rebelled now against the Kaiser who fled to Holland. The armistice was signed by Germany, and the war was over!

Very well, indeed, I remember that Armistice Day. While I was on duty, busily washing medicine bottles and putting up magnesium sulphate solution bottles on the shelves at the Dispensary that morning, all of a sudden, I heard an uproar resounding through the mile-long corridors. In order to learn what it was all about, I stepped out into the corridor. There I saw Corporal Cullinane, the Irish gentleman pharmacist, rushing down toward me saying, "War's over, war is over now, comrade Charr! Germany signed the armistice at eleven o'clock! Major Greer has just received a telegram from Washington!"

"Oh, yes? The war's over — so soon? Hurrah! Hurrah! And we won the war! Hurrah! Hurrah! Hurrah!" I cheered.

Yes, the war was over, and was over sooner than expected, even before we had the chance to go over to see what the actual battle line looked like, and no doubt a lot of our men were sorely disappointed. Nevertheless, everyone was happy that the terrible war was over now, and we were soon to be returning home, back to our normal life and endeavor.

After returning from my two weeks' furlough, visiting with some Park College people who were working at the Du Pont Powder Plant on the Cumberland River near Nashville, Tennessee, I enjoyed the last few days in the camp with my friends before I was mustered out from the United States Army. The disbandment order had been received from Washington and the men were being prepared to be mustered out by taking a checking-out physical examination. I was with the first batch to receive the Honorable Discharge certificate. Mine reads as follows:

"Honorable Discharge from the Army of the United States

"This is to certify that Easurk Emsen Charr, #2579684, Private First Class, Medical Department, U. S. Army, as a Testimonial of Honest and Faithful Service is hereby Honorably Discharged from the military service of the

United States by reason of Authority Telegram
A. G. O. November 15, 1918, . . . etc.

> (Signed) M. M. Greer
> Major, Medical Corps,
> Commanding."

On the reverse side it reads:

"Inducted into the United States Army April
15, 1918 — born in Korea — Age 24 — sallow
complexion — 5 ft. 4 in. — Occupation: Student
— Character: Excellent — Remarks: Service
honest and faithful — No A.W.O.L. — No
sickness in hospital, under G. A. 45-14 — Honorably discharged by authority of Telegram
A.G.O. Nov. 15, 1918 as set forth in Par. 3,
G.O. 305, Headquarters: Camp A. A. Humphreys, Virginia, Dec. 28, 1918.

> (Signed) Robert R. Linden
> Captain, Sanitary Corps
> Commanding Det. Med. Dept."

17

My Alma Mater

With Pomona, California, the place of my Local Draft Board, as my destination, I was furnished with transportation fare at two cents a mile, plus sixty dollars in bonus. I was paid in cash in two fifty-dollar bills and sizable loose change. That was the first time in my life I had ever seen or possessed such big denominations! So now I was ready to travel from the Atlantic seaboard to the Pacific Coast with my Honorable Discharge paper securely tucked away in my blouse pocket. Oh, yes, I was still in the army uniform with a V-shaped red chevron sewed on my sleeve, showing that I was a discharged soldier.

My first stop was in the national capital city of Washington where I enjoyed the New Year's holiday and the first two weeks of peaceful and easy civilian life without the bugler disturbing my sweet slumber early in the mornings or washing the medicine bottles during the day time. I slept all that I wanted and ate some things that were more tasty and varied than the army beans. I stayed at a cozy place right on Pennsylvania Avenue, a few doors above a "Y" hut and diagonally opposite the old Knickerbocker theatre. It was a combination lodging and boarding place; that is, it had sleeping rooms upstairs and a cafeteria on the ground floor. There were many others, all in service uniform, quartered there also.

To stay and enjoy life in Washington, however,

was an expensive proposition, I found out. My first fifty dollar bill was changed on the third day at the Knickerbocker theatre on Pennsylvania Avenue. When I presented it at the box office, the pretty cashier said to me, "Ah! Soldier, you've got lots of money — a fifty dollar bill!"

"Oh, that's nothing. I've got another one like that right here," I said, showing it to her.

I was so proud of myself to have so much money in my pocket, but it did not last very long. In two weeks' time all that first fifty dollars were gone, and it had me worried. Just then, I received a letter from Dr. Hawley, the new president of Park College, advising me to return to Park for the second semester which was scheduled to begin early in February, 1919. Thinking of seeing the dear old campus again and meeting my dear old schoolmates there, I packed and left Washington for the last time on my way back to Parkville, Missouri.

On my way, I stopped over at Akron, Ohio, to see my bosom friend, Changhai, whom I had left in San Francisco several years ago. He had come East and was now employed at one of the rubber factories there during the war. He was one of the score of Korean nationals making rubber shoes and boots while many of the former employees were drafted into the armed forces of the United States. Among them were three other old friends of mine who were my fellow sojourners from Pyeng Yang to Honolulu back in 1904.

I was indeed glad to see Changhai once again and to enjoy mutual friendship together again as we had out in San Francisco. Of course, we had written to each other often while I was in the army camp, and he had asked me to drop in to see him on my way back to school. Here, now, we met and went together for some ten days while I stopped there. I met him again in Chicago a few years later.

Traveling on a Baltimore and Ohio train from Akron to Chicago, and on the Burlington and Chicago train, I arrived at Parkville one sunny afternoon. Meeting hardly anyone on my way, I walked straight up the many steps of the many terraces toward the campus. Oh, it certainly was good to see the dearly familiar buildings, standing out so beautifully, and seeming to smile a greeting to me. When I looked up at the Mackay tower on the upper terrace, the clock showed it was a little after twelve. No wonder I had seen hardly a soul abroad on the campus. It was lunch time, and everyone was in the dining halls, of course.

When I reached the level of the campus, the closest building was the Alumni Hall to my left where I had had my last meal on the morning of the day when I left for my army camp. Now, as I turned my eyes from the clock tower I heard a sweet familiar voice issuing from the upper story window of the Alumni Hall, calling, "HELLO! OH, HELLO E. E.!" I looked up and saw a girl's hand waving from the dining room window. Of course, I knew who it was, readily, and I responded, "OH, HELLO THERE! HELLO M. E.!"

"Come right up, E. E., we're waiting for you," she said.

She was one of the finest and friendliest young women I had ever known on the campus. At times we were classmates, and we went to the social gatherings together often, before and after this. Naturally we wrote to each other quite often while I was in my camp down in Virginia. Why, kindly Mrs.

Goodson, her matron, had placed me next to Mary at her own table on that morning of my departure, some ten months ago, so that I could enjoy my last breakfast with her. And here she was now, the very first person to greet me back. Was I happy! Sergeant Johnson of my old camp did not know that I really had a "girl friend" up in Missouri when he asked me "Who's your girl friend you're going to see down in Tennessee?" when I was going down there on my furlough. Mary Elizabeth was a very fine girl and I liked her very much!

Now I was back in school, and back to normalcy. So were the nations of the world going back to their home soil from the battle fields of Flanders, and the peace conference was being held at Versailles. The Allies went home happy because they had won the war. Even the vanquished enemy nations were happy in displacing autocracy in favor of democracy for which the world was now made safe. And, although not directly involved in the war for the survival of democracy, all the subject nations of the world were also happy that the "Self-determination" principle of President Wilson was thought applicable to them all. Korea, my native country, was one of them.

I was a great little Korean patriot. I was so patriotic that everywhere I went to and to everyone whom I met, I talked about Korea and her plight. One strange thing I discovered, though, was that the average American was ignorant of geography. Very few people knew where Korea was located on the map. Naturally, I have always been mistaken for either a Chinese, or a Japanese, or even for a Filipino. And did that make me mad, one might ask. No, indeed. They made me smile, instead. Well, they made me smile to think that some Americans had taught me geography back in Korea years ago, and here in America I was trying to teach some other Americans the geography lessons which I had learned long ago.

The only American people who know Korea best, something of her people and customs, her history as well as her geography, are the Christians. It was the Christians who had sent out the missionaries to Korea away back in 1883, and through the missionaries they have learned of that once "Hermit Kingdom" that so many others were so ignorant of. Magazine articles and books were written by the missionaries, relating to the progress of their Evangelical work that was being done among the strange people of the least known country in the world. It was through a few of these books which I bought from the Student Volunteer Convention in Kansas City that I had learned many things of my native land which I had not known before.

I had not been back in school for more than some five weeks when one day I read some startling, tragic news of my home land. On March 1, 1919, Korea had declared independence of Japan, having been inspired by the "Self-determination" principle of President Wilson. What followed were blood-curdling scenes enacted by the brutal Japanese in Korea. *

I was a Korean patriot. So were other Korean students on the campus, including my good friend, George Paik. We, in America, we thought, must do something to help the helpless people back in our homeland. Naturally, we thought of asking for both the assistance and prayers of the millions of American Christians, especially our fellow students in the Christian colleges and universities. We sent out a circular to hundreds of churches and schools through the country. The following letter was written and printed by myself:

"Parkville, Mo.,
March 20, 1919.

"TO OUR CHRISTIAN FRIENDS:

"We the Korean Christian students at Park College, representing the Christian Koreans in America, sincerely and earnestly appeal to the Christian people of the United States of America for your deepest sympathy and earnest prayers on behalf of Korea our native country.

"For today is the most critical moment in Korea. The life of the nation is at stake and Christianity is being trodden upon under the power of darkness. Korea has declared its independence of Japan and Japan utterly denies it. Korea is bleeding today at the point of the Japanese sword. While the Peace Conference is being held in France the world doesn't seem to comprehend that a nation of twenty million inhabitants is being brutally subjugated. The following is some of the tragic news we have received through the special cable reaching the Chicago Daily News from Peking, China:

'The Japanese are committing brutalities equal only to those committed by the Germans in France and Belgium. They are attempting to plaec the blame on the missionaries. Probably it will never be known how many persons have been killed in the last two weeks, but the total must be very large. Soldiers are said to have cut off the hands of the school girls for holding up manifestoes. Many innocent

persons have been bayonetted by the enraged
soldiers. Christian Churches have been
wrecked and missionaries have been insulted.
Some have been treated so badly that it is
feared that their lives may be endangered. It
is believed that an attempt is being made to
drive them out of Korea. The situation de-
mands the world's notice and inquiry! Late
reports indicate that probably 10,000 Koreans
have been already massacred by the Japanese
in cold blood in two days!'

"Oh! Let us ask you, fellow Christians and
friends, how would you feel, if your beloved
country were garrisoned with foreign troops; if
the Revolutionary War of 1776, in which the
United States asserted their independence of
Great Britain, had been unsuccessful; if the lives
of your loved ones and your fellow-countrymen
had been lost and properties despoiled by an
invading army; if your president was deposed
and imprisoned by an alien power; if your
churches were wrecked and the Christians were
mutilated and murdered in cold blood by the enraged enemy soldiers for being patriots for
their fatherland?

"Will you now, fellow Christians and friends,
pray for us, sympathize with us and help us to
obtain the right and freedom of our native
country? Will you not give practical expression
to your sympathy by writing to your Congress-
man and Senator at Washington urging that the
United States come to the rescue of this shame-
fully down-trodden but liberty-loving nation?"

Sympathetic responses were coming forthwith

from our Christian friends all over the nation. "The Continent," a national church periodical, responded most heartily and commented on the "pertinent questions" asked in the circular as to how the Americans would feel if they were in the place of the Koreans. The Kansas City Star had this article printed:

"Declaring that the treatment of the people of Korea by the Japanese was on a par with the methods used by the Turks against the Armenians and the Huns against the Belgians, the Rev. Grant A. Robbins, pastor of the Linwood Boulevard Methodist Episcopal Church, scored the great world powers for permitting such a condition of affairs to exist, in a sermon yesterday.

" 'The people of Korea are crying out for religious freedom and the right to govern themselves,' he said, 'and their pleas go unheard by the so-called Christian nations, who now have representatives sitting at the peace table in Paris, with the envoys from the country that is responsible for Korean desolation. Men at the peace conference are aware of what is taking place in the Far East, but no one has made any known attempt to stop this crime against humanity,' he said."

Some time later I was given a chance to present the case of Korea to an American audience. The minister of Parkville Presbyterian Church, Dr. Moore, invited me to speak on Korea in his church one Sunday evening. Accepting the invitation, I had my speech all written out and memorized as was practiced by the forensic students in the college. It was my first experience in speaking to an American audience, yet, I thought I did pretty well, judging by the kindly reception given me by the audience. Mine was an opening speech to a stereopticon lecture. Since then, I was invited to repeat my set speech, time and again, at different churches in the neighboring towns and cities in Kansas and Missouri. Honestly, I was received and feted like an unofficial ambassador from that "Hermit Kingdom" of Korea. Dr. Bailey, of the Westport Presbyterian Church in Kansas City, remarked that I was quite an orator.   *

It was during these visits to the churches that I found a new friend whom I always remember more than many others. One Sunday evening, at the Central Presbyterian Church in Kansas City, I met the late Mr. W. M. Bunting, a businessman of that city. After listening to my message, he became interested in me so deeply that he pledged to help me finish my schooling until I was ready to enter a medical college. He did help me greatly during all four years at Park College until I was graduated from it.

At Christmas time every year, Mr. Bunting remembered me kindly by sending me a beautfiul necktie. One Christmas day, I was invited out to his family reunion dinner at his lovely home in the Country Club district. His kindly mother and his brother's (Mr. George B.) families were present there. Another brother of his, Mr. Frank B. of Ontario, Canada, whom I never had the pleasure of meeting, also became interested in me through him, all because of brotherly love in Christ, and helped me along with his brother. These good people wished me to become a medical missionary back to my native country, just as much as I myself had aspired. But, it was not to be. Heaven seemed to have decreed otherwise. I tried hard to become a doctor, but it was something which I was destined not to be, in spite of all my effort.

In the fall of that year, in 1919, I entered college as a Freshman with the military service credit of twelve hours granted to me in advance toward graduation. Bible, English, Biology, Chemistry, and Physics were the five subjects which I took. They were mostly pre-medical subjects, since I intended to study medicine. By no means were they light subjects for me, and I had to dig very hard. From my own experience, I found out that the harder I dug, the easier it became, and nothing could mar the smiles on my face at any time.

One morning in my room at the new Copley-Thaw dormitory, I happened to pick up a copy of the Kansas City Star to which my roommate, Andrew Layman, subscribed. My eyes were fixed on a news item which interested me deeply. I was so intently interested in it that I read it over a dozen times, so surprising and so inspiring was the news to me. I said to myself, "Well, well, what do you know about that? Can it be true? A Japanese, it says, was granted American citizenship! And of all places, it was given to him in the heart of the anti-Japanese State of California. If a Japanese got it, why not I?"

In substance, the article said that a Federal Court in Los Angeles, California, had granted American citizenship to a Japanese, named so and so, on the ground that he served in the armed forces of the United States during the War.

Just then, my roommate came in. He was one of the most popular students on the campus and a son of a minister and himself a ministerial student. He was a Junior in the college and a fellow member of a literary club, to which I was invited by him to join.

When I showed the news item to him, he said, "Oh, say, this is good news for you in a way, Emsen. For it means that you, too, as a veteran, will have the same privilege to acquire American citizenship as this Japanese fellow has!" And he suggested that I should consult Dean Sanders who could advise me just what to do and how to go about it in an orderly manner. I agreed with him.

It happened to be Monday morning, and I found Dean Sanders in his office in the Mackay Hall. When I showed him the news clipping and expressed my view of my own case in the light of the precedent set by the Federal judge in California in granting American citizenship to a Japanese veteran, he agreed with me one hundred percent. "Why, certainly, this is a good precedent set for you whereby you can be benefited. According to this report, this Japanese was granted American citizenship because he was an American soldier, a World War veteran. So are you! There can be no two different interpretations of the same identical Federal Law, no matter which Court you should go to in this country." And he said he was going to write to Mr. Cameron Orr, a Park College Alumnus, a lawyer, and he was then the U. S. District Attorney in Kansas City, for information relative to this case.

A few days later, Dean Sanders called me into his office and told me that he had received a letter, together with a booklet containing all the naturalization laws and regulations, from Mr. Orr with regard to my citizenship matter. In Mr. Orr's letter, he advised that my case could be heard in a Circuit Court which was scheduled to be in session at St. Joseph, Missouri, in a couple of weeks. To do so, I was to file my application or petition with the clerk of the naturalization bureau there before that time, and I would need two witnesses with me.

That sounded good to me, and I was indeed happy. I told Dean Sanders that Andy Layman had already promised to be a witness, and he said, "That's fine. I'll take you and Andrew to St. Joseph next Monday. I'll be the other witness for you, and don't you worry about the expenses. I will take care of them for both of you."

So, on the following Monday, the three of us made a trip to the Federal Court Building in St. Joseph and I had filed my petition for naturalization. And, a few months later, the court decision was made and handed down to me, not at the Circuit Court in St. Joseph, but at the Federal District Court in Kansas City. I was denied citizenship on the ground that I was an Oriental who was never eligible to American citizenship regardless of my veteran status.

There was a first page report on my case in the Kansas City Star at the time, and the court's ruling was recorded in a bulky volume of naturalization laws relating to the veterans of the World War which I read a few years later. It certainly was a big puzzle to me to read in the same paper about two persons of the same background, with the same qualifications and claims, and under the same Federal Law, who received treatment of opposite results—one was taken, the other was rejected. There was inconsistency there, I thought.

When a foreigner is in Rome, he may do as the Romans do, but when there are a number of foreigners in Rome at the same time, there may be a Cosmopolitan Club there for the purpose of mutual friendship as fellow-foreigners as well as for the purpose of exchanging their views and opinions formed of their observations and experiences which they may have had while they are in Rome. And, no doubt, there was the first such club founded by the Greeks, called Cosmopolitan, meaning "World Citizen."

There were quite a few foreign students at Park College, as there had been almost every year, and there was a Cosmopolitan Club in existence as in the other colleges and universities in the United States. Following the older brother organizations long established, it had adopted for its motto "Above All Nations is Humanity." Of course, all the foreign students were eligible to the membership and there were one or two elected from the native Americans and an honorary member from the members of the faculty.

The very first gathering of the Cosmopolitan Club to which I was invited was held at the home of Mr. and Mrs. Edwin Knapp one evening in the spring of 1914. Dr. Wolfe, the Acting President of the college, and Mrs. Wolfe were present, along with several foreign students and a few others who were my fellow printers in the college press. Mr. Knapp was my boss, you remember, and Mrs. Knapp was on the editorial staff of the Kansas City Evening Journal. They took great interest in our club, and honored us that night with refreshments and entertained us with phonograph music and the printing office quartet.

Naturally, there were some short speeches made, and can you imagine that I made one, too! I had a prepared speech all written out and memorized for some such occasion. Having heard William Jennings Bryan's oratory twice already, I admired him so much that I had the ambition to be an orator myself. I thought I had a good subject to talk about, but I

could not find the appropriate words to express myself in correct English style. The only Korean scholar who could help me with this, I thought, was Dr. Syngman Rhee from Princeton University, Ex-President of the Republic of Korea, who was then in Honolulu directing educational work among the Koreans there. So I wrote him a letter asking him to write an oration in English for me. What he said in his reply was truly remarkable. He said, in substance, "Please be advised, young man, that you should first learn to speak English before trying to deliver an oration
* like William Jennings Bryan."

Therefore, that maiden speech of mine that night was the fruit of my diligent learning of English during the past six months in school, and I thought they thought I was another "Silver-tongued orator of the Platte." I was applauded most heartily by my audience! My subject was on Korea, which I knew something about, and I was the only Korean there at the time.

Upon my return from the war, I found that the Cosmopolitan Club had grown larger. There were four Koreans at one time: George Paik, formerly President of Union Christian College in Seoul and Ex-Minister of Education for the Republic of Korea government; Daniel Lee, now a dentist in California; William Lee and Sungwhan Cho who have since returned to Korea, and myself; six Chinese — Bown Tsiang, brother of Dr. Tingfu Tsiang, a former Park College student and now the Chinese delegate to the United Nations; Suya Yang, Chang, Nan, Sarah Liang, and Glenn Ginn; three Japanese — two from Hawaii, Sasaki and Hasegawa, and Okino from Japan; George Shimoon, a Persian; Renjilian, Armenian; Slavko Crnkovich, now Frederick Lawrence

Park since his naturalization, a Yugoslavian; Tadeo Caro, a Filipino; six Puerto Ricans — Gallardo, Acosta, Irrizary, Lemeres, Quintana and Avilles; one Greek named Yohanas from Macedonia. Then there were American-born Morris Zutrau from the Bronx, now a minister in San Francisco, and Peter Masei from Pittsburgh, the former a Hebrew and the latter an Italian, both my classmates in the Academy, and Sam Pettigrew, a full-blooded Navajo Indian from Arizona.

As soon as the "war to end all wars" was ended, there began a series of minor wars which flared up from the Near East to the Far East, the fire of hatreds blazing from Smyrna to Seoul, between the Reds and Whites in Russia, and between the Blacks and Whites in Chicago. While at the Peace Conference in Paris, George Clemenceau was crucifying President Wilson's Principle of Self-determination upon the cross of selfish national interests when he cynically growled "God was content with Ten Commandments, Wilson must have Fourteen!" The Japanese gendarmerie were crucifying the Korean Christians who only shouted "Mansei, Korean Independence!"   *

The majority of the club membership being unofficial representatives of the so-called "subject peoples" and with the events and incidents of the war still fresh in their minds, there were frequent discussions on international politics at our meetings. How much I enjoyed listening to and participating in the friendly debates among our cosmopolitan group.

The most eventful college year I had at Park was during my Junior year in 1922. It was an eventful year, the year of the Disarmament Conference in Washington. H. G. Wells was in this country then, writing articles in the newspapers, commenting on

the progress of the conference, in general, and ex-
horting America's responsbiility as a world leader,
in particular. I admired this great Englishman for
his idealism and liberalism. I compared him with
Rudyard Kipling. If Kipling was an imperialist,
Wells was a missionary, I thought. The former
preached to the United States on the "White Man's
Burden," the latter on "A World State" in which
Uncle Sam was to be the rightful leader.

About a month prior to the Commencement time,
the American History Essay contest was announced
by Professor Magers of the History department
through "The Stylus," the students' publication. It
was open only to the students of the American History class and was sponsored by the D. A. R. Galesburg, Illinois, chapter, of which Mrs. George A.
Lawrence, daughter of the founder of Park College,
was a member, giving prizes to the winners once
every year on the commencement day.

I was one of the American History students.
George Paik was another. To be sure, I was the first
Korean student at Park, but George was the first
Korean student to graduate from Park. He was a
Senior then. It was in this class that Professor Magers took me as an example when we were discussing
the Constitution of the United States. Pointing to
me, he used to say to the class, "You see, the points
of the laws of the United States were so strict that
although Charr is a World War veteran, who was
ready to give his very life for Uncle Sam, he was
denied American citizenship for the second time because of the Chinese exclusion statute."

"United States and the Far East" was one of the
subjects given to write on in the essay contest and
that was my choice, for naturally I was interested in

it. So, I wrote an essay on that subject, and George wrote on something else. We were roommates that year so we knew very well what each other was doing. One morning shortly before Commencement day, George told me he had dreamed a dream, and in his dream, he said, I was the winner of the American History Essay Contest! My essay had been written a month or so before, and I had practically forgotten all about it. Smiling, I said to him, "Please quit kidding me, George, that's impossible. How could I possibly be a winner as there are smarter students and more capable writers than I in the class? Don't you remember that I flunked out in the last examination and I had to make it up? Really, George, I would like to see you win."

On the day before the Commencement Day, on my way from the Post Office downtown, I happened to meet Dean Sanders, who, too, was walking toward the campus. In the midst of our general conversation, he said to me rather suddenly but casually, "Emsen, you wrote an essay on American History, didn't you?"

"Yes, sir, I did. But why do you ask?" I inquired.

He replied, "Oh, nothing, I just wanted to know."

That was all he said, simply as a passing remark. However, it made me curious to know why he asked me that. When I told George about it back in my room, he said to me, "Of course, Dean Sanders is in a position to know who the winners will be on Commencement Day, and what did I tell you about my dream? You won a prize last year on 'Why you came to Park,' offered by Mrs. Hawley, don't you remember?"

Particularly, I remember the Commencement Day of that year. It was a fine, sunny day during the first week of June. The chapel was filled to capacity. The graduating class of men and women in cap and gown, including George Paik himself, occupied the front pews of the two middle sections, on the ground floor facing the platform. The remainder of the floor was taken up by the more elderly people of the village and the visitors from distant parts. Among others, there were the two Blair brothers from Korea. The gallery upstairs was occupied almost entirely by the student body of both the college and academy. I happened to sit with Uncle Walter Wolfe in a pew on the west end row on the first floor.

The platform was graced by the members of the faculty and the honored guests, all arrayed in cap and gown. The honored guest and principal speaker of the Commencement exercises was none other than the Honorable Arthur M. Hyde, the Governor of the State of Missouri, who later became the Secretary of Agriculture in President Hoover's administration. Upon him was conferred that day the honorary degree of Doctor of Laws.

Following the presentation of diplomas to the candidates of the graduating class by President Hawley, the awarding of prizes began. Dr. Fred Tower, executive secretary of the college, was the master of ceremonies. At this juncture, whether or not I believed in George's dream, I could not help but feel somewhat excited, to tell the truth. So I waited rather tensely and nervously. Uncle Walter did not notice it, perhaps, not knowing the cause of my inward agitation.

To make the matter aggravating to my agitated mental condition, the History prizes were withheld to the last. When it came though, it was dramatic. There were three prizes given, starting with the third prize. If George's dream were true, I was not the

third prize winner. Neither was I the second prize
winner. After the second prize was announced and
given away, I thought there was a slight pause displayed by Dr. Tower. Maybe he did so in order to
be dramatic. Perusing the envelope containing the
prize money of fifteen dollars to be awarded next,
he looked around the audience with smiling eyes and
humorous mouth, and said something like this: "In
my hand now I hold the name of the winner of the
first prize. It is not a common name, though. (And
I thought it was George Paik's name, and George
thought it was mine, and we smiled at each other.)
"Yet, evidently this foreign student knows more about
American history than do the Americans. What is
more, this young man is loved by the American
daughters! (Applause in the audience.) The first
prize of fifteen dollars offered by the Galesburg
chapter of the Daughters of the American Revolution goes to the winner, E. Emsen Charr! The winner will please come forward and receive the prize."

Trembling with emotion, in the midst of loud applause, I rose from my seat, walked out to the aisle,
up the side steps to the platform, and received the
envelope from Dr. Tower, thanking him in an almost
inaudible voice.

Like everyone else in the audience, Uncle Walter,
all in smiles and almost tears, too, welcomed me back
to his side. More than any others in the audience he
had good reasons to be especially happy over my
success. He had been my Sunday School teacher
every year while I was in the college, and I had
known him ever since I knew Dr. Wolfe, his brother.
Particularly in this connection, it was gratifying to
him because I had read my essay for his criticism before it was submitted to Professor Magers.

My friend, George Paik, was the first Korean student to graduate from Park College, and I congratulated him on his graduation. He did the same to me on the honor which I received that day. George's dream came true, and we were both winners, evening up the score.

During my senior year, I worked for Dean Sanders in his office, after having spent practically all the rest of the time in the college printing office. My work in the Dean's office consisted of recording the students' grades in the books and lettering on the diplomas in the old English style, the names of the candidates for graduation. And, of course, I made my own diploma with my name written on it with my own hand.

On the day of my graduation, in June of 1923, I received my diploma, and along with it I was awarded another prize in the American History essay contest. It was not the first prize again as it was the year before though. It was only the second prize, but still, it was good enough, I thought. After the conclusion of the Commencement exercises, Mrs. A. L. Wolfe came rushing up to me and said, "Let me congratulate you, Emsen, I was so glad to see you get your diploma and an honor besides. I am proud of you. Now that you are about to go away from us, I wish you all the good luck and success in the world. We will always think of you and pray for you."

Was I happy that day? Yes, I was in a way — I can't say that I wasn't. Still, I was more sad than happy to think of leaving the dear old campus where I had spent the happiest days of my life. I did not realize until that day, why so many former graduates looked the same way as I did on that day. I had witnessed some of them actually shedding tears on their last days on the campus. So did I, for I loved Park College and everything and everybody that was associated with it. Park College meant so much to me. May God bless her in educating thousands of others who went before me and those who have followed me. May God bless my Alma Mater! Park College celebrated its Diamond Jubilee in June, 1950.

18

To Be or Not to Be a Doctor

Now I was a college graduate! Ten years ago I had left California for Park College, and now I was back in California visiting with my cousin who had sent for me. I was glad to see him and his wife and they were glad to see me back as a college graduate. And soon after my arrival there, my cousin's sister, Esther, arrived from the old country. It was shortly before the Oriental immigration closed in 1924. She came with her nephew, my eldest cousin's only son. Of course, my cousin had sent for both of them. Esther taught the girls' mission schools in Pyeng Yang and in Taegu in South Korea.

It was quite a family reunion here after having been separated in the two worlds for so many years. Esther was two years younger than I, and having no sister of my own living, she was just like my own sister to me. Indeed, I was very glad to see her and talk to her. And her nephew, who was only a small boy when I left home, was now a full grown youth. Having pictured him as my little brother who was about his age, made me realize I was that much older.

Esther told me of my mother and brother. She said my brother was a printer in Pyeng Yang as I was a printer at Park College press. And she said my widowed mother, who was being taken care of by my brother and the kindly relatives, was counting days and months in expecting me to return home as a learned doctor, as I had often told her I was going to be a medical missionary back to my native land some day soon.

Now, my original intention in going to California was to come back East to pursue my medical course in the fall of that year. But the news from home now changed my mind about it for the time being. I decided to work for a few months in order to make some money to help my mother a little. I worked in my cousin's place as a janitor in Pasadena when he gave his own job to me and went to Los Angeles to go into a grocery business with a Korean friend of his. And, while I was working there, an old Korean friend of mine remarked, "Ah, how lucky is the I. Magnin Company to have a college graduate janitor!" And I replied, "Well, I'll be lucky if I can get a janitor job when I'll be at the Medical College in Kansas next spring."

In the latter part of the following January, once again I left California for the East. Upon arrival in Kansas City, I paid Mr. Bunting a brief visit at his downtown office on Walnut Street, not far from the YMCA, and told him I was on my way to Lawrence, Kansas, to enroll at the University of Kansas Medical College. Wasn't he happy to hear me say that to him! He knew very well that I had always wanted to study medicine in order to become a medical missionary, and he endorsed it heartily. I told him that I intended to work my way through the medical school just as I had done at Park College. He wished me luck in securing a job and in studying medicine, saying, however, that in case I needed any assistance I should not hesitate to let him know about it. At the time he had his own son in an Eastern college, he told me.

Of course, I did not forget to make a trip to Park

College campus before I went to Kansas. I was glad to see the campus again and to meet my dear friends there, the students as well as the members of the faculty and their families and the townfolk. When they heard I was going to a medical school, they all expected to see me back some day as a doctor.

I finally arrived on the University of Kansas campus in Lawrence, Kansas, early in February, in 1924, just in time to enroll for the second semester. It was the first time I had ever been to a university campus. The buildings were larger and more numerous than they were at Park, and there was a bigger student body. I found two former Park College students already there, and I was glad to see them when I was a stranger on that big campus.

As soon as I had enrolled in the medical school, I looked for a part time job for my board and room. Through the Commons and all over the downtown cafes and restaurants and boarding houses, I went hunting for some work to do, but I could find nothing. Finally, I went to the dean's office and asked for his assistance in locating a job for me, but neither could he find anything for me in two weeks' time. There was not even a janitor job to be found. I was told I had come too late for a job. All the available jobs were already taken by the others who had come at the beginning of the school year.

All the cash money which I had was expended in my long distance travel, for my tuition and fees, and for my room and board during that time. Now I was scared. Up in my small attic room which I had rented in an elderly lady's house, back of the campus, on the north side of the hill, I sat down, listlessly worrying myself. I had come clear back from California thinking I could make a go of it somehow.

Now here I was lost, penniless, and hopeless. Had I
known of this predicament, I would not have come
here in the first place at that time of the year. Had
I listened to my cousin and gone into the grocery
business with him I would have been better off, I
thought. He did not approve of my further study
because he told me he could not afford to finance my
medical study, which required large sums of money.
Besides, he was called upon constantly by the folks
back home for financial assistance which drained his
meager saving from his hard labor. He had said to
me that I had enough education already, and that I
could be of help to him in his grocery business which
he had just started.

Now I found I could no longer stay in school
there, nor could I come away from there with no
money left for my train fare. I thought the only
party from whom I could expect any assistance was
from Mr. Bunting in Kansas City. I wrote him a
letter telling him of my sad predicament, and asking
him for his kindly advice. He sent me a handsome
check for twenty-five dollars by return mail, advising
me not to be discouraged so easily, but to be patient
and trust in the Lord.

Thanking him for his timely assistance and kindly
advice, I was greatly encouraged. After school hours
every day, I renewed my job hunt, roaming all
over the town again, from door to door, from shop
to shop, from one end of the town to the other, from
the campus down to the railway station. But nothing
doing! It seemed to me there were more people
working for someone else than there were places to
employ them. At least, I was one too many.

If I am not mistaken, I think it was one Sunday
morning (February 3, 1924) when I bought a morn-

ing paper with a big headline, "Ex-President Wood-row Wilson Dead." In my attic room I read with great interest the life history of the great man who was my Commander-in-Chief during the First World War. I had admired him greatly before, now I sor-rowed for him deeply. "Has his principle of 'Self-Determination' and his idea of the League of Na-tions died with him, too?" I wondered. He was a disappointed man. So was I just then. Of course, his disappointment was greater than mine, yet mine was great enough for me to bear, nonetheless. Right here my life's ambition had been shattered to shreds just because of lack of money. The check from Mr. Bunting was about to give out, with no possibility whatsoever of replenishing it from any other source. What else could I do but quit the school and go somewhere to make some money, for the train fare would be gone in no time?

I left school, and went back to Kansas City, Mis-souri. Here with Mr. Bunting's help, I tried to find something to do until the school opened again in the fall. I was no luckier here in job hunting than I was at Lawrence. I thought then there was no place like Park College which was to me like my home, sweet home, and the people in it like my home folk. I wrote to Dean Sanders, asking him if he could find some-thing for me to do on the campus for my room and board for a while until I located a place to go next.

"Why, certainly," replied Dean Sanders. "I talked to Dr. Hawley about your problem and he said that it could be arranged for you. You can have your old job back in my office, making diplomas for this year's graduating class. Come right on out. We'll be glad to have you back with us and you can stay with us as long as you want to."

Is it any wonder that my thoughts always turned to Park whenever I was happy, and more so, perhaps, whenever I was in distress? More than thirty years have passed since I left my Alma Mater, but my fond memories of her grow fonder as the years go by. I returned to Park and stayed there until the middle of May. While there, I wrote to my good old Korean friend, Changhai, who was then in Chicago operating a cafeteria. He wrote back and said, "My dear friend, come at once to Chicago. Medical schools aplenty here. Plenty of jobs, also. I want you here. What are you waiting for?"

Once again I left Park (I've never been back since) and went to Chicago with the train fare borrowed from a Parkville bank endorsed by Dean Sanders himself. Chicago was the biggest city I had ever seen. I had passed through it once before on the train on my way back to Park from Washington. I had been with Changhai last at Akron, Ohio, and here in Chicago we met once again. One comforting thought which I entertained was that silver and gold had I none but worthy friends had I many, among the Americans as well as the Koreans in America.

Changhai was operating a cafeteria in Chicago on Jackson Boulevard, and how I wished it were in Lawrence instead, so that I could work for him and continue my medical studies there. But, indeed, there were many medical schools here in Chicago, and just as good, if not better. Any one of them will do for me, I thought, and I was confidently happy then. There wouldn't be any more unsuccessful job hunting either, for I was given a part-time job in my friend's cafeteria as soon as I arrived there. For some time I worked for another man, an old acquaintance of mine named Kim, as a dishwasher at the Washington

Cafeteria on Washington Street near Wells Street.

Soon it was vacation time, and dozens of Korean students arrived in the city from colleges and universities of the Middle West for the summer. There were a few old-timers already there in cafeteria and restaurant businesses in Chicago. The two groups united, making quite a settlement of their own. From time to time, there were social and patriotic meetings held in one of those cafeterias after the business hours in the evenings. During the summer months, outdoor picnics were enjoyed together on the beaches in Evanston or out in the city parks.

One day I received a letter from my mother saying, "My son, when are you coming home? How soon are you going to be a doctor? My, it takes you so long! If it takes you too long to be a regular doctor, why don't you study pharmacy instead? Here in Korea, a pharmacist is just like a doctor — even better, and he makes more money than a doctor can. 'So and so' in Pyeng Yang became rich by selling only quinine and black ointment. It's the medicine that's in demand here. Hurry, hurry, my son. Bring with you plenty of quinine if you can't bring anything else with you. Return home quickly and get settled here. You are old enough to have married long ago. Your little brother married two years ago and he's got a boy three months old already. I'm longing to see you come home soon and get married, too. There are lots of girls here waiting for an American-educated man like you."

I read the letter to my friend Changhai, and he said to me, "I think what your mother says about studying pharmacy when you can't possibly study medicine is quite true. I agree with her. Yes, why don't you take up pharmacy instead of a regular medical course? It wouldn't take you much time to study that, and if you like, you can go to school during the daytime and come to work at my new place on Howard Street after the school hours when I need you most. How about it, Emsen?"

"To be a doctor has been my ambition all my life," I said, "and the sole purpose in my coming to America. Now to think of studying to be a mere pharmacist is something I had never dreamed of before. Though, come to think of it, pharmacy, too, is a study of medicine, isn't it? So when you can't have the best, you'd better try the second best, eh? Yes, I think I'll take my mother's and your advice and take up pharmacy. If an opportunity offers itself in the future, I can still learn to be a regular doctor, can't I? Then, as a doctor I can write my own prescription, and as a pharmacist I can fill out my own prescription!"

So I enrolled in the School of Pharmacy of the University of Illinois Medical College, located near the County Hospital, and lived in a rooming house nearby. I studied hard and worked hard until ten o'clock at night at the north end of the city. In fact, I worked harder than I studied, and more time was spent in work and on the streetcars than I could find time to study my lessons, except in classrooms. And, consequently, I failed in half of the subjects which I took in my first semester examination and was compelled to leave school!

Thus, I lost my medical ambition; instead I found a great friend. Through a Korean student friend of mine, I met the late Dr. J. Paul Goode, Professor of Geography at the University of Chicago and the author of "Goode's School Atlas," and worked for him as a topographic draftsman.

"So you are a veteran, too," he said. "Then you must be an American citizen now, I suppose."

"No, sir, I'm not," I replied. "I tried to become naturalized twice but failed both times because I was told I was not entitled to it under the Oriental exclusion law. However, I've read about a Japanese veteran in Los Angeles, California, who was granted American citizenship by a Federal Court there."

"Is that right? Can you imagine that? That doesn't sound reasonable to me. Oriental or Occidental, an American war veteran is more than an ordinary citizen, I should think. You say a Japanese veteran was granted citizenship by one Federal Court and you were denied by another Federal Court? There is inconsistency there some place. It can't be that the court considered that you were good enough to have been an American soldier, but not good enough to be an American citizen. Rather the reverse is often the case, I know. Of course, I am not familiar with the naturalization laws, but I know of a professor of our law school in the university who can advise me on that. I am going to call him up tonight and ask him if he can help you get your American citizenship at the Federal Court here," he said.

Professor Goode was making some maps for the Keystone View Company's lantern slides which were used in the schools. In his employ, I worked all that winter of 1925 to May of the following year. Upon completion of those maps, I was transferred to the Editorial offices of the Rand McNally & Company downtown. I was put to work on his school atlas which was then being revised and enlarged for the second edition.

So, the answer was that I was not destined to be a doctor. Instead, I found a friend, a job, and romance!

19

Lotus Flower

If I was not lucky in medicine, I was lucky in love. She was like a flower in full bloom, and even prettier. She was a Korean student from Dubuque, Iowa, vacationing in Chicago during that summer of 1927. I saw her at a student gathering for the first time and fell in love with her at first sight, even before I knew who she was or what her name was. She was a very attractive-looking girl, and she was admired and pursued by several Korean students; so much so that I had no opportunity to get acquainted with her all the time she was in Chicago. I found out later that her name was Nien-wha, or Lotus Flower! In school she was known as Evelyn Kim.

It was on the University of Dubuque campus during the New Year holidays that I really met her for the first time and became acquainted with her. She was sweet, she was lovely. I adored her, and I loved her. During the following Easter holiday season, I paid her another visit. Here we met more privately this time than before, and we were engaged to be married during the coming summer.

Back in Chicago I wrote her letters and she wrote back. I told her how much I loved her and she told me she loved me, too, and also my handwriting! We wrote to each other every single day. I was getting my mail through the editorial rooms of the Rand McNally where I was working. One day Miss Hammitt's secretary, who brought me the letters every day, whispered in my ear, "Why, Mr. Charr, you are receiving a letter every day from the same writer. I notice it is feminine handwriting! I think you are in love, aren't you? Tell me, confidentially, is she pretty? What's her name?"

"Yes, she is, and her name is Lotus Flower," I whispered back to her.

"Ah, what a pretty name! She must be as pretty as her name indicates. When's your wedding going to be, if I may ask?" Miss Bonar inquired.

"You'll hear from me as soon as I see Dr. Goode. You see, I am going to tell him that I'm going to marry the girl I love and that he is going to be her godfather and will give her to me in marriage," I told her, confidentially.

As soon as her school closed early in June, Nienwha came to meet me in Chicago and the very first thing I did for her was to buy her a white-gold diamond ring at the Peacock Jewelry Store on State Street. I slipped it on her finger there in front of the counter. That was the engagement ring, of course. And wasn't she pleased! I bought a wedding ring at the same time.

The two of us then went together to pay our respects to Dr. Goode at his home on Dorchester Street near the Midway campus. When I presented my fiancee to him as my June bride-to-be and told him that her Korean name was Lotus Flower and her American name was Evelyn Kim, he beamed and said to her, "Oh, how nice! How interesting! Miss Lotus Flower! I'm very glad to know you. 'What's in a name?', someone has said, but your name fits you perfectly, I should say. A very charming bride-to-be, indeed." And he asked me, "How soon are you going to marry, may I ask?"

"CONGRATULATIONS!

Best wishes for happiness
    We offer you!
May this gold be the symbol
    Of sunshine life through
May you journey together
    With never a jar;
Joy, peace, glory, honor
    Attend both named Charr!
Our remembrance we're sending
    in two tiny parts,
And may God bless this union
    Of two loving hearts!"

ceremony now being over, Professor Goode
few snapshots of us and then escorted us to
adrangle Club for the wedding dinner which
promised us. The party was composed of the
d Mrs. Merrifield, Professor Goode himself
sister, Mrs. Palmer, and the two of us. (Hon.
. Paul Goode, formerly a member of the Illi-
ate Legislature, had passed away the year be-
met Professor Goode.) It was a quiet family
in which we could enjoy our privacy and a
acquaintance. You see, we had never before
e minister who united us in holy matrimony and
he first time we had met Mrs. Merrifield who
lestined to become the godmother of the bride.
s here at the table that we became acquainted
he first time and we have since become lifelong
ds. I still have preserved the place cards used at
able in Professor Goode's own handwriting. On
card, it says, "The Groom"; on the other, "The
e."

"As soon as you will select a date for us, if you will," I said.

"Oh, that would be easy enough, I think," he said, and looking up at the calendar hanging on the wall, he said, "How about next Sunday, June the 10th?"

"That will be just fine," both of us responded readily.

"You have a minister of your own choice to officiate, I suppose?" he asked.

"No, sir, we haven't," I replied. "I want you to be the bride's godfather at our wedding and . . ."

"All right, I'll be very glad to act as one for the very charming bride-to-be, if you want me. As for a minister, you say you haven't one. Well, I will have one for you. He is a great friend of mine, a professor of the School of Divinity of the University of Chicago, Rev. Fred Merrifield. I will ask him tonight to see if we can use the Thorndike Hilton memorial chapel on the university campus. I will call you in the morning and tell you what arrangement I will then have made for you."

He made us so happy that neither of us could find suitable words to thank him adequately. The next morning he called me on the phone and told me that everything was arranged as planned the day before, and then some more, he said. He said he would give us a private wedding dinner following the wedding ceremony at the Quadrangle, the Faculty members' clubhouse on the campus!

Evelyn and I were busy making preparations day and night, for we had only four days in which to do it all, and we had to do everything by ourselves, with advice obtained from Professor Goode and his sister, Mrs. Palmer, and from Changhai, and his wife, Bertha. The invitations were written for us by Dr.

Goode, and I had them printed and mailed to our friends and to my cousins in California. Next, we had to go downtown on a shopping tour. It was fun, indeed, for us to search and shop for our own wedding at the big department stores on State and Dearborn Streets. What did we know about wedding trousseaux, anyway? There were so many other things to get besides the wedding gown. The first thing I bought was a large hat-box in order to put everything in it. And what high prices I had to pay for everything that year! It was the year before the stock market crash! I did not, however, thank God, have to borrow any money from anyone for our wedding!

My mother would be happy to learn that I was getting married, according to her own wishes, although not in her presence back in my native city. She would be satisfied to know that when I could not become a doctor, not even a pharmacist, I married a nurse! Evelyn was a trained nurse, you see, and she, too, had come to America to become a doctor. Now, will the two would-be doctors, teamed together, make a real doctor somehow, just as two minus quantities added together make it a positive?

I had never seen a day more tranquil and beautiful than was that day of June 10, 1928, when it dawned upon us on our wedding day, except the day when I received my diploma from Park College, five years before. Rising early with the dawn, I set out for the home of my friend, Changhai, and his wife, Bertha, where Evelyn was staying. Of course, Changhai was to be my best man and Bertha was to be the maid of honor. Miss Virginia Sone, who was Evelyn's schoolmate at Dubuque and fiancee of the brother of Baron Yun Tshiho of Seoul, and Helene Kang,

an American-born bridesmaids. For there were Helen lovely children of t it complete, Miss Seoul, Korea, was t sion.

Now when they w place and all ready, I them! Honestly, that I rode in a taxi! We campus, stopping direc Hilton Memorial Cha and the Rev. and Mrs good-sized crowd of ou us. Still others were a If I am not mistaken, I ental couple married in tl we were the first Korean city of Chicago, other Kor all Eurasian.

Our wedding ceremony Indeed, there were gathere Korean and American, fillin flowing, who had come to se them was a goodly company from the editorial rooms of t were my fellow-workers there McNally people were some had ever known while I was w years. They brought up a wedc pact containing two bright piec panied by a beautiful poem whic sixteen sweet persons. It read

The only Korean women found in the East were students from Korea. My wife was such a student. She had come to America as a student just two years before our marriage. It was at our wedding dinner table at the Quadrangle Club that day that Mrs. Merrifield said to her, "Now that you are married, you have to live here in Chicago with your husband, and as I hear from Dr. Goode, you have to go to school since you came to this country as a student. Now, my child, have you decided what school you will attend, may I ask?"

"Not yet, Mrs. Merrifield," I answered for my wife. "You see, we were just thinking of looking for a school for her to go to this fall, but really we have no idea as to which school she will attend when the time comes in the fall."

"I see," said Mrs. Merrifield, who had already taken deep interest in my bride. "Well, in that case, I think I can find just the kind of school to which you would like to have her go. I would like very much to have her come to my school."

"Your school?" I inquired, with happy surprise.

"Yes, my school, where I teach. It is a private girl's school not far from here," she said with affectionate smiles.

"Oh, mother!" said my bride. She addressed Mrs. Merrifield as though the beautiful lady she had just met was like her own mother. Why shouldn't she? Her own mother could not have been sweeter to her than this very kindly lady who was destined to become her benefactress during the years to come.

"That will be fine!" I said. "Indeed it was the most urgent problem facing us at this time, and now you have solved it for us! I am very grateful to you for it. Of course, it being a private school, it may be a little more expensive for her to go there than to a public school, wouldn't it?" I asked her.

"Oh, that! Ordinarily, it would be the case, yes. But maybe I can arrange that for you, too. You see, a scholarship is available there, at least one every year. I'll see Miss Loring, the principal, and talk to her tomorrow. I am quite sure I will get it for you."

She did get the scholarship for Evelyn the very next day, and told us about it when we dropped by her home to pay her and her family a visit. Both Rev. Merrifield and Mrs. Merrifield were graduates of the University of Chicago, and they had a lovely home and family. Their eldest son, Ted, was a law student at the University at the time. Charles, Margaret, and the twins, Bruce and Marshall (the latter a girl), were their younger children. Theirs was one of the finest Christian families that I had the good fortune to know intimately. If I were to say they were more dear to me and mine than some of my own relatives, I would not be exaggerating the least, let me assure you. It is true that my young bride found her Goode father made her feel good, and her Merrifield mother made her heart merry, indeed.

When fall came, my wife was enrolled in the Kenwood-Loring School, located opposite the St. James Methodist Church in the Kenwood district, and we lived near there with an American family. Mrs. Merrifield taught her English there and Miss Loring, the very fine lady, loved her, too. She liked the school and her teachers and schoolmates who were so friendly to her right from the start until the time she was graduated two years later.

On Sunday evenings we found great pleasure at the International Student Club at the Ida Noyes Hall

on the University campus which Mr. Merrifield and
Dr. Goode had introduced to us. As water finds its
level, we humans, too, by nature, find our own group
and environment where we find enjoyment in mutual
association and interest. So did we here at the club
where all the foreign students attending the many
schools in the city gathered once every week and enjoyed the hospitalities offered by the university and
the interesting programs presented under the direc-
torship of Mr. Bruce W. Dickson, the able and genial
gentleman whom I have known very well since then.
It was at one of those pleasant Sunday evening gatherings that I had the pleasure of meeting for the first
time the President of the University of Chicago, Dr.
Hutchins, the nationally-known great educator.

In June, two years later, my wife was graduated
from her school. Unforgettable were her graduation
exercises held one evening in the St. James Methodist
Church across the street from her school. It was a
gorgeous ceremony, to say the least. And all the flowers and more flowers, and, oh, they were so lovely!
And, who do you suppose furnished her with all
those many beautiful flowers? None other than her
godfather and godmother, Professor Goode and
Mrs. Merrifield! And that was not all. A graduation present of twenty-dollar gold pieces from each
of them, besides!

At the conclusion of the graduation exercises, Rev.
and Mrs. Merrifield and Professor Goode, who were
present in the audience, came forward to congratulate Evelyn. Weren't they happy to see her happy!
They made me happy, indeed, and I was grateful to
them for their great kindnesses. Before I had the
opportunity to say to them a word of my gratitude,
Mrs. Merrifield said to my wife and me, "Oh, before

I forget, I want to ask you if you would like to come over and stay in our house while we are gone during the summer?"

"Your house?" I asked.

"Yes, if you like. You see, we are going out to Estes Park in Colorado in a few days and we would like to have you come and live more comfortably. I know you will soon need more room in order to accommodate a new arrival in your family," Mrs. Merrifield said to me, the last sentence in a whisper. (Professor Goode had invited us to his summer home in Shelby, Michigan, the previous summer.)

To be sure, we knew a baby was coming, and coming real soon. Our first baby girl was born at the Lying-in Hospital while we lived at the beautiful Merrifield home located on Kimbark Avenue near the University. And she was attended by a lady doctor from the Billings Hospital who had been engaged for us by Mrs. Merrifield before leaving for Colorado. And, of course, our baby was named "Anna Pauline," after Mrs. Anna Marshall Merrifield and Professor J. Paul Goode.

A loving cup and a baby's spoon, both made of silver and gold, with her name inscribed on them, were given to their namesake by Mrs. Merrifield and Professor Goode. They are the most highly prized treasures of our possessions. They were beautiful to look at then, and they are the reminders of the gracious givers thereof now.

When the school time came in the fall, my wife was supposed to be in school but she could not with an infant daughter only five weeks old. Realizing this, Mrs. Merrifield, who was an English teacher, kindly arranged with her school to make my wife a special student specializing in English, which my wife

"As soon as you will select a date for us, if you will," I said.

"Oh, that would be easy enough, I think," he said, and looking up at the calendar hanging on the wall, he said, "How about next Sunday, June the 10th?"

"That will be just fine," both of us responded readily.

"You have a minister of your own choice to officiate, I suppose?" he asked.

"No, sir, we haven't," I replied. "I want you to be the bride's godfather at our wedding and . . ."

"All right, I'll be very glad to act as one for the very charming bride-to-be, if you want me. As for a minister, you say you haven't one. Well, I will have one for you. He is a great friend of mine, a professor of the School of Divinity of the University of Chicago, Rev. Fred Merrifield. I will ask him tonight to see if we can use the Thorndike Hilton memorial chapel on the university campus. I will call you in the morning and tell you what arrangement I will then have made for you."

He made us so happy that neither of us could find suitable words to thank him adequately. The next morning he called me on the phone and told me that everything was arranged as planned the day before, and then some more, he said. He said he would give us a private wedding dinner following the wedding ceremony at the Quadrangle, the Faculty members' clubhouse on the campus!

Evelyn and I were busy making preparations day and night, for we had only four days in which to do it all, and we had to do everything by ourselves, with advice obtained from Professor Goode and his sister, Mrs. Palmer, and from Changhai, and his wife, Bertha. The invitations were written for us by Dr.

Goode, and I had them printed and mailed to our friends and to my cousins in California. Next, we had to go downtown on a shopping tour. It was fun, indeed, for us to search and shop for our own wedding at the big department stores on State and Dearborn Streets. What did we know about wedding trousseaux, anyway? There were so many other things to get besides the wedding gown. The first thing I bought was a large hat-box in order to put everything in it. And what high prices I had to pay for everything that year! It was the year before the stock market crash! I did not, however, thank God, have to borrow any money from anyone for our wedding!

My mother would be happy to learn that I was getting married, according to her own wishes, although not in her presence back in my native city. She would be satisfied to know that when I could not become a doctor, not even a pharmacist, I married a nurse! Evelyn was a trained nurse, you see, and she, too, had come to America to become a doctor. Now, will the two would-be doctors, teamed together, make a real doctor somehow, just as two minus quantities added together make it a positive?

I had never seen a day more tranquil and beautiful than was that day of June 10, 1928, when it dawned upon us on our wedding day, except the day when I received my diploma from Park College, five years before. Rising early with the dawn, I set out for the home of my friend, Changhai, and his wife, Bertha, where Evelyn was staying. Of course, Changhai was to be my best man and Bertha was to be the maid of honor. Miss Virginia Sone, who was Evelyn's schoolmate at Dubuque and fiancee of the brother of Baron Yun Tshiho of Seoul, and Helene Kang, an American-born friend of ours, were to be the bridesmaids. For a flower girl and a ring bearer, there were Helen Chun and Jerome Kim, the two lovely children of the Eurasian parentage. To make it complete, Miss Yun Sungduk of Ewa School of Seoul, Korea, was to furnish the music for the occasion.

Now when they were all assembled at my friend's place and all ready, I called the taxicabs — three of them! Honestly, that was the first time in my life that I rode in a taxi! We dashed down to the Midway campus, stopping directly in front of the Thorndike Hilton Memorial Chapel where Professor Goode and the Rev. and Mrs. Merrifield, together with a good-sized crowd of our friends, were waiting for us. Still others were arriving from all directions. If I am not mistaken, I think we were the first Oriental couple married in that chapel, and I know that we were the first Korean couple ever married in the city of Chicago, other Korean marriages having been all Eurasian.

Our wedding ceremony took place at high noon. Indeed, there were gathered a host of my friends, Korean and American, filling up the chapel to overflowing, who had come to see our wedding. Among them was a goodly company of ladies and gentlemen from the editorial rooms of the Rand McNally, who were my fellow-workers there. Honestly, the Rand McNally people were some of the finest whom I had ever known while I was with them for over five years. They brought up a wedding present — a compact containing two bright pieces of gold — accompanied by a beautiful poem which was undersigned by sixteen sweet persons. It read as follows:

"Congratulations!

Best wishes for happiness
        We offer you!
May this gold be the symbol
        Of sunshine life through
May you journey together
        With never a jar;
Joy, peace, glory, honor
        Attend both named Charr!
Our remembrance we're sending
        in two tiny parts,
And may God bless this union
        Of two loving hearts!"

The ceremony now being over, Professor Gooue took a few snapshots of us and then escorted us to the Quadrangle Club for the wedding dinner which he had promised us. The party was composed of the Rev. and Mrs. Merrifield, Professor Goode himself and his sister, Mrs. Palmer, and the two of us. (Hon. Mrs. J. Paul Goode, formerly a member of the Illinois State Legislature, had passed away the year before I met Professor Goode.) It was a quiet family affair in which we could enjoy our privacy and a closer acquaintance. You see, we had never before met the minister who united us in holy matrimony and also the first time we had met Mrs. Merrifield who was destined to become the godmother of the bride. It was here at the table that we became acquainted for the first time and we have since become lifelong friends. I still have preserved the place cards used at the table in Professor Goode's own handwriting. On one card, it says, "The Groom"; on the other, "The Bride."

needed. So a year passed without an incident, and we were very grateful to her godmother for that.

Realizing the predicament she was in, Mrs. Merrifield told me that my wife could not possibly go to school all her life as a married woman and as the mother of a young child, and there must be something done about that before long. That was timely advice, I knew, and of course that problem was uppermost in my mind all the time. When I brought up the question to Professor Goode one day, he said to me, "Oh, that! I'm sorry that I had forgotten all about it. Yes, I remember the case, very well. Your wife's problem could be solved somehow, I think, if you became a naturalized citizen as a World War veteran. I will speak to my friend, the law professor, and see if he can help me to help you. That's about the only way I can see out for her. I will see him in the morning and you will hear from me or from him directly."

The very next afternoon, while I was at work at the Rand McNally office, a youngish looking gentleman came in to see me. I have forgotten his name. He said he had come from the University Law School at the request of Professor Goode to accompany me to the Naturalization Bureau at the Federal Building. Wasn't I excited! So to the Naturalization Bureau I went for the third time. If that old Korean saying were true, I might be successful this time, I thought.

The Federal Building was only two blocks away, at the corner of Clark Street and Jackson Boulevard. I remembered that building very well. I had taken a U. S. Civil Service examination for Postal Service there in 1925, obtained a fairly high rating, and also passed a physical examination successfully, only to be refused an appointment because I was not a citizen, although I was a veteran.

My friend introduced me to a Naturalization official, a dignified and elderly looking gentleman. I cannot recall whether he was an examiner or the commissioner himself. When the question of my eligibility to American citizenship came up, the official shook his head saying, "No, this man is not eligible to citizenship under any circumstances. I know very well the case involving a Japanese down in Virginia during the war and while he was in an Army Camp. He was not admitted to citizenship under the Chinese exclusion law which covers all the Orientals." I wondered if he was not referring to myself and to my own case.

"But how about the other Japanese veteran who was granted citizenship by a Federal Court in Los Angeles?" I put in.

"Oh, we wouldn't know about that," he said, and that was all. As a rule, it occurred to me, the officials never care to discuss any point of decision handed down by other courts of which they were not in favor, quoting only the points which they believed as correct interpretations. When my friend called his attention to the special regulation which was in force during the war that "Anyone who served in the armed forces of the United States be given citizenship," the official said, "Oh, that's out of date now, as the life of that special regulation expired with the return of the last soldier of the Army of Occupation several years ago. At any rate, the regulations did not apply to this man's case. You see, there is the great principle embodied in the Chinese exclusion law. It purported to prevent the influx of the Asiatic millions to

America. The recent immigration laws help to carry
out that principle."   *

"I understand perfectly, sir," said my friend. "It
is conclusive. The principle of the basic law is to be
considered," he concluded, and thanking the official,
my friend led me out of the building.

My third try in quest of American citizenship had
failed, too. Would there be a fourth try some day?
If so, when and where and how? Why didn't I try
in Los Angeles, California? Wouldn't the same
court that had granted citizenship to a Japanese
grant the same to me? But it would be too late now,
I thought. My disappointment this time was two-
fold, in that I was now refused citizenship for the
third time, which seemed final, and, consequently, the
solution of my wife's problem seemed more remote
than ever. There was only one alternative left to
her. She could continue her education indefinitely as
long as she could. Nothing was wrong in that as I
saw scores of gray-haired students attending the University year in and year out in quest of more and
more knowledge, digging ever deeper into all the mysteries yet unearthed. She could yet become a doctor
and I could follow her footsteps, too. But how long?
That was the question.

20
The Depression Era

My luck had turned in the opposite direction once again. Indeed, those were some of the gloomiest days in my life. Even for my optimistic nature, they were too hard to bear. In the fall of that year, I lost my job with Rand McNally as a draftsman. The work on "Goode's School Atlas" had just been completed, and I was made a victim of the great depression like hundreds of thousands of others all over the land. The financial panic of 1908, which I had suffered at Salt Lake City, was nothing as compared to this one. Need I tell the bitter experiences of it as if no one else knew anything about it? It was so bad that I knew of quite a few Korean students who were rounded up by the Immigration authorities during those days and shipped back to Korea when they were discovered working on part-time jobs at their fellow-countrymen's restaurants and cafeterias. It appeared that these students were supposed to finance their education here with money brought over from their homeland as if they were the sons of American millionaires. The fact of the matter was that jobs were so scarce that when the American citizens themselves were out of work and even the veterans were selling apples on the street corners, it was the policy of the government at the time to eliminate the foreign element from this country as much as possible in order that the few jobs taken away from it were made available to the American citizens.

I, too, found that jobs were indeed scarce. For three months after I lost my job, I looked all over the city, making out an application for a job at every map-making and publishing concern, but all in vain. Maybe it was because they were not making any maps anymore, for no one was going to buy any maps, because no one had any jobs to make any money, because nobody was giving any job to anyone, because everybody was going around in a circle, and not getting anywhere. One thing that everybody asked me was whether I was an American citizen. That was always the first question they asked me, and I had to say, "No, but I am a World War veteran." It made no difference for other millions of citizens were standing in the bread and soup lines and thousands of other veterans were in the bonus march to Washington. Citizen or not a citizen, there were no jobs to be had, that was all there was to it.

That being the case, I was advised by Professor Goode and Rev. Merrifield, as by Horace Greeley, of old, to go West where at least our grocery bill would be smaller and other living costs would be less. Therefore, we decided to return to California — good old California — and Rev. Merrifield kindly secured for us half-fare train tickets to San Francisco. We were indeed sorry to leave these good people behind, especially Professor Goode who was ill for quite some time and also my friend, Changhai, who, too, was seriously ill at the time. Both of them passed away soon after we left.

On the day of our departure, the Rev. and Mrs. Merrifield, the latter with her small namesake clasped to her bosom, took us to the station in a taxi on that cold day in November, 1931, to bid us farewell. My wife and her godmother bade farewell to each other with tears in their eyes.

For the first time in nineteen years, I returned to San Francisco, this time with my family. Here, in 1913, two years before the Panama-Pacific World's Fair held there, I had met Dr. George S. McCune who sent me East to Park College. In 1931, I was sent back West to San Francisco. This romantic city of San Francisco was the city of my dreams in my boyhood days in Korea. "San Francisco, here I come," I sang in my heart when I first landed there in 1905. "San Francisco, here I come back," I sang in my heart that day when the train pulled into the Townsend Street Station. I was glad to be back in San Francisco for I had a rendezvous with her. I loved her, and she loved me. Once leaving her behind, I had gone clear across the continent to the banks of the Potomac River. Now I had come clear back to her, to the Golden Gate. I was glad indeed to return to San Francisco. There was now a small Korean community, too, and we were met by my cousin, Esther, who was now the wife of the pastor of the Korean Methodist Church, Rev. S. S. Whang, an old schoolmate of mine in Pyeng Yang, and her nephew, and several old friends.

The city looked more beautiful than ever before. A great change had taken place while I was away. San Francisco was rebuilt; San Francisco was reborn. The old city hall was gone. What a beautiful new civic center there was now on Van Ness Avenue, with the two War Memorials — the Veterans Building and the Opera House which was destined to become the cradle of the United Nations! The old Barbary Coast was no more and the old Chinatown had its face lifted. The Treasure Island was emerging out of the bay as the site of the coming Golden Gate International Exposition to celebrate the completion of the two great bridges — the Bay Bridge, seven miles long, and the Golden Gate Bridge, the greatest single span in the world.

The people, in general, had become most friendly to all, fellow-Americans and foreigners alike. The city had become the playground of the nation, the city of the world's fairs, the city of national conventions, and most recently, the scene of the birth of the United Nations. "The city that knows how" to do great things, the city that the whole world knows, the city that is beautiful by nature, the city that I loved the best. I was first landed here in San Francisco. Here I lived the longest. Here I joined the American Legion, which proved to be my Big Brother and champion. Here two cousins of mine were buried. Here two children of mine were born. Here I was born as an American citizen. It is no wonder that although I left her many times on business, I always returned to her. I loved San Francisco because she was my lucky star!

Well, now that I was in the city that knew how to do things, I ought to know how I was going to make a living. But how? For this city, too, was engulfed in the throes of that terrible depression just then. Just as back in Chicago, jobs were scarce and I could not find a thing, not even a janitor job. Begging for a job was worse than begging for bread, I discovered. Neither had a beggar a choice, nor had I a choice for a job. Finally, I went to a barber college and learned the trade for five months until I was graduated and obtained a State license as an apprentice barber, and then worked in my nephew's shop in the heart of Chinatown.

I was all dressed up now in a snow white smock which made me look like a surgeon. Having failed to become a doctor as I had intended when I first landed in San Francisco, I was now only a barber in surgeon's smock. What a cruel fate! But, I learned from the barber college text book that there was a close relationship between a barber and a surgeon. In fact, in the olden days, when there were no surgeons, the barbers were the surgons, it said. Maybe that's why the barbers and the surgeons are dressed alike today. Had I lived a few centuries back, I could have passed for a surgeon then, I thought.

To me, the year of 1932 was the most excruciating period of my life, full of heartaches and sad and bad news. I lost two great friends, a loving cousin of mine, almost lost my loving and dear wife. Professor Goode and Changhai of Chicago passed away soon after I arrived in San Francisco, and my cousin, Esther, died five months later. My wife was ordered deported to Korea by the Immigration authorities following the birth of our boy. That's when my Big Brother, the American Legion, came into the picture to save my family.

21

My Big Brother, the American Legion

As soon as we arrived in San Francisco, I joined the Cathay Post No. 384, of the American Legion, and my wife joined the Cathay Unit of the American Legion Auxiliary, Department of California. My wife was attending a music school while I was at the Barber college. As was the case back in Chicago, when the school began in the fall of that year, my wife was not in condition to resume her school work for she was expecting another child in September.

Taking Benjamin Franklin's advice that "honesty is the best policy," for I was an honest person, I wrote to the office of the Commissioner General of Immigration Bureau in Washington, petitioning that, under the circumstances, Lotus Flower, now as a veteran's wife, be excused until such time when she would be able to continue her school again. I thought that my petition should be given some consideration which would be more reasonable with my wife, and I was praying to hear good news from Washington.

When the news came, it was the very least that I expected. It came like a thunderbolt from clear skies. The Immigration authorities immediately began my wife's deportation proceedings. They sent an inspector from the dreaded Angel Island Immigration Station to my place to investigate the case and to interview my wife personally. Were we not scared! Honestly, it was the first time in my life I was made to feel as though I had committed a crime of some sort! All I had done was to marry a young woman of my own race and nationality who had come here as a student. It was against the Federal law. If I had married an American woman, it would have been against the law of the State of California. I was in a state of awful dilemma!

The inspector wanted to know how we were married, how she attended school since, how old our first child was, how soon our second child was expected, what was her home address in Korea, and so forth. He paid us two visits and we paid him as many visits at his office in the old Appraisals Building.

When I told the inspector that I was a World War veteran of the United States Army and asked him if the authorities would give a little consideration to a veteran's wife, he said, "Hardly. They might if you were an American citizen." When I told him I was a Legionnaire, and asked him if the Legion could not help me out, he said, "Oh, yes, I should think so. If I were you, I would seek the Legion's assistance." He said he was sorry for me and would like to see me do something about it before it was too late. Really, he was sympathetic toward us, and my honesty paid dividends in a way. Knowing and trusting that I was an honest man, my wife was left free all the time at my own cognizance.

My first thought was to go and see my Big Brother, the American Legion for two things — the American citizenship matter, and the immigration case. I went to Comrade Jim Fisk, the Department Adjutant of the American Legion, at his office in the Veterans Building for his advice and assistance. It was the first time I had ever met him, but I found him to be a very friendly and scholarly gentleman. He was glad to know that I was a member of the Cathay Post, for the Chinese post was organized in 1930 with the assistance of the San Francisco Post No. 1 and was loved by the whole department. In fact, those two posts were like twin brothers in that they held joint installation ceremonies and joint banquets annually. How they loved each other!

I talked to Comrade Fisk about the naturalization matter before mentioning anything about the immigration case directly, thinking that my naturalization would take care of the other automatically. I told him quite fully my experiences in vain attempts to become naturalized three times already, whereas a Japanese veteran in Los Angeles and a number of Korean and Chinese veterans in Hawaii were granted citizenship long before that. He agreed with me that I had the same right and privilege as any other Oriental veteran to become an American citizen. He said, however, that he did not know the subject matter any too well, and referred me to Comrade James Espey, an attorney-at-law and a member of the Americanization Committee of the County Council, who could advise me more expertly than he could.

Immediately, I paid Comrade Espey a visit at his law office in the Mills Building. Yes, he was a lawyer, and a Legionnaire, or a Legionnaire lawyer. I could not have found a better adviser than he. He was able to understand my problem with sympathy and could counsel me expertly, and I found him to be a delightful person, easy to talk with. I presented my case to him in a straightforward manner. Both the naturalization and immigration case went together with me as was the case with the set-up of the twin bureaus in the same labor department. I wanted to be a naturalized citizen in order to solve my wife's immigration case.

To my great dismay, Comrade Espey at first said to me that the naturalization question was out. He explained that the interpretation of that law affecting the Oriental veterans had now long since been definitely established against them, and unless and until there was made a new law more specifically in their favor, there was no chance whatsoever left for me in any Federal Court. He promised, however, that he would do his best to make an appeal to the Commissioner General of the Immigration Bureau in Washington in behalf of my wife as deserving some consideration as a veteran's wife. Well, if he could do that successfully, that was all I wanted, and with his promise of success, I came away hopefully happy that day.

Nothing further was heard until after our baby was born in the latter part of September. I was informed however, by the inspector that my wife would be given six weeks' time following the birth of the child in which to get ready to leave the country. Without fail, that dreaded order came, ordering my wife to surrender herself at the Angel Island station, of all days, on November 11, to be deported back to the old country! "Surrender on November 11!" As if she was Germany of 1918. Oh, what a sad Armistice Day was in store for me that year!

A week before that dreaded Armistice Day, I made a trip to the Angel Island station for an interview with the commissioner there. I wondered then how, why, when, and who ever named it "Angel Island." A more dreaded place than that island I had never visited until that day. At the entrance of the office, I met an official wearing an American Legion button on his lapel. Greeting him as a comrade, and telling him that I was a member of Cathay Post, I showed him the letter of deportation order and told him I wished to see the commissioner. Comrade Smith was his name, I think. He read the letter and said to me, "Oh, my, is it you?" I explained to him that it was not I, but my wife who was concerned.

"Oh, that's too bad, Comrade Charr, but, of course, I don't understand anything about it. I'll take you to the commissioner. I wish you good luck," he said and took me to the commissioner, and left.

"Well," said the commissioner, "Did you bring your wife with you?"

"No, sir," I answered. "I could not bring her with me because she is not well. That's why I've come over to ask you if you will postpone the date of her deportation."

"Is that so? Well, I'll send a government doctor over to examine her to know just how she is. It will be sometime tomorrow," he said.

Finding nothing more to be said or done there, I hurried back across the San Francisco Bay on a small government boat, with leaden heart and ashen face. The tigers never scared me when I was a small boy, but the immigration law scared me that day! As soon as I arrived in the city, I went straight to Comrade Espey's office and asked him if he had any good news from Washington. He told me he had written to Washington on the very day I interviewed him for the first time, but he had not yet received any word. Then I told him about my trip to Angel Island, saying, "Now, Mr. Espey, the commissioner is going to send a government doctor over tomorrow to examine my wife's health, and if the doctor finds her quite strong enough to travel, they will take her away for sure, won't they? Please tell me what I'd better do."

"Of course, I'll tell you what to do," he replied. "I have been thinking, and I've got an idea. The matter is very urgent and time is too short. We need more time to do anything. In order to gain time, there's only one thing left for us to do just now. I want you to rush over to Comrade Jim Fisk and ask him to send a wire to the Commissioner General of Immigration in Washington, asking for a sixty day stay of the deportation order owing to Mrs. Charr's illness. You understand, of course, that I am not trying to pass the buck or anything like that. The truth of the matter is that the authorities in Washington would not listen to you or to me, personally, but surely will listen to Jim who represents the American Legion of the department of California."

"I understand you perfectly," I said, "and I'll do just as you say."

So I paid Adjutant Fisk my second visit. As soon as he saw me walk into his office, he greeted me ever so cordially, saying, "Well, Comrade Charr, how are you and what can I do for you this time? You seem to be in a hurry for something very important. Can it be something about the naturalization matter?"

"No, indeed, Mr. Fisk," I said, "it isn't that this time. But there is something else which is really very important that I want you to do for me just now. Mr. Espey sent me to you with his compliments." Saying this, I pulled from my pocket the deportation order and handed it to him. "Please read this," I said.

"Oh! Oh! This is too bad, indeed. How in the world has this happened to Mrs. Charr? I didn't know anything about it until this minute. This is very important. Please tell me all about it, if you will," he said.

I told him the whole true story, including my trip to Angel Island. I did not forget to remind him of the pledge which I had made to my wife before we were married that if anything should happen to her with regard to the Immigration law, the American Legion, of which I was a member in Parkville, Missouri, would be able to help her to stay in America.

"Why, certainly, we will do all that we can to assist our comrade who is in distress. But I can't think just exactly what to do right now. What does Comrade Espey want me to do for you? What did he say?"

"He wants you to send a wire to the Commissioner General of the Immigration Bureau in Washington, asking for a sixty day stay of the deportation order against Mrs. Charr who is still ill," I replied.

"He did? I'll certainly do that for you. Why didn't you say so in the first place?" Saying this, he walked over to his secretary's desk and said, "Please take a wire and send it right off. This is urgently important:

'To Commissioner General
of Immigration Bureau,
Washington, D. C.

'Kindly grant Mrs. Charr, formerly Miss Nien-
wha Kim, a sixty day stay of her deportation
order owing to her illness. This is a worthy
cause.

> James K. Fisk,
> Adjutant, Department of
>   California
> The American Legion
> 117 Veterans Building
> San Francisco, California.' "

"Thank you ever so much, Mr. Fisk. You are indeed my Big Brother, representing the American Legion," I said.

"We are glad to help, comrade," he told me. "I
sincerely hope that everything will come out all right.
Please don't hesitate to call on me any time when
there is anything we can do for you."

Thanking him again, I left and relayed the news
back to Comrade Espey, my counsel. He said he was
glad and that he would write another letter to Washington that day. On returning home, I told my wife
everything that my big brother, the American Legion, was doing for us, and she was gratefully happy
to realize then that the American Legion was cham-
pioning her cause, confident that everything would be
all right soon. I told her, too, that a government
doctor was coming to see her the next day.

Comrade Fisk had been the Department Adjutant
continuously over a dozen years already then, and
Comrade Espey was the Chairman of the American-

ism Committee of the County Council of San Francisco, of which I was a member the following year.

The next day, later in the afternoon, a government doctor from Angel Island came to examine my wife's health. I was out, and my wife was all alone in the house on Jackson Street with two little children — a two-year-old girl and the baby boy only six weeks old. I had been in and out of the house a dozen times that day waiting for the doctor to come. When I stepped in, the doctor was already in the house and I saw him in the kitchen rinsing off his thermometer after taking my wife's temperature.

"Oh, the doctor's here already," I said to my wife who was in bed. I walked into the kitchen then and said, "Oh, how do you do, doctor."

Turning around, he looked at me and at the American Legion button on my lapel, and said to me with a smile on his face, "Oh, how do you do? I see you are a Legionnaire!"

"Yes, I am, Colonel," I said, noticing the insignia on his shoulder band.

"I'm a veteran myself," he explained. "I was an army doctor in the World War and still am now."

"So I see, Colonel," I said. "How interesting! All the officers in my camp were doctors down at Camp A. A. Humphreys, Virginia. You see, I was in the Army Medical Corps and with the base hospital there. I had intended to study the medical profession myself when I was in school in Missouri. However, before becoming a doctor I met my wife in Chicago and married her there. She had come from Korea, my native country, as a student. That's how she's been caught in the dragnet of the immigration law, and the government is going to deport her back to the old country."

"Yes, I know," he said. "It is too bad."

"By the way, how is my wife now, Colonel?" I asked him.

"Oh, your wife is not too well. She's got some fever and her pulse is not normal. She is not in condition to travel on a long journey only six weeks after childbirth. I will report that as soon as I get back to the office and I will have to recommend a stay of sixty days for her," he said to me.

"Sixty days! Thank you, Colonel," I exclaimed. "Do you know that's exactly the thing our adjutant, Jim Fisk, did for her yesterday when he wired to the Commissioner General in Washington?"

"He did!" he said, pleasantly surprised. "That's just fine. I know him very well and I am glad to learn now that you have found the right channel. I was about to suggest to you to do that very thing. Ordinarily, of course, I am not supposed to advise anyone in a case like this as a government official doing his duty, but you are different, and you have already done wisely. You are a veteran and a Legionnaire. It is unthinkable that the government which you have served as a soldier should break up your home in this fashion. And a student can't always be a student. What's an education for? She has to get married and have children sooner or later, which is no crime, is it? And she'll have to take care of her children's education pretty soon, won't she?"

"You are right, absolutely," I responded, "and I want to thank you for your words of comfort when we are in trouble."

"Not at all, not at all," he said. "I haven't done a thing. I was saying that you were doing the right thing through the American Legion. If I were you, I would write the National Commander a long letter

— make it strong and elaborate, you know what I mean — appealing urgently for immediate help. Nobody will listen to you as an individual, but will listen to him because he's got the American Legion behind him," he advised me just before leaving my house, and I said I would follow his advice.

Now it was proved beyond any doubt that my original idea that the American Legion was going to be my champion was correct. That very night I started writing letters. The first letter was written to the Commander of my own Cathay Post, to Commander Wong K. Jean, thinking it would be the more orderly manner of procedure, and I delivered the letter to him in person. As a result of that, an executive meeting was held at his home the following evening, and through Comrade Gus Ringold of San Francisco Post, an attorney, they made an appeal to Honorable Florence Kahn, the Congresswoman in Washington who represented their district, to intercede in my behalf.

Next I wrote a really strong and elaborate letter to all the important people in American Legion circles, simultaneously. You see, I was a soldier, although I carried no gun, believing in the military science that to attain an important objective is to act quickly and attack in force simultaneously from all sides. I had to, for I was in a very "tight spot." The letter was dated November 11, 1932, and was addressed to National Commander Louis A. Johnson; to John T. Winterich, editor of the American Legion Magazine; to National President of the American Legion Auxiliary, Mrs. S. Alford Blackburn, in my wife's name; to the Department Commander, Warren Atherton; and to the Department Adjutant, James K. Fisk. It was more like a circular — the contents being similar. The letter to the National Commander was as follows:

"November 11, 1932.

"Mr. Louis A. Johnson,
National Commander,
The American Legion Headquarters,
Indianapolis, Indiana.

"My dear Commander:

"As a fellow comrade of the American Legion, may I plead with you for your generous consideration and kindest cooperation in my behalf? For I am in dire need for your hundred percent support, knowing that you represent this great organization of yours and mine which has tremendous influence in civic matters and stands for the things that are just and right in the eyes of every citizen of these United States.

"By birth I am a native of Korea, and I came to America as early as 1905. I have lived here ever since and served in the United States Army with you in the late war. I was stationed at Camp A. A. Humphreys, Virginia. I have been educated in this country from grammar school up, graduating from Park College, Parkville, Missouri, in 1923. Indeed, I have lived more than the half of my life here in America, and truly, I know I have done my duty as any American citizen would have done. Yet I am much aggrieved to say that I am still an alien because I have been denied American citizenship for being an Asiatic who is not eligible to that privilege in spite of the fact that I had volunteered into the military service of this country. During

the war there was a special regulation provided
to naturalize 'any alien who served in the United
States military service,' and I know several Orientals who were naturalized on their military
record by some judges, but unfortunately I was
denied citizenship by a federal judge in Kansas
City who interpreted the same identical law so
differently than did others.

"And now here is the very urgent matter to
which I wish to call your special attention for
your generous consideration and recommendation. Some five years ago back in Chicago, I
married a Korean girl who came here as a student. We now have two children, one of them
is only six weeks old. Even after our marriage
my wife always maintained her status of student,
continuing her studies until last June. But realizing that she can no longer maintain her student life under the circumstances, I had written
to the Commissioner General of the Immigration Service in Washington, petitioning him to
excuse my wife from attending school for a
while at least, considering she is the wife of a
veteran. But, alas! Contrary to all my expectations, he ordered my wife's deportation with
her six weeks old child. She was ordered to surrender on this very memorable day — this Armistice Day, but thank God, it was due to the
timely help of our Department Adjutant James
K. Fisk that a sixty day stay has been secured, I
think. My wife came here in 1926 under the
maiden name of Nien-wha (Evelyn) Kim.

"I had promised my wife when we were married that the American Legion would be able to
make her free from the immigration law and let

her stay in America which is my adopted country and to which country I gave my military service.

"I sincerely hope that you do not think I am asking too much. Is it too much for me to ask this government to give me some freedom inasmuch as I have freely given my life and all to this country as a soldier at the time of great need? Is it too much for me to ask this government to let the mother of the two potential American citizens stay with them in their native country which is America? Or would it be too much for me to ask this great organization of ours to extend its helping hand to influence the immigration authority in Washington to consider my case with some favor? Do you not think I deserve some consideration? Do you not think I have some right to ask for such a favor from this government in return for my military service?

"With your kind approval will you please recommend this case immediately to the proper authority in Washington and see to it that some justice be done so that your own comrade's wife can stay here? And you can't imagine how grateful my family would be to you, if you will do this great human kindness in my behalf. If you will do this for me and for my family, your name and deed will be remembered in all the days of our life.

"Thanking you in advance,

"Very respectfully yours,

(Signed)

E. Emsen Charr
Historian, Cathay Post 384,
Department of California,
The Amercan Legion."

I was desperately in need of all the available help
that could be gathered around me from every direction I could think of. The more the better, I thought.
First, politically, then socially, and now educationally,
also. More than once before Dean Sanders of my
Alma Mater had helped me out of my troubles. I
was now in a real man-sized trouble. Under any circumstances, it was my duty as well as my desire to
inform him of the tough predicament in which I was
then. So, I wrote him a letter, too. When writing to
him, I also thought of writing to Secretary of Agriculture, Arthur M. Hyde, who was one man in Washington who knew me personally. You will remember
that he, as the Governor of the State of Missouri, delivered the Commencement address on Park College's
Commencement day in 1922, and the honorary degree of Doctor of Laws was conferred upon him
when I received my first prize award of the American History essay given by the Daughters of the
American Revolution.

The very first response to my letters came from
Dean Sanders a week later. He said he was going
to do his best to help me in my hour of urgent need
and that he had already written to Vice-President
Charles Curtis who was his fellow-townsman in To-
peka, Kansas, before coming to Park College. The

first response from Washington was from the office of the Secretary of Agriculture, dated November 26, 1932, and was as follows:

"Dear Mr. Charr:

"Acknowledgment is made of your letter of November 11, outlining the problem which now confronts you relative to your wife's stay in the United States. Secretary Hyde is away and is not expected to return to Washington for several days. In the meantime, I am taking your case up with the Department of Labor to see what, if anything, may be done to assist you.

"You will realize that the immigration laws are very strict and the Department of Labor has little discretion in cases of this character. If there is anything the Department can do, I assure you it will be glad to render assistance.

"We appreciate fully your plight and sympathize with you.

"Very truly yours,

(Signed)
E. N. Meador,
Assistant to the Secretary."

A day later I received another very encouraging letter from the editor of the American Legion Magazine in New York. The letter reads:

"Dear Mr. Charr:

"I have read with deep interest and sympathy your letter of November 11 which was addressed to our Chicago office but should have been addressed to New York. I do not believe that much delay has been caused thereby, however.

"It seems to me from reading your very clear statement of your case that you are absolutely in the right. I must admit that I say this without being any too familiar with the actual technicalities of the law involved. I want to say, in addition, that if you have people like Jim Fisk helping you, you are certainly doing all you can on your side, and you may be sure that Mr. Fisk and his associates will do all they can on theirs.

"I am taking the liberty of sending your letter to the Legion's National Legislative Committee in Washington. This is in no sense a passing of the buck. The Legislative Committee is fully conversant with the law in the case, and I know they can give you expert advice.

"You may expect to hear from them or from me within a few days. I am asking the Legislative Committee to keep me informed of the situation as I am definitely interested.

"With all good wishes, and the hope that your troubles may soon be satisfactorily settled, I am

"Yours sincerely,

(Signed)
John T. Winterich, Editor."

This good letter was followed the next day by that of National Commander Louis A. Johnson, written from the National Headquarters in Indianapolis, which reads:

"Dear Comrade Charr:

"I have your letter of November eleventh, and, inasmuch as the case already has been taken up through the channel of the State Department of the American Legion, I am taking the liberty of forwarding your letter to James K. Fisk, the Adjutant, asking him to pursue the matter.
"If he has need of service by the Legion, nationally, I am sure you can count on his taking the matter up with our proper representatives in Washington, D. C.

"With kind regards, I am

"Very sincerely yours,

(Signed) Louis Johnson
National Commander."

Another letter dated December 3 was received by my wife from The American Legion Auxiliary, National Headquarters in Indianapolis which reads:

"Dear Mrs. Charr:

"Your letter of November twentieth addressed to Mrs. S. A. Blackburn, National President of the American Legion Auxiliary, has been referred to the writer for reply.
"I am taking this matter up with our Washington representatives and we will give you any assistance that we can.

"Yours very truly,

(Signed)
Remster A. Bingham
General Counsel."

Still another letter, dated December 3, arrived from the American Legion National Legislative Committee in Washington, D. C. It reads as follows:

"Dear Mr. Charr:

"Your letter of November 11 has been referred from Mr. Winterich to me for attention.

"Please be advised that this matter has been presented to Mr. Harry E. Hull, Commissioner General of Immigration here, and just as soon as we have received his reply, we will pass the word on to you.

"I sincerely hope that we will be able to find a way in which to aid you at this time.

"Very truly yours,

(Signed)
John Thomas Taylor,
National Legislative Committee
The American Legion."

In the meantime, one afternoon a reporter, Mr. E. V. McQuade of the San Francisco News, came to my place with a staff photographer, asking for an interview on the case. He said he had come from the San Francisco News at the request of the American Legion executives and the representatives of the Bay Region Park College Alumni Association who wished to help me out of my trouble. "Ah, now I see my Big Brother and my Alma Mater are coming to rescue my family!" I said to myself. Yes, I realized then that I had started the ball rolling all right. On the following afternoon in the San Francisco News a two-column article, along with a photograph of my family, appeared on the third page, top center, and was headlined:

"U. S. Officials Trying to Deport Co-ed Wife of War Veteran; Two Children Face Suffering

.   .   .   .

Many Leading Citizens Join in Fight on Latest Federal Abuse

.   .   .   .

The Nation he served honorably as a soldier . . . etc., etc."

The San Francisco Chronicle followed suit by publishing the same article in its morning issue. Many people read it even before I did. Some of the Park College people were the first to call on us or write us letters about the newspaper account of our troubles, expressing their sympathy and praying for a happy outcome of the case now widely known. Among them were Jennie Nicholson of Park, who was now Mrs. Morris Zutrau, my classmate at Park College Academy, and Hilda Bloom, my classmate of the College Biology class.

On that same afternoon, the good tidings of joy and happiness ushered into my famly through my counsel, Comrade James Espey. As I was busy working in my nephew's barber shop, I saw him coming in with a happy grin on his face. I sensed that he was a bearer of good news for me, else he would not have come to see me in person. Greeting me ever so courteously, he said, "Well, Comrade Charr, I've good news for you at last. Here's a copy of the letter which I have just received from Washington

which I want you to read." Saying this, he handed it
to me. The letter reads:

"Dear Sir:

"In reply to your letter of November 30, 1932,
you are informed that the Department has entered an order staying indefinitely the deportation of Nienwha Kim, or Lotus Flower Kim,
now Mrs. E. Emsen Charr.

"Respectfully yours,

(Signed)
H. E. Hull
Commissioner General."

Oh, I was happy! Honestly, I was so happy that I
thought I would faint. It was the happiest moment
of my life. And how grateful I was to the bearer
of that glad tiding, my friend and counsel, Comrade
Espey! Thanking him for the good news which he
brought and putting on my hat and coat, I told him
I must dash up to my house to show the letter to my
wife. He said, "Oh, Mrs. Charr has read it already.
You see, I went up to your house first. Mrs. Charr
sent me down here to give you the letter. Let me
congratulate you and Mrs. Charr. And I wish you
a very Happy New Year!"

Early the next morning the mailman brought us
an official letter from the Angel Island station, dated
December 29, 1932, and addressed to Mrs. Charr:

"Madam:

"With further reference to your case, the following quoted letter has been received from the

Bureau of Immigration, Washington, D. C. under the date of December 22, instant:

"Referring to your file No. 12020/20890, you are advised that the deportation of Nien-wha Kim or Lotus Flower Kim, now Mrs. E. Emsen Charr be stayed indefinitely."

"Respectfully,

(Signed)
E. H. Hoff,
Acting Commissioner of
Immigration,
San Francisco District."

On the following day, another letter from the American Legion Legislative Committee in Washington arrived, dated December 27, which read:

"My dear Mr. Charr:

"Relative further to the deportation proceedings against your wife, the following response to my contact in your behalf was received today from Mr. Harry E. Hull, Commissioner General of Immigration:

" 'You are informed that the department has entered an order staying the deportation of Nien-wha Kim or Lotus Flower Kim, now Mrs. E. Emsen Charr indefinitely.'

"I was very glad to be of service to you in this

matter and if I can assist you further at any time, do not hesitate to write me.

"Very truly yours,

(Signed)
John Thomas Taylor
Vice Chairman
National Legislative Committee
The American Legion."

On the following day a letter from the American Legion Magazine, Editorial offices in New York, dated December 28, was as follows:

"Dear Mr. Charr:

"You have doubtless already heard from John Thomas Taylor, Vice-Chairman of the Legion's National Legislative Committee in Washington, and you know that the Commissioner General of Immigration has sent him the following message:

"'You are informed that the department has entered an order staying the deportation of Nien-wha Kim or Lotus Flower Kim, now Mrs. E. Emsen Charr, indefinitely.'

"I want to congratulate you and Mrs. Charr on this happy outcome of your difficulties. I hope that everything will be straightened out satisfactorily, including the matter of your own admission to citizenship. As I wrote you before, I do not know too much about the technical qualifications involved, but I believe now so much progress has been made that your worries are well on the way toward getting over. Please call on me or on Mr. Taylor direct any time you feel we can be of service to you.

"I know you are in the best possible hands if Jim Fisk is looking after you at the San Francisco end, and I know you feel exactly the same way about it. If you happen to see Jim, please give him my very best regards, and tell him I am proud of the way he is carrying on.

"With all good wishes to you and Mrs. Charr,

Yours sincerely,

(Signed)
John T. Winterich, Editor."

Honestly, in all my life I had never received a more interesting letter of this nature than this one from the Editor of the American Legion Magazine. I had never become a doctor, but this man was more than a doctor to my aching heart. Not an iota of medicine was necessary. Just an encouraging word of his seemed to have cured all my troubles, one after another. He must be a very interesting man, I know, because he said to me now, "I hope that everything will be straightened out satisfactorily, including the matter of your own admission to citizenship." And he said that confidently because he had the great organization behind him, and the organization had a grand person with great talent and magnanimous heart to represent it.

Dean Sanders of Park College was happy to learn the good news through the intercession of Vice President Curtis to whom he had written in my behalf. Congresswoman Florence Kahn, answering my letter of gratitude to her for her part in bringing about this happy event, wrote from Washington:

"Dear Mr. Charr:

"This is to acknowledge receipt of your very kind letter of January 18 and to assure you that I was very glad to do what I could in your behalf. The immigration laws of the United States are extremely rigid, and, unfortunately in some cases, work great inconvenience and even hardship on individuals. However, after reviewing the facts in your case the Secretary of Labor, Hon. Wm. N. Doak, directed that permission to remain in the United States for an indefinite period be given.

"With best wishes, I am

"Sincerely yours,
(Signed)
Florence P. Kahn, M.C."

And now last but not least, a very nice letter from the American Legion Auxiliary National Headquarters, dated January 10, 1933, was as follows:

"Dear Mr. Charr:

"I have intended to write to you to express my pleasure at the good news that the Department of Immigration stayed the deportation of your wife indefinitely. I was so very glad that you called my attention to this distressing situation and through the National Legislative Committee of the American Legion we could be of service to you.

"I shall be wishing for you much happiness in

the year 1933 and if I can assist you further at
any time, do not hesitate to write.

"Very truly yours,

(Signed)
Laura B. Blackburn
Mrs. S. Alford Blackburn
National President."

So my Big Brother, as well as my Big Sister cham-
pioned my cause, thus fulfilling the pledge made in
the preamble to the American Legion constitution "to
consecrate and sanctify our comradeship by our devotion to mutual helpfulness."

Thus ended the most perplexing problem of my
life, removing the lingering pain from my side, with
the invaluable assistance and good advice rendered by
the circle of my worthy friends. You can very well
imagine all the indescribable sufferings which I had
gone through during those five long years of my otherwise happy married life — the ever present mental
agony of suspense and uncertainty that had dark-
ened the sunshine of my days and kept me awake at
nights. Believe it or not, as in the case of the famous
Chinese author of the "One Thousand Character
Chinese Primer," which I have told you about, my
worries, too, had turned my jet black hair half gray
during those trying days and wakeful hours. Of
course, my wife shared the ordeal with me.

Now, though, we were happy, very happy indeed.
Yes, it was a very happy new year for us. Oh, how
much more beautiful is the dawn after the night of
storm, and how much more bright is the sun when the
dark clouds have rolled away! I felt as though a
load of mountain had been lifted off my chest and as

if I were Lazarus of old, rising out of his grave!
And my hair seemed to look as black as ever.

Good news, too, like misery, came not singly. Good
news, too, loved company, it seemed. One was now
an accomplished fact; the other, just as good, in the
light of what had been accomplished — the matter of
my admission to citizenship. That was not all. The
birth of our boy, the second child, which was the immediate cause for concern instead of a good reason
for rejoicing, was now to be celebrated.

To climax the happy events crowding into the once
troubled hearth, a celebration was thought appropriate and in order. We decided to give a party at the
Canton Cafe in the heart of Chinatown, my comrades
of the Cathay Post assisting me most heartily. Comrade Commander Wong K. Jean and Comrade Adjutant Lee Poo (Lee being his last name), and the
Unit President Lily Jean and Secretary Dorothy
Chan, were responsible for its success.

To the party were invited the entire membership
of the Cathay Post and the Cathay Unit, Comrades
James C. Espey and Gus Ringole of San Francisco
Post No. 1, and Department Adjutant James K.
Fisk; Mr. E. V. McQuade of the San Francisco
News; and the Park College friends, Rev. Philip
Payne, Rev. and Mrs. Paul Arnold Peterson, Rev.
and Mrs. Morris Zutrau, Mr. and Mrs. Charles
Schermerhorn, Mr. Merle Scott, and Miss Hilda
Bloom. "Once a friend, always a friend" and "a
friend in need, a friend in deed" were they all, and
we were happy to have enjoyed with them an evening
of warm friendship over a cup of oolong tea, "bird's
nest" soup, and what not of the now famous Chinese
chop suey dishes. And my good comrades of Cathay
Post pinned on me a 14-carat gold American Legion

button that night, and the Auxiliary made my wife the Unit's president a year later.

Now, I was happy, but I was poor, and who wasn't at the height of the great depression years? I was happy now that my wife was free to stay with me in America, but I was out of a job. My barber business was not any too good. It did not quite buy me a bag of rice to feed the four mouths of my family or pay the house rent which was only eighteen dollars a month, which I tried to pay in three installments. An old Korean friend of mine said to me, "Don't you worry about that, my friend. Don't you remember the Korean saying that 'never a live man's mouth be covered with cobwebs.' We are all poor, but we can get along somehow. Now that your family is being kept intact, that's the main thing."

Fortunately, taking the kindly advice given me by * Mr. Wm. Chester Rowell, of the San Francisco Chronicle, I had registered at the WPA or Works Progress Administration office on Oak Street, applying for a draftsman job on the Forest Modeling Project. The forest models were to be exhibited at the coming Golden Gate International Exposition. I was assigned to that job a short time later which paid me fifty-four dollars a month to start. At the start, the modeling was done at the Ferry Building, but soon moved into the new National Forest Service office in the Phelan Building on Market Street at Grant Avenue. It was just right walking distance from my house, and one should have seen me strutting gaily and sprightly down to my work every morning with a broad smile on my face. I was one of the hundreds of thousands of the army of unemployed all over the land who were made happy by the benevolent government in the administration of President Franklin D.

Roosevelt, which gave them something to live on when the times were hard. And, what a nice place to work with such a fine group of the Forest Service personnel like Arthur Bell, my immediate supervisor, and Don Jackson, Hank Klamm, and Chief Sedelmeyer, and others!

Oh, how terrible was that long depression! Whether true or not, it was my impression that even during the wartime I had never seen such scared looks and deathly pallor on the faces of the people as I saw during the depression days. In fact, the people at home during the terrible war looked to me as though they were rather happy and jolly because there was plenty of work to do and a chance to make plenty of money with which to buy many things, if not everything — food, clothes, shelter, and even some luxuries and entertainment.

Hence, history repeating itself, the common man of today, the poor man who is in the big majority, who lives from hand to mouth, from day to day, when his livelihood is cut off from the bare necessities of life, is seen to wear that unmistakable sign of hunger in his face. The WPA changed that complexion of the great multitudes of the people, citizens and aliens alike, including myself, in those miserable days of the depression era.

22

A Citizen of the United States

Though I was poor, yet I was happy. Then, too, I was secretly happy in anticipation of another happy event to follow soon, as was encouraged by Mr. John T. Winterich, the editor of the American Legion Magazine. "If only now I can get the American citizenship as he said I might, I won't have to be a barber any longer, nor on the WPA project, and I could get a civil service job as a draftsman," I thought and prayed. That was my sole ambition from that time on.

One day I received a letter from Mr. Winterich of New York, in which he said in part: "Have you made any progress with your citizenship efforts? The government has just issued a very bulky digest of Federal laws relating to the veterans of wars of the United States which has a lot to say about citizenship. I am sure you will find a copy of this in Jim Fisk's office. The material on citizenship is in Chapter XIII, pages 345 and 353, Section 991-1040. I am sure you will find your questions answered in this chapter."

Expecting to find in the book something new, I rushed down to the Department Adjutant's office in the veterans building and asked Mr. Fisk if he had a copy of that book. He said he did and took it out of his library shelves and handed it to me. I sat down and turned to Chapter XIII and started to read through those pages. Soon my eyes were glued to a paragraph under a title "Historical Note."

What do you suppose I read there? Why, I read my own name in full, printed there in black and white! Was I surprised! I could not have imagined that I was quite as famous as that to have a place in such a big historical document. But my name was there, with the correct spelling, too. It was used there as an example to illustrate that although I was a United States World War veteran, I was denied citizenship by the Federal Court in Kansas City in 1922, because I was an Oriental and was subjected to the so-called Chinese Exclusion Law.   *

Taking great interest in my case, I knew that Mr. Winterich was studying the naturalization laws when he came upon my very name in the digest, discovering that I was the same person who was rejected citizenship, which I had complained about in my letter relating to my wife's immigration case. Knowing now the history of my case and the laws as they existed, then he saw no avenue of hope for me except by making a new law specifically to include me in it. Yes, the digest answered my questions all right, beyond any doubt. There was nothing to be done in my favor under that existing statute. I had known that all the time, of course.

But what about the other cases involving those Oriental veterans who were granted citizenship during and after the war? It was strange the book had not said a word about this. I was personally acquainted with at least six different cases, including four Koreans and one Chinese who were naturalized, two in California and the rest in Hawaii, and a Japanese in Los Angeles of whom I had read about in the Kansas City Star. The government obviously did not wish to contradict itself by mentioning the facts about the opposite views of the same law.

During the following year, in the fall of 1934, good news was whispered to me one day in China-town, San Francisco. As I was walking along near Grant Avenue and Clay Street, I came face to face with Comrade Dr. Changwha Lee who had just re-turned from the Miami National Convention of the American Legion.

"Hello, Doc, I'm glad to see you back. Did you have a good time and enjoy your trip?" I greeted him.

"Yes, indeed, Comrade Charr," he said. "And I've got good news for you. I know you'll be interested."

"Oh, yes? What good news? Please tell me."

"Well, can't you guess what it could be?" he re-plied. "I think you're going to get your citizenship pretty soon. At least I hope so. You see, the con-vention passed a resolution proposed by several de-partments to petition the Congress to enact a law to naturalize all the veterans who have not been given citizenship heretofore. That means you are one of them. Of course, Congress will respond to the wishes of the American Legion, especially on matters of this nature, I know, and I know you will get it this time."

Indeed, it was good news to me, and it was now just as good as if it were already done. I had said that many times before. I knew who started the ball rolling, too. Weren't they really swell people? Weren't they truly my Big Brothers! Now that my Big Brother was out to make of me a citizen of the United States by proposing a new law, I was all ex-cited, counting the days and weeks until it became a reality. I realized that it must take quite some time, and I waited and waited for six months to hear the final good news. However, it was not forthcoming, so I wrote to my friend, Mr. Winterich in New York, asking him about the prospect of the new naturalization law. The following letter was received from Colonel John Thomas Taylor, in Washington, on May 14, 1935:

"My dear Mr. Charr:

"Mr. Winterich has forwarded me your letter of April 25, in which you make inquiry relative to H. R. 7170 reported to the House, April 26, 1935. This bill, as you know, carried out our Miami resolution to permit naturalization of Oriental veterans who served honorably with the American forces. This bill is on the House calendar and will come up some time in the near future under unanimous consent.

"You may rest assured that we will make every effort to have this legislation passed during the present session of Congress. But, of course, there is no way for me to tell at this time whether or not we will be successful in our efforts. I will advise you when this bill passes the House.

"Sincerely yours,

John Thomas Taylor
National Legislative Committee
The American Legion."

From this letter, then, I learned for sure that the bill was in Congress, and I knew it would become a public law shortly because the American Legion will never fail to get justice done. It had already done it once for me a short time before. It would do it once

again for me in this, I believed. Colonel Doer's pre-
dictions would come true—you will remember him as
my commanding officer at Camp Humphreys, Virginia, who had foretold of a mighty veterans' organization to be formed and which would sponsor a law
to make an American citizen of me.

How prophetic were his words when finally I received a letter from Washington, dated June 25, 1935,
It read:

> "My dear Mr. Charr:
>
> "For your information I am attaching hereto a
> copy of public law which permits the naturaliza-
> tion of certain resident alien World War veter-
> ans.
>
> "I thought you would be interested in this bill,
> as some time ago I helped to get for your wife
> a stay of deportation.
>
> > "Sincerely yours,
> >
> > (Signed)
> > John Thomas Taylor,
> > Vice-Chairman
> > National Legislative Committee
> > The American Legion."

Was I happy! I was elated! "At last, now I'm
going to be an American citizen this time! This law
is made to order specifically for me and there wouldn't
be any more adverse interpretations nor any technical arguments about it, pro and con," I said to myself. I could hardly wait until the morning to file my
petition for citizenship at the Post Office Building in
downtown. Honestly, I was so excited about it that

I could not sleep that night. Now I realized that my long letter written to my Big Brother "killed two birds with one stone"—first, the immigration case, and now my citizenship.

When I rushed down to the Naturalization Bureau offices in the Post Office Building, I found I was the first and earliest customer there. No doubt about that, I was the very first person to apply for citizenship since that new law was passed. Greeting the lady clerk at the desk, I told her that I wanted to file my petition as a veteran under the newly enacted law. She replied that she had heard of some such law being recently passed but that as yet neither any instructions nor a printed copy of the law had been received from Washington. Thereupon I showed her the letter from Colonel John Thomas Taylor, together with the printed copy of the public law, the sequence of H. R. 7170. Wasn't she surprised to see a man carrying a law on himself to be administered there where they did not yet have one of their own!

First she read the letter and then the printed copy which filled a page, and said to me, "Oh, my, you are lucky. You certainly are entitled to citizenship all right, according to this, and how quickly you got this copy! You are better off than we are. You see, we haven't received it yet. May I take this inside and show it to the examiner? I know he will be glad to see it. I'll be back in a minute."

She said I was lucky. Of course, I was, but perhaps she did not know it was the fourth time which was my lucky number. In the three previous attempts I had gone to the law which was made fundamentally and conclusively against me. This time, I took the law with me in my hand, made specifically and especially for me. So, how could I fail this time?

The lady came back shortly and informed me that I could now file my petition in the examiner's office. I filled out the form, answering all the questions asked, including my military service record. Some of the questions were rather hard for me to answer readily from memory. I was asked on what steamer I had come, in what port I had arrived, on what day, month and year, who my fellow passengers were, where I lived, for whom I worked, and so on and so forth. I found out later, though, that my memory was proved to be pretty good after a period of thirty years, exactly correct as to the month and date. I had arrived in San Francisco on June 26, 1905. Wasn't that a wonderful coincidence, too!

In any ordinary case, naturalization cannot take place until seven years after the "Declaration of Intention," or "First Paper," has been filed. In my case, this was not necessary. I had lived here long enough already. Besides, according to the law, mine was to come two in one—the first and second papers both together at once, and free of charge!

Four months later, on November 18, 1935, I received a mimeographed form letter from the Chicago office of the Naturalization Bureau, asking me to write to my witnesses, Mr. Andrew McNally of the Rand McNally & Company, who was my employer there, and Mr. Bruce W. Dickson of the University of Chicago, who were to testify for me as to my residence and character during a part of the past five years. So I did, and so did they, and I was very grateful to them for their kind services given on my behalf. In San Francisco, I had two other witnesses with me. Morris Zutrau and Charles Schermerhorn, who were my schoolmates at Park College, also testified for me at the San Francisco office. That being done, I was given citizenship training lessons, successfully passed the oral examination given in a private office in the Federal Building, and I was ready to receive the certificate of my citizenship.

January 6, 1936, was my birthday as an American citizen. Only four days before that was my natural birthday. As the fourth time was my lucky number, January was my lucky month, too. Early that morning I was ordered to appear in the United States District Court, located on the top floor of the same building, presided over by Judge Harold Louderback. When I arrived there, I found myself one among nearly one hundred other candidates lined up in the long corridor waiting for the court room to open. Because I was the only Oriental there, I looked conspicuous and some of the crowd eyed me with surprise, I thought. Was I embarrassed? I should say not. I was proud of myself!

The court opened at length and we were ushered into the august, beflagged court room. I walked in with the rest, but following in the rear. When I stepped just inside the doorway, I heard the doorkeeper standing there whispering to the examiner, saying, "Say, that man, an Oriental, how come he is here?" And I heard the examiner, a very fine gentleman, answered him, saying, "But, he is a veteran and a new law entitles him to citizenship now."

When we were all inside, the judge appeared from behind the dais and sat down on the bench, and we were motioned by the attendants to be seated. The clerk stood up and read out loudly the long list of names of the candidates who were qualified to receive the certificates of citizenship. I was thrilled to my bones when I heard my own name mentioned as a successful candidate. What a change of emotion I experienced then as compared to the time in another court when I was not even permitted into the court which denied my Naturalization privilege!

Then, at the direction of the clerk of the court, we all arose and took the oath of allegiance, as follows:

> "I hereby declare, on oath, that I absolutely and entirely renounce and abjure all allegiance and fidelity to any foreign prince, potentate, state or sovereignty, and particularly to ———, of whom I have heretofore been a subject (or citizen); that I will support and defend the Constitution and laws of the United States of America against all enemies, foreign and domestic; that I will bear true faith and allegiance to the same; and that I take this obligation freely and without any mental reservation or purpose of evasion: SO HELP ME GOD."

The certificates were not given out in the court at that time. I was notified to appear on a designated date and hour at the office of the clerk, bringing two witnesses with me, to receive my certificate sealed and signed by the clerk and also signed by myself, with a photograph of myself attached to it.

Handing me the certificate, the clerk with a friendly handshake congratulated me and I thanked him. So did my friends, Morris and Charles. Indeed, they had done me a great service twice as my witnesses and were happy to see me happy. From Park College campus to the Federal Court here, we had walked side by side, then as fellow-students, and now as fellow-citizens. In all cases, my Big Brother and my Alma Mater had proved conclusively to be my twin champions. They saw to it that I became an American citizen, the former sponsoring the law for me, and the latter assisting me in the application of that law.

At Cathay Post meeting one evening, I was called upon to tell the audience of Chinese veterans, some of whom were not yet citizens, of my experiences in the naturalization procedure. Comrade Adjutant Lee Poo himself, was still an alien then, but acquired his citizenship soon after I obtained mine. Comrade Past Commander Otto Hintermann, of San Francisco Post No. 1, who was present, said to me, "Congratulations, Comrade Charr. At last, you've gotten your citizenship eighteen years after your honorable discharge from the United States Army! Well, you certainly earned it and you truly deserve it. I am glad that you have it now."

"Thank you, Comrade Hintermann," I said. "Yes, I earned it the hard way, like everything else that I have ever earned. It is for that very reason I will value it more highly than would some others. I'll try to be a good law-abiding citizen of these United States, and I will ever be gratefully loyal to the American Legion that has helped me out of difficult problems, time after time."

The Preamble to the Constitution of the American Legion reads: — "For God and country, we associate ourselves together for the following purposes: To uphold and defend the Constitution of the United States of America; to maintain law and order; to foster and perpetuate a one hundred percent Americanism; to preserve the memories and incidents of our associations in the Great Wars; to inculcate a sense of individual obligation to the community, state, and nation; to combat the autocracy of both the classes and the masses; to make right master of might; to promote peace and goodwill on earth; to safeguard and transmit to posterity the principles of justice, freedom and democracy; to consecrate and sanctify our comradeship by our devotion to mutual helpfulness."

It is no wonder that I am proud of my Big Brother, the American Legion, the champion of justice, freedom and democracy, and of one hundred percent Americanism.

When I received the certificate of my citizenship that day, I was reminded of one of the most soul-inspiring passages in a book of the Old Testament — the story of Ruth, the Moabitess, following Naomi, her mother-in-law into the land of Judah. Ruth said to Naomi, "Whither thou goest, I will go; where thou lodgest, I will lodge; thy people shall be my people, and thy God, my God; where thou diest, will I die, and there will I be buried; the Lord do so to me, and more also, if ought but death part thee and me!"

What loyalty! What devotion! I admired Ruth. Oh, how so eloquently had she expressed my thoughts! And, I said to Uncle Sam, "I love thee with all my heart. I pledge my allegiance to thee and I will cherish thee always in peace and in war. Thy flag shall be my flag; thy country, my country; thy God, my God; thy people, my people; till the end of my life will I dwell with thee in this sweet land of 'Freedom, Equality, Justice, and Humanity'; and so will my children and my children's children after me!"

Then, too, I was reminded of ex-President Calvin Coolidge's address to the American Legion national convention at Omaha, October 6, 1925. He said, "Whether one traces his Americanism back three centuries to the Mayflower, or three years to the steerage, is not half as important as whether his Americanism of today is real and genuine. No matter by what variant crafts we came here, we are all now in the same boat."

"True Americanism," said Theodore Roosevelt, "is a question of spirit, conviction, and purpose, not of creed or birthplace."

"Ah, that certainly includes me, too," I said to myself, and sang joyously and prayerfully,

"God bless America
My home, sweet home."

Indeed, my wonderful dream came true wonderfully in more ways than I had ever dreamed!

23

Twenty Years
in U.S. Civil Service

As soon as I became an American citizen, I wasted no time in applying for a Federal Civil Service examination. Ever since I had been with the National Forest Service, I was very much interested in the history of the Service that administers some 180,000,000 acres of timber-land in 32 States and Alaska and Puerto Rico. I was especially interested in the art of map-making techniques, all free-hand drawing and lettering beautifully done by the expert draftsmen in the San Francisco office.

But, during the depression era, even the government positions were scarce, too, and naturally, there were no examinations forthcoming. The first successful examination which I took on November 10, 1938, resulted in the rating and average percentage of 93.00, including 5-point veterans preference. But, there was no position open for me just then. I took another examination in June, 1939, and this time I was fortunate to be given my first appointment on November 7, 1939, as an Assistant Engineering Draftsman, SP-4, $1,620 per annum, with the U. S. Department of Agriculture, Soil Conservation Service with its regional headquarters in Berkeley, California. I was directed to report for duty at its area headquarters at Yerington, Nevada, on February 21, 1940.

Thus, my Civil Service career began as a man of the soil from Yerington, Nevada, to the newly reorganized regional headquarters in Portland, Oregon, in 1942, making the soil survey and farm plan maps and charts covering the five Pacific Coast states and Alaska and Hawaii. So I was just like my father and the old folks back in Korea who were dirt farmers. The only difference was that I was just a pen-and-ink farmer. We in the Service worked eight hours a day and six days a week during the war.

A soil scientist friend of mine, Dr. Hafenrichter, said that two and one-half acres of cultivated land is needed per person to maintain our standard of living. There were three and one-half acres per person of cultivated land in the United States in 1937, only three acres in 1947, and it will be only two and one-half acres in 1970, which is the minimum required. There were only one and one-half acres per person in Europe in 1947, less than one acre in China and India in 1947, making the world averages of one and three-quarters acres in 1947. It must be much less than that now.

The sites of the ancient civilizations had flourished in the soil-rich river valleys of the Nile, of the Jordan, of the Euphrates and the Tigris, of the Hwang-ho and the Yangtze, of the Indus and the Ganges, of the Tiber, the Po, and the Danube. One of the earliest inventions of man was the ploughshare for tilling the soil in search of food. Indeed, food was the first and foremost item on the list of the necessities of life. That was why the famine-stricken children of Israel had journeyed into Egypt in search of food, and that was how the hungry legions of Napoleon Bonaparte, retreating from the ruins of Moscow, had cried "Food, Food" on their way homeward. Of the Four Horsemen of the Apocalypse, beware of the child of man starving to death in the very arms of his Mother Earth for lack of food from the soil!

Hence, the Soil Conservation Service — a very good cause, indeed. I am proud of myself to say that I was in that Service for more than ten years, and was awarded a ten-year service button by the Department of Agriculture sometime before I was transferred to the Bonneville Power Administration. My fellow workers in the Cartographic Section gave me a farewell gift just before I left. In Civil Service, as well as in other industries, one has to look around from one agency to another to find more suitable or better paying positions.

During the depression era, while I was working on the WPA project in San Francisco, the Federal government initiated construction of the Bonneville and Grand Coulee dams, primarily to create employment. By the Bonneville Project Act of August 20, 1937, the Bonneville Power Administration, under the jurisdiction of the Department of the Interior, became the Federal agency for marketing the power generated by Bonneville Dam and other Federal dams for the benefit of the general public. The power is sold at a wholesale rate. A customer can obtain one kilowatt 24 hours a day, 365 days of the year, for $17.50. In 1956, the residential and rural kilowatt hour rate in Massachusetts was $3.48; in New York, $3.16; in Illinois, $3.00; in Minnesota, $3.03; it was only $1.15 in Washington, $1.17 in Tennessee under T.V.A., and $1.29 in Oregon. In that same year, Bonneville supplied 63.5 percent of the total energy generated by the utilities of the northwest region. It sold 28.4 billion kilowatt-hours in 1958 and its net revenues were $101,761,383 from sales of power, the

largest since the start in 1938, according to a BPA
informational folder as revised in 1959. The reve-
nue is turned into the United States Treasury, and
Congress appropriates funds annually for the main-
tenance and expansion of the Bonneville project. It
is a self-liquidating government business for the benefit of all concerned.

For over four years, I was busy drawing maps and
graphs showing the Bonneville grid system consisting
of 7,200 circuit miles of transmission lines and 178
substation road maps from Hungry Horse in Mon-
tana to Gold Beach in Oregon, from Spokane to Port
Angeles in Washington, from Grand Coulee in the
upper reaches of the Columbia basin to the mouth of
the great Columbia River at Astoria. As of July 1,
1956, BPA had 2,297 employees.

It so happened that soon after I joined the Soil
Conservation Service at Yerington, Nevada, my wife
and I were invited to the S. C. S. banquet held in
town, and were welcomed into a fine circle of good
people. The Lyon County Post of the American Legion and the Ladies Auxiliary there also welcomed us
into their midst, and we enjoyed our comradeship together while we lived there for two and a half years.

The same thing happened to us when I joined the
Bonneville Power Administration. There was a big
Bonneville banquet held here honoring the ten-year
service Bonneville employees, and I was honored as
the baby of the family. I was then only three days
old in Bonneville. It was arranged by the Personnel
Officer and Program Chairman, the Past Commander
of Columbia Power Post #120, the American Legion, Department of Oregon, Comrade Commander
Howard Strawn, that my wife and I were presented
on the platform and were received most graciously by

"Pop" Sheriff, the Master of Ceremonies, and by Dr. Paul J. Raver, the Bonneville Power Administrator himself, who presented a corsage to Mrs. Charr.

Four years later, when I was being transferred to the Bureau of Indian Affairs, my friends in the Drafting and Graphics section gave me a wonderful farewell party with an angel food cake baked by June and a year's subscription of U. S. News and World Report magazine by Gordon. Expressing my gratitude, I said to them that I had intended to stay with them for that ten-year service honor, but that I found there was no room left for me to grow up to be ten years old. So, like the show that must go on, I must move on up to the top floor of the eight-story high Interior Building in which all the Interior agencies are located. Well, I hope no one would think I am bragging, because if I were bragging, I was bragging about the wonderful people with whom I have been associated.

As a student of American history, I was deeply interested to learn more about it ever since I entered the Bureau of Indian Affairs. From the booklet written by George C. Wells, and issued by the Educational Branch of the Bureau, I have learned many interesting facts concerning the relationship between the government of the United States and the original natives of this great new country of ours.

"There are many misconceptions about Indians and the Bureau of Indian Affairs," says the booklet. "Indians are people with about the same variety of characteristics as any other group. The more one knows about Indians, the greater is his admiration for them such as was expressed by Benjamin Franklin in 'Poor Richard's Almanac' nearly 200 years ago." Well, I have met some of them, I work with some of them, and I like them and admire them whether they may be so-called "Legal Indians," "Biological Indians," or "Cultural Indians." They remind me of the very first Indians that I saw at the Sherman Institute in Arlington, a suburb of Riverside, California, near where I picked oranges in 1905. They were some of the handsomest and intelligent looking young Indians that I ever saw. They must have been the "Biological Indians." And I saw the Haskell Institute from a distance while I was in Lawrence, Kansas, and the Indian school at Stewart, Nevada near Carson City.

Soon after I entered the Indian Service, I had the rare privilege of visiting some of the Indian Reservations—the Warm Springs Reservation on the Deschutes River in North central Oregon, the Yakima Reservation in Washington, the Fort Hall Reservation in Idaho, and the reservations in Arizona, the largest in number and in extent of the Indian Reservations there since the days of Indian Territory when I first landed in San Francisco in 1905. The Indian Territory of Oklahoma became a state in 1907, and New Mexico and Arizona became the youngest states in 1912. Now, the States of Alaska and Hawaii are the youngest. And, just as it is in California, the Indian Reservations in Arizona have the strong Spanish influence in their names, such as San Carlos, Gila River, Mojave, Navajo, etc. the letters "j" and "g" are pronounced like an "h."

As my work is in the irrigation section of the Service, I was particularly interested to learn that Indians practiced irrigation from the United States to Chile. There were about 150 miles of irrigation ditches in Salt River Valley of Arizona before Columbus discovered America in 1492. "Indians have given more to civilization than most people think," the booklet goes on to say, in the art of domesticating wild plants and of growing corn, white potatoes, sweet potatoes, tobacco, tomatoes, onions, peanuts, pineapples, pumpkins, squash, and so forth. Tobacco is one of the most important cash crops.

There were more than 200 different tribes in the United States, and the Indian population in the United States was 343,410 in 25 states, according to the 1950 census. The largest total of 65,761 was in Arizona; 53,769 in Oklahoma; 41,901 in New Mexico; 23,344 in the Dakotas; the smallest was 14 in Delaware in 1940, none there in 1950; the smallest in 1950 was 30 in Vermont.

The Bureau of Indian Affairs has a long history back of it, much longer than most of the other Federal agencies. It was first created in the War Department in 1824, then it was transferred to the Interior Department in 1849. The Commissioner of Indian Affairs is appointed by the President, and under him there are eleven area directors who are responsible to the Commissioner for all the Bureau activities in their respective areas, and superintendents are in charge of Indian Agencies, non-reservation schools, hospitals, and independent irrigation projects. In 1952 there were 18 non-reservation schools, 31 reservation schools, 41 Navajo community schools, and 140 day schools in reservations; and there were 94 day schools and three boarding schools in Alaska, making a total of 237 schools maintained by the Bureau of Indian Affairs. The Portland Area headquarters is located in the Interior Building along with other agencies of the Interior Department.

Of course, the Federal employees, too, have their organizations much the same way as any other labor unions have. The National Federation of Federal

Employees is one, and the American Federation of Government Employees is another. The one thing which is different from any labor union is that, by Federal law and by their own constitution, they cannot engage in or support strikes against the United States Government, nor can they be outspoken partisans in any national elections. I have been with N.F.F.E. for 15 years and with A.F.G.E. for five years.

The National Federation of Federal Employees was organized in 1917, and it celebrated its 40th anniversary at a dinner held on September 17, 1957, at the Mayflower Hotel in Washington with more than 700 persons in attendance, including members of Congress, many high ranking Federal executives and key personnel officials of many departments and agencies. A telegram from the President of the United States was as follows:

"Please give my greetings to the officers and members of the National Federation of Federal Employees gathered in celebration of their 40th anniversary. Our Government is served well and devotedly by its civilian employees. In fulfilling their daily responsibilities, the men and women of your organization have established a splendid tradition and contributed much to the strength of the national community. Congratulations and best wishes,

Dwight D. Eisenhower."

Another message from Secretary of the Interior Fred A. Seaton which said in part:

"The steady growth and influence of the
NFFE during the past four decades has been
marked by energetic and intelligent support of
progressive policies in behalf of improved personnel management in the Federal Government.
The NFFE has contributed much to the realization of employee goals and to the efficiency of
government operations. Based on the record of
accomplishment, your contributions will grow in-
creasingly in matters pertaining to those high
principles on which this Republic is founded —
a vigilant regard for human liberty, a wise concern for human welfare, and a ceaseless effort
for human progress."

Three years ago we celebrated the Diamond Jubilee of the Federal Civil Service — 75 years of service
to America — 1883-1958. In recognition of this occasion the President issued the following proclama-
tion:

"Whereas the Federal Civil Service System
was established by the Civil Service Act of January 16, 1883, and will be seventy-five years old
on January 16, 1958; and whereas the seventy-
fifth anniversary of the Civil Service Act is an
appropriate time to salute the Civil Service of
the United States and to increase public knowledge and understanding of its importance in our
system of self-government; now, therefore, I,
Dwight D. Eisenhower, President of the United
States of America, do hereby call upon the people of the United States to participate in the
observance of the seventy-fifth anniversary of
the Civil Service Act on January 16, 1958, and
throughout the ensuing years."

During the last Christmas season, I was awarded a "TEN YEAR SERVICE" button with a citation by the Department of the Interior. Now, together with the "TEN YEAR SERVICE" button awarded me by the Department of Agriculture ten years ago, it makes me a 20-YEAR employee of the Federal Government. I am very grateful that I have been privileged to serve the Government of the people, by the people, and for the people of the United States of America, my country, my home.

"In fulfilling their daily responsibilities," as said the President, one should watch and see what a bee-hive of a place is the Interior Building where more than a thousand Federal employees, men and women, of all ages, are eternally busy like the busy bees. I am one of them. I had witnessed some similar scenes in the government buildings every time I visited Washington during the Great War in 1918 and 1919.

On Sundays of course, I go to the First Presbyterian Church to hear Dr. Paul Wright, Moderator of the General Assembly, and Dr. Ward Davis, who was a Junior, and Mrs. Davis, formerly Miss Eva Williams, who was a sophomore in college when I was a First Year student in Park College Academy in 1913. Dr. Davis and I picked tomatoes together once in the Park College vegetable garden, and Mrs. Davis taught my English class one semester, I remember. Dr. Davis is now retired.

On Monday and Tuesday evenings every other week, each month, I would attend the American Legion meetings and enjoy our comradeship together immensely. I carry two membership cards of the American Legion. One might wonder why, but I do because I love the American Legion, my Big Brother.

They are the Portland Post No. 1 card with two stickers on — "MEMBER 31 YEARS" and "EARLY BIRD," and the Columbia Power Post No. 120 card with "EARLY BIRD" sticker every year. My membership was transferred from Cathay Post No. 384 in San Francisco to Portland Post in 1942, and I joined the latter Post when I was with the Bonneville Power Administration.

Thus, providentially or incidentally, I am in close touch with both my Alma Mater and my Big Brother, and I feel very fortunate, indeed, spiritually and patriotically, socially and intellectually.

Epilogue

Ever since the end of World War II, I had dreamed of making a round-trip to my native land to pay my long over-due visit to my mother who was still living before Pearl Harbor, and to my little brother who lived with her. Just then I learned of several Korean students in this country who were employed as Korean interpreters back in Korea during the American Military Government in South Korea. And, thinking that there was an excellent chance for me to visit my mother and brother if I got an appointment as an interpreter, I had made an application for such a position to the proper authorities in 1947. But, I was turned down because of my age. The age limit for foreign service was from eighteen to fifty, and I was just one year too old for FOREIGN service to my native land!

But, it is too late now! My long-widowed mother died twelve summers ago, before I had the opportunity to see her once more and to say to her, "Hello, mother, it is I, you remember, your raven-haired little boy you sent away to America, now come back a gray-haired old man. It has been such a long time, hasn't it, mother?"

My Big Uncle has long since passed away, followed by my Big Aunt. So Charr Chosey, the Generous, the leader of the house of Charr, who sent me to America, is no more; nor is my Big Aunt, who loved me as one of her own sons and sent me away with her youngest son. So is gone my cousin's wife who died in San Francisco in 1944, and my cousin who passed away at Riverside in 1956 and was buried in Pasadena where he spent most of his later years. My scholar cousin, who was an exile in China, holding an important office in the Korean Provisional Government in Chunking, also died in exile there just ten days after Japan signed the surrender terms on the U.S.S. Missouri in Tokyo Bay. His wife and a son survived him and lived in Seoul. My Middle Uncle died at old age, and his daughter, Faith, and my brother still lived in Pyeng Yang. My oldest cousins were still farmers, and the only son of the oldest who had come to America with his aunt Esther is now living in Los Angeles with his American-born Korean wife and two daughters both now married. My brother's son had joined his cousin in Seoul and both were in school there before the start of the Korean War, and both were drafted into the Republic of Korea Army and both were killed in battle.

Of the pioneer missionaries whom I knew long ago, I have no knowledge except for Mrs. George Shannon McCune (Helen B. McAfee McCune) who, following the death of Dr. McCune several years ago, lived with her married daughter in Wisconsin until she passed away some years ago and was buried in her family cemetery in Parkville, Missouri.

The late Mr. Ahn Changho, the great Korean patriot and educator, and my good friend, was captured by Japanese spies while he was the head of the Korean exile government when in Shanghai, China, and was taken to Seoul where he died in the Japanese prison in 1938. His wife and children are living in Los Angeles. His oldest son, Philip Ahn of the movies in Hollywood, was in the U. S. Navy during the late war, and his eldest daughter, Susan, was a WAVE and saw service overseas in Europe.

Our eldest child, Anna Pauline, with her B.A. degree from Park College, my own Alma Mater, and her M.A. degree from Oberlin College, has been with the cancer research laboratories of the University of Chicago for the past four years. On Washington's birthday, 1958, she was married to a Korean scholar at the same chapel where my own wedding took place thirty years ago and is now mother of a boy and a girl. Our son, Philip, a graduate of the University of Oregon Dental School in 1956 was a captain in the U. S. Air Force, stationed at Yokota Air Base in Japan for the past two years, has just returned home last year and is now practicing his profession here in Portland. And, Flora, the baby of the family, who, too, was born in San Francisco, with two years of college work in Portland State College and secretarial training, was for four years a medical secretary at the Veterans Hospital here in our hometown of Portland, Oregon. She was married five years ago to a Chinese-American ex-GI and is now mother of a girl.

This story has a very happy ending, indeed. For supremely happy was my Lotus Flower when her greatest ambition and fondest aspirations were fulfilled to her heart's desire. On December 11, 1958 in ceremonies before the United States District Judge Solomon's court here in Portland, Oregon, Lotus Flower has become an American citizen under the new naturalization law. And, it made my family a hundred percent American!

And now that I have lived for the past eighteen sweet years here in this lovely City of Roses, in the State of Oregon, where all our children were educated and grown up to manhood and womanhood, and where now Lotus Flower is born as an American citizen, I have the right to claim myself as an Oregonian. And, naturally, together with the native sons and daughters of Oregon, I have celebrated the Oregon Centennial in 1959!

May God bless the State of Oregon and all the United States of America, my country, my home!

THE END

Notes

Hulbert was one of the early Presbyterian missionaries to Korea. Charr met Hulbert in California in 1908 and again in college in 1920.

41 Choi Jay-woo (Ch'oe Che-u), the founder of the Dong-Hak (Tonghak), was executed by the government in 1862 for sedition.

44 The 1882 Treaty was negotiated by Admiral Robert W. Shufeldt, for the American side, and Li Hung-chang, a Chinese statesman acting on behalf of Korea.

46 Underwood and Moffett (Charr misspelled the latter's name) were two of the early Presbyterian missionaries in Korea. Underwood was the founder of Yonsei University in Seoul, where L. George Paik, Charr's college classmate, later served as president.

72 "Croi" should be spelled "Choi."

85 By coincidence, Charr spent the latter half of his life in Portland.

87 The eye disease was probably trachoma, a contagious but relatively easy to spot and treat condition that a number of immigrants from Korea suffered from at the turn of the century. It was a significant cause for medical rejection from entering the United States.

93 The Independence Club existed from 1896 to 1898, until Emperor Kojong and his conservative advisors opposed it because it called for greater public representation in the government.

94 An Ch'ang-ho shortly left for California, where he founded the Hŭngsadan, or Young Korean Academy, to work for the renovation of Korea through gradualist measures of economic growth, education, and the development of moral character. Charr met An in San Francisco in 1905.

94 Noble was one of the missionaries who approved of Koreans going to America.

97 "Swallon" should be spelled "Swallen."

98 Charr later worked for Rand McNally in Chicago.

102 In the 1590s, invasions by the Japanese warrior leader Toyotomi Hideyoshi devastated Korea.

106 Wages for sugar plantation work were about seventy cents a day or about sixteen dollars a month for twenty-six days of work.

106 See Charr's passport (included among the illustrations in this book). He is listed as fifteen years old when he was actually ten.

107 Classical Chinese studies were traditionally studied by the country's *yangban* elite.

111 Chinnamp'o, now known as Namp'o, is a seaport city on the northwestern coast of Korea. Emigrants would leave from there for Japan, where they would transfer to larger transpacific steamers.

112 The correct name of the agency was the East-West Development Company (Tong-Sŏ Kaebal Hoesa), which had offices in the major cities and ports in Korea. It was managed by David Deshler. See also page 115, where Charr again mistakenly identified the agency as the Hawaii Development Company.

116 Although Charr identified the *Ohayo Maru* as a Japanese ship, it was in fact the *Ohio*, owned and operated by the recruiter David Deshler, whose hometown was Columbus, Ohio.

116 Emigration from Korea to Hawaii continued until the spring of the following year.

117 Chemulp'o was the old name for Inch'ŏn, a port city about thirty miles west of Seoul, the capital.

122 The person referred to here is Chŏng In-su, who had worked for Deshler when he was associated with the Unsan mines in northwest Korea. When Deshler began the recruiting enterprise he took Chŏng along with him.

126 Charr is referring here to the creole language, or "pidgin English," a combination of several different languages that was spoken by most of the nationalities on the plantations.

139 This sentiment, directed primarily against the Japanese, led the Japanese government to prevent Koreans from going to Hawaii.

144 His first organization was the Chinmokhoe (Associ-

ation to Cultivate Friendships), followed by the Kongnip Hyŏphoe (Cooperative Association). The Korean National Association (also know as the Kungminhoe) was founded in 1909.

144 Charr is referring to Durham White Stevens, an American employed by Japan's foreign ministry who was assassinated in San Francisco in 1908 (not 1907) by a Korean immigrant, Chang In-hwan. Stevens was on a lecture tour of the United States to praise Japanese actions in Korea, not on a secret mission to Washington.

165 Charr was indeed the first Korean to attend the academy (the high school attached to the college), and he continued his education at Park College, where he was the second Korean to be graduated. The first was L. George Paik (Paek Lak-jun), who entered in 1918, graduated in 1922, and achieved prominence as a scholar after writing *The History of Protestant Missions in Korea, 1832–1910* (P'yŏngyang: Union Christian College Press, 1927; 2d ed., Seoul: Yonsei University Press, 1970).

170 Park College became affiliated with the Church of Jesus Christ of Latter-Day Saints in the 1970s.

180 Koreans both inside and outside Korea, believing that Wilsonian self-determination would lead to independence from Japan, launched the March First Movement of 1919 to proclaim their independence. Wilson, however, was not referring to Korea because the United States and Japan were cobelligerents during World War I.

203 Charr is referring to the March First Movement, or Samil Undong.

207 Charr had joined a nationwide organization called the League of the Friends of Korea.

210 Two Supreme Court cases, *Ozawa v. U.S.* 260 U.S. 189 (1922) and *U.S. v. Thind* 261 U.S. 204 (1923) confirmed that Asians were ineligible for citizenship.

212 Syngman Rhee (Yi Sŭng-man) was the leader of one of the nationalist organizations in Hawaii, the

Dongjihoe, or Comrades' Society. He later served as president of the Republic of Korea from 1948 to 1960.

213 Mansei literally means "ten thousand years" and is equivalent to the Japanese "Banzai." In this context it means "May Korean independence last forever!"

241 This is a reference to the Immigration Act of 1924.

274 "Wm. Chester Rowell" should be "Chester H. Powell."

277 The citation is *Petition of Easurk Emsen Charr*, 273 Fed. 207 (1921) in Missouri. A similar case in California was *In re En Sk Song*, 271 Fed. 23 (1921). Both grew out of legislation enabling certain war veterans to become naturalized citizens and affirmed the ineligibility of Koreans for naturalization. Forty-four Koreans in Hawaii were naturalized under the same legislation, but their naturalization was subsequently voided.

Index

Puerto Ricans, 126
Pusan, 117
Pyeng-an-do (province), 15,
    29, 74, 106
Pyeng-Yang, 15, 17, 21, 24,
    29–30, 32, 46, 51–52, 55,
    58–59, 61, 64–66, 68, 70,
    74–76, 78–79, 88–89, 92–93,
    99–100, 108–9, 113–15, 119,
    121, 129, 132, 137, 143, 149,
    159, 176–77, 179, 200, 220,
    226, 244, 300

Qai-ja-dyung Pavilion, 93

Rand McNally, 228–29, 233,
    239, 242
Ray-surk, 108
Red Sea, 54
Revolutionary War (U.S.), 205
Rhee, Dr. Syngman, 212
Roosevelt, Theodore, 155
Ruling class society, 39
Russian: cossacks, 100; scout,
    101
Russian Hill, 132
Russo-Japanese War, 42, 70, 103
Ruth, story of, 286

Saloon Alley. See Sool-mak-gol
Salvation Army, 142
Salvation Institute, 39
Sanders, Dean, 209–10, 215,
    218, 224–25, 261, 270
San Francisco, 118, 125, 128–
    29, 131–32, 136, 142, 144,
    150, 152–53, 158–59, 164,
    168, 180, 187, 200, 243–47,
    265, 278, 282, 288, 290, 299
San Francisco Chronicle, 266, 274
Sang-nom ("commoners"), 39
Sang-soo-goo Gate, 83, 97
Scholars, 27

Selective Service (U.S.), 178
Seoul, 20, 29, 39, 42, 46, 51,
    70, 91, 94, 212–13, 300
Seven Point Treaty, 144
Shanghai, 41
Shang-soo-gu Gate, 63
Shintoism, 36
Shoongsil Academy, 177
Shoongsil Middle School, 89,
    94, 96
Sho-woo-mul, 55, 58, 69, 77
Sino-Japanese War (1894), 15,
    100
Smithsonian Institution, 187
Soil Conservation Service
    (U.S.), 288, 290–91
Sool-mak-gol, 58, 60, 62, 66,
    177
South Korea, 134
Statue of Liberty, 44
Student Volunteer Conven-
    tion, 173, 203
Sul-see-dang-gol Street, 90
Sun-Chun, 15, 64
Sur Jai-pil, Dr., 93–94
Swallen, Reverend, 97, 99–100
Swallon, Reverend. See
    Swallen, Reverend

Taegu, 220
Taft, William Howard, 155
"Tai-Pyung-Ga," 41
Tai-won-goon, Regent Prince,
    40
Taoism, 36–37
Telegraph Hill, 132
Ten Commandments, 47–48,
    51–52, 139
Tien-ju-hak-jang, 56
Ting-Fu Tsiang, 167
Tokyo Bay, 117
Tong-Myeng Wang, 30
True Man. See Jin-In

EASURK EMSEN CHARR, who emigrated to the United States from Korea in 1904 at the age of ten, was a career civil servant (engineering draftsman) for the U.S. Departments of Agriculture and the Interior until his retirement in 1964. He died in 1986.

WAYNE PATTERSON, a professor of history at St. Norbert College in DePere, Wisconsin, has been a visiting professor of Korean and Japanese history at a number of universities throughout the United States. The author or editor of eight books, including *The Korean Frontier in America: Immigration to Hawaii, 1896–1910,* he is working on a history of first-generation Koreans in Hawaii between 1903 and 1953.